T0365917

LIVING FAITH DAILY
IN SPIRIT
AND
IN TRUTH

This Is the Day the Lord Has Entrusted to Me; Let Me Live My Faith as Best as I Can

Rev. Benjamin A. Vima

Order this book online at www.trafford.com
or email orders@trafford.com

Most Trafford titles are also available at major online book retailers.

All scriptural quotations are from the New American Bible Revised Version
(NABRE) and a few from the New American Bible (NAB) and the International
Commission on English in the Liturgy Corporation Translation (ICELCT).

New American Bible (Revised Edition) (NABRE)

Scripture texts, prefaces, introductions, footnotes and cross references used in this work
are taken from the New American Bible, revised edition © 2010, 1991, 1986, 1970
Confraternity of Christian Doctrine, Inc., Washington, DC All Rights Reserved.

Scripture quotations marked NASB are taken from the New American
Standard Bible®, Copyright © 1960, 1962, 1963, 1968, 1971, 1972, 1973,
1975, 1977, 1995 by The Lockman Foundation. Used by permission.

Print information available on the last page.

ISBN: 978-1-4907-9249-1 (sc)
ISBN: 978-1-4907-9250-7 (e)

Library of Congress Control Number: 2018966610

Trafford rev. 12/11/2018

 www.trafford.com

North America & international
toll-free: 1 888 232 4444 (USA & Canada)
fax: 812 355 4082

DEDICATION

I warmly dedicate this work to all the seminarians and candidates who are pursuing earnestly and anxiously the realization of becoming spiritual leaders in the world. Church is eagerly waiting for their arrival as servants of God to offer new face-lift to her damaged image.

Rev. Benjamin A. Vima

CONTENTS

INTRODUCTION

Dear readers,

I present this book for your spiritual needs as you strive to genuinely live your faith daily as disciples of Jesus. With the church, I uphold a relentless faith and hope in the efficacy of the Word of God as the writer of the letter to the Hebrews states, "Indeed, the word of God is living and effective, sharper than any two-edged sword, penetrating even between soul and spirit, joints and marrow, and able to discern reflections and thoughts of the heart" (Heb. 4:12). And I too daily repeat the Word from Psalm 119 as my continuous ejaculatory prayer: "Your word is a lamp for my feet, a light for my path."

Above all, I esteem the Word that, coming from heaven, has become flesh as my spiritual and social guide to live my faith daily in my Master's way, in spirit, and in truth. As Tertullian, an ecclesiastical writer, has confirmed in his treatise *On the Prescription of Heretics*, I join the club of millions of Jesus's disciples in believing that "our Lord Jesus Christ himself declared what he was, what he had been, how he was carrying out his Father's will, what obligations he demanded of men. This he did during his earthly life, either publicly to the crowds or privately to his disciples." That truth is profusely proclaimed in all the NT books.

Accordingly, all of us—the disciples of Jesus—are committed daily to listening, reading, and meditating the sayings and deeds of the Master and, above all, trying to live up to his expectation. This is because we are indeed smart enough to know through our Master that "one does not live by bread alone, but by every word that comes forth from the mouth of God" (Matt. 4:4).

The second dimension of my conviction with which I labored for this work in my ministry of writing is that I join our Master and his messengers in concentrating on the importance of "today" as the only day designed by the Creator for me to live the discipled life for him. There is a valid reason why we are advised by many sages that we must learn to live one day at a time. God, in Jesus, emphasizes in the Bible the importance of today. I follow faithfully Jesus's instruction about the extraordinary value of "this day." "Do not worry about tomorrow; tomorrow will take care of itself. Sufficient for a day is its own evil" (Matt. 6:34). St. Augustine, in his explanation of the Lord's Prayer, writes, "When we say: *Give us this day our daily bread,* in saying *this day* we mean 'in this world.'" We may certainly take his interpretation as we talk about *living faith daily.* Yes, while we concentrate on our daily schedule with the Lord, we too can state that we live our faith in this world. After death when we reach heaven, we don't need the virtue of faith or any of its teachings and practices because we will be seeing the Lord face-to-face.

However, I am concerned more with living daily my faith—the faith I believe in, the faith I am baptized to, and the faith with which I fulfill the demands of my Master in his service. I am strong in my conviction that the only day I am given to live in the only world I am entrusted with is today, "this day." I too am reminded of this factual heavenly truth when I recite in Psalm

118 the verses "This is the day the Lord has made; let us rejoice in it and be glad. Lord, grant salvation! Lord, grant good fortune!" (24–25). The psalmist invites us to rejoice and be glad about this day, the unique chance offered to us by the Lord; plus, he cries out in that joyful spirit that the Lord may bestow salvation to us (in Hebrew, hosanna) on this precious day.

We know undoubtedly that the prerequisite to covet and enjoy God's gift of salvation is to live our faith "this day" according to the divine teachings and admonitions. Very aptly therefore, applying such hilarious spirit and perspective about this day, I have subtitled this work with "This is the Day the Lord has entrusted to me. Let me live my faith as best as I can." The Bible suggests to me that it doesn't say, "This is the year, the decade, or the life that the Lord has made." We are exhorted to rejoice and be glad on this day. And as an expansion, it relates "this day" with "this person"—the person whom we are encountering on this day and in this situation.

Today is the only chance entrusted to me; yesterday is gone, and tomorrow is no guarantee. Hence, we should be prudent enough to make a difference in this available day. Most of us retain a wrong approach toward our past, present, and future— exaggerating yesterday, overanxious about tomorrow, and underrating today. In opposition, many spiritual writers—being enlightened by God's Word—have been teaching us about the extraordinary value of today. They insist that everything happening within today's twenty-four hours will never ever be replicated tomorrow. And they too tell us that it is left to us how we either benefit out of this day or destroy ourselves by being careless and abusive toward it. Every bit of fortune or misfortune of today largely depends on how we shape, mold, and groom our attitudes, habits, perceptions, and behaviors, which arouse actions, reactions, or "proactions" from the world around us. Therefore, our elders have encouraged us to do every day the ordinary things in an extraordinary way.

It is on such above-listed convictions this book is structured. And therefore, my main reason for writing this work is this: just as I am striving to be an extraordinary disciple of Jesus at least one day at a time, according to my Master's demand, echoing in my heart and mind uninterruptedly "If you remain in my word, you will truly be my disciples" (John 8:31b), so too my readers may enjoy the fuller life of the Master in their today.

Though this book may not be an icebreaker because it is my tenth one, still, you will find that it will be a deliberate but humble effort of sharpening more the two-edged sword of God. As you take and read it, you may be surrounded by many ice storms and tornadoes in the spiritual valley of your lives. I request you to go through the chapters slowly and meditatively and listen to God carefully. Never open this book with a certain biased age-old attitude. If you do it, I warn you, you will be muddling yourself; instead of profiting, you will end up broke in spiritual assets.

One more thing you should remember: don't brand me a leftist, rightist, or centrist. I want to be truthful to myself, to my faith and tradition, and to the signs of the times. Please never be afraid of smiling, laughing, and giggling as you read each article of this book. God is a God of joy and happiness. There are certain things we have to laugh at, including our own phony and puny self. God loves such lighthearted but enlivening laughter.

Finally, I want to stress that my priority in my writing ministry is to take care of the faith and spirituality of my readers, who are destined already by the Creator and the Redeemer to be "God's good news" in walking, talking, and serving. Kindly cooperate with the Holy Spirit. He will guide you and remove from you your coldness and indifference to God's call to be his effective, efficient, and faithful disciples in this postmodern age.

Praying for you with love,
Rev. Benjamin A. Vima

CHAPTER I

BEGIN THE DAY WITH TRUST TO SHOVE OFF "STARTING TROUBLES"

1. Well Begun, Half-Done
But a Blessed Start Fully Done

*This is the day the Lord has made; let
us rejoice in it and be glad.*
—Ps. 118:24

"**W**ell begun, half-done" is a golden rule pronounced
by ancient sages for successful people who get very
good results in their life. I always remember this maxim
whenever I start something new in my life. In anything
I do or perform, I am very keen on the starting point.
Many times, I struggle at the beginning of my day, my
week, my month, and surely my New Year. I call this
"a starting trouble." But once I choose that important
moment of starting with a right perspective and
attitude, everything seems to be okay.

The same is true in the lives of successful men and
women. They always begin their undertakings with
great interest, full of trust and hope, being blessed
by God and their neighbors. They make sure their
efforts start at a good time and good place with good
opportunity, good plan, and sufficient finance, plus
with good attitudes and efficient helping hands. Once
they begin their business with these blessings, the entire
project reaches its completion as they have willed.
Every day of life should start well so that the rest of the
year will be happy and fruitful.

While humanity is prone to seeking secular ways
and means to make their start perfect, we Christians—
instead of making recourse to human power or any
worldly wisdom—want all that we begin to be filled

with the Lord's graces and blessings. According to our Christian faith, as God blessed the OT people of God through his messengers and elders, we too have been blessed by God abundantly through our faith-filled adherence and commitment to his love call, plus through our active participation ritually and actually in his church's discipleship. We discover that our God's blessings are triple: priestly, kingly, and prophetic.

The first one is priestly blessing: In the book of Numbers (6:22–27), God tells Moses that he is imparting the power to Aaron and his sons to bless his people. Aaron and his sons have been chosen by God and anointed by him to act as priests in his name. In other words, they have been chosen to be the channel of blessing from God to the people. "So shall they invoke my name upon the Israelites, and I will bless them," says the Lord. Each one of us, through our baptism, is called to act like a priest between God and our community. Just as Jesus has become the priest of God, so we are made into priests through our baptismal anointing. We hold a power to bless each other as mother, father, brother, sister, husband, wife, leader, friend.

Second is a kingly blessing: Paul, in his letter to Galatians (4:4–7), makes us aware of our identity and our birthright. Through our baptism as Christians, we have become sons and daughters of God. We, like Christ, have inherited the power and dignity to be called the children of God. Just as Christ has become the Son of God and inherited the kingly blessing from his Father, so too we inherit the kingly power from God. That is the blessing inherited from God. Kingliness is usually an inheritance of power and throne. We, as adopted children of God, have received already the blessing from our Father—the ability to control, to manage, to maintain, to lead, to solve, to fix, and to empower others with the same power.

And the third blessing is a prophetic one: We firmly believe that our God, who has spoken in the past to our ancestors through the prophets, has spoken to us in these last days through the Son (Heb. 1:1–2). Everything about Jesus's future has been prophetically told in the scriptures. So every day Jesus and his followers, specially his parents, have lived their lives in accordance with those prophetic promises.

Consequently, they have been liberated from undue anxieties about their past, present, and future. In the same way, the Lord also has prophetically promised about us and for us in the scriptures. Before our conception, he has written our names in his life's book. He has designed a beautiful and fruitful future for every one of us. He too has promised to be with us till the end of ages. This is a great prophetic blessing for us. Therefore, with Paul, we are fully convinced that "all things work for good for those who love God, who are called according to his purpose" (Rom. 8:28–39).

By our baptism and our sincere adherence and commitment to his love call, we have been blessed with the priestly, kingly, and prophetic blessings from God. So let us bless ourselves with this positive faith thinking at every moment of starting any of our daily accomplishments. So many unexpected things may have jolted us, shaken us, or shocked us in the past. But still, we hold on to the words of God about his blessings. Let us hand over the past and the future to the Almighty. The present only should be in our eyes.

While we drive our cars, we do not look back constantly to be safe; we only see what is coming back to us through the side or rear mirrors. So shall we use the past as a side effect to our future orchestra. The past failures and even sins will assist us in straightening out our attitudes and our decision-making. As the Lord exhorts us, let us not be overanxious about the future, which is solely in his hands. The only day given to us by God is this day, this week, and this year. The promised blessings are there in abundance. God is blessing us with the ability to bless others, the power to lead and manage, and the luck to hold an eternally propitious word of fortune; we are predestined for good and good alone to enjoy everything that is good born out of his love.

2. Start Everything with Providential Calculation

The Lord bless you and keep you!
—Num. 6:24

We are humans gifted with rationality and intelligence. Unlike animals or birds, we are anxious about how, why, and how long we survive and live our lives. From the day of humanity's origin, humans have attempted to calculate their living period in this world, how to avoid the curses of life, and how to enjoy its blessings in that period.

Many make a natural calculation, which is based on the stars in which we are conceived and born. Horoscope, astrology, numerology, and palm reading are some of the sciences generated out of such anxious calculation. Some others use an artificial calculation through which, in ancient period, humans have calculated and measured their living time by the sun's movement, even by the shadow its light has created on the ground. Gradually, with the help of astronomy and mathematics, each nation and race has created their own calculation called calendar, which contains years, seasons, months, days, hours, and seconds and now even light-years (and megabytes and gigabytes) and so on.

There is also a third calculation in the circle of religious and spiritual humans, which is called "providential calculation." According to this, we are told that, at one time, the Supreme Spiritual Being has created the entire universe; every being on the earth begins its life from him and ends in him. Though he lives in a timeless time, he recognizes and appreciates every kind of calculation of time we have introduced and are following. Only he knows fully well our beginning and our end. Though he has created a cyclic system for other beings and materials, he has denied it in the lives of humans. There is only one birth and one death. Humans' lives are journeying in a one-way traffic. Above all, he is concerned about our limitation of worrying too much about our lifetime.

It is this providential calculation that most of us apply to our life as it progresses from womb to tomb. From scriptures, it has been confirmed that everything existing in this universe moves and has its being only according to God's calculation. Our time, hour, day, and year are in his timeless time. He performs marvelous deeds in his own time and place. When we listen to Paul's way of calculating his and the entire human race's life, we are encouraged to go forward from one year to another and from one day to another with the relentless hope that there is always a bright tomorrow reserved for us, thanks to the providence of our Abba, Father.

Most importantly, we should be convinced that such providential calculation lets us realize our life's predestined abundant design. It also enlivens us to uphold our own positive calculation about earthly life. We begin to perceive with rationality and see through all that has happened in the past and still happening today and behind everything and every event the unthinkable love-based, providential hand of God leading us as he has promised.

3. In God, the Immanuel, We Trust

If God is for us, who can be against us?
—Rom. 8:31b

At every dawn as we get up from sleep, we bid goodbye to the previous day and say hello to the new one. We are stepping into another milestone as we march on toward our heavenly home. We know when we have started this journey but are unaware of when and where this march of ours will come to a halt. However, we are sure conventionally that each step leads us to a place where all our dreams will come true, the dreams of never-ending life, ever-blissful environment, and unchanging love experience.

Commonly, analytic people like me may begin the day with mixed feelings. There is a feeling of gratitude and happiness for the previous day because of having been spared from accidents, deaths, or cruel illness and for having been left unharmed by natural disasters. Happiness fills some of us because so much has been forgiven, and we are not punished despite all our blunders, bad habits, and misbehavior. Many among us may be overwhelmed with joy that, despite all the prophecies and predictions of doom and terror, humanity—especially the place we live in—has still been kept in balance between war and peace, disaster and prosperity, crime and sanctity, violence and kindness, and terrorism and charity.

There is also a certain feeling of sadness if we have lost our loved ones by death or have broken our friendship by divorce and conflict, and there may be others who feel sad because they have missed good opportunities to improve, to gain, to do good. Surely, most of us will be feeling sorry because we have hurt our friends and relatives and sometimes messed up their lives. We feel ashamed for making wrong decisions; plus, we feel unhappy for the dreams and plans that have not been realized or have ended up in failure.

Undoubtedly, almost all of us are anxious and fearful about the future of this new day. We ask certain questions about it with anxiety: Will our dreams and plans be accomplished at least today? Will our chronic or terminal disease or any other illness continue bothering us or be healed? What about our family problems—the irritable habits of our loved ones, their stubborn temperament, their unpredictable behavior, our job, our house, and our savings?

To get over with or to get even with these mixed emotions and feelings, each one of us chooses different ways. To escape from these inner troubles, many make use of some perverted acts like alcoholism, workaholism, doing drugs, or simply being couch potatoes, lying down in bed or watching TV for hours and so on. Unarguably, all those listed are excessive and forbidden fruits. However, as committed Christians, what should we do to cope with such "starting troubles" lawfully and fruitfully?

First, we should look for the almighty presence of God as Immanuel in ourselves. Second, we must remind ourselves, as we start the day, of Jesus's promise: "And behold, I am with you always, until the end of the age" (Matt. 28:20b). Third, before leaving from home to work, we have to take a few minutes in front of the Immanuel and pour out to him all our feelings— especially those of fear, anxiety, remorse, and shame— and express our sincere appreciation for all that he has done in previous days, months, and years in our lives. Besides, we must surrender ourselves and every moment of the new day at his feet and resolve to stay on his lap throughout the day as our strength, our mighty rock, our fortress, our stronghold, and our high tower.

4. Settling in the Covenantal Ark of Fulfillment

This is the time of fulfillment . . . believe in the Gospel.
—Mark 1:15

To any human born and bred in this world, life is nothing but a battlefield between godly people and satanic ones. And the Word, who has become flesh and lived in our midst, has not been exempted at all. In the light of the Bible, we realize that the entire life of Jesus has been a warfare. To introduce his life of strife, like a foreword in a book, all the four Gospel writers have included a narration about his intense fight with the devil. It is an event happening in the desert where Jesus has spent forty days in prayer and penance. One of the evangelists, Mark, plainly puts it, "Jesus remained in the desert for forty days, tempted by Satan" (Mark 1:12–15).

During those days, besides feeling the absence of relationships, Jesus would have been feeling lonely gazing out at a wilderness and its emptiness and surely suffering out of its inclement climate, staying night and day among wild animals. Together with such evils, the devil gave him hard time. To portray his horrible battle with the evil, the Gospels narrated three temptations. According to Mark, Jesus passed through his life's warfare successfully as he went through the forty-day struggles against Satan. With Jesus's remarkable success in his battle with evil, as we read in Hebrews, he was made a role model, a sympathizer, and even the source of eternal salvation to all humans (Heb. 4:15–16, 5:1–10).

Like Jesus, we too are tempted, we are tossed around, we are broken to pieces, we are wounded, we are crucified, we are misunderstood, we are diagnosed with different kinds of unheard-of brand-new diseases, and we are struck down by natural calamities and other social and political problems as wars and terrorism. Besides all these, we as Christians join Christ in fighting against Satan, who deploys his legion of evil spirits that are inside and outside us.

To cope with this hectic life situation, to live in peace and joy in the midst of problems and temptations, and to win our life's battle, the Spirit of God in the Bible suggests one important and very efficacious ammunition. Peter underlines this necessary ammunition, saying, "Be sober and vigilant. Your opponent the devil is prowling around like a roaring lion looking for someone to devour.

Resist him, steadfast in faith" (1 Pet. 5:8–9). What is this faith we should hold on to? I am convinced that it is nothing but staying put in the ark of God.

As Jesus and God's messengers have stayed put to the movement of God's Spirit, we are told to choose willingly and remain faithfully in the ark of God's covenantal love and Spirit wherever our life situates us. Noah and his family, for instance, have been saved from deluge by staying in the ark (Gen. 9:8–15). Like them, we will be saved and reach our victory if we too stay inside the ark of the covenant. Our God is proclaimed in the Bible as the guaranteed covenant partner to humans. He has always desired to build his relationship with us through a covenant of love. The OT ark of the covenant is the symbol of such love-based relationship. As Jesus has always been led by the Spirit, even to the desert encounters, the Spirit wants us to be led to enter freely and stay firmly inside the ark that Jesus has built for us, the church (1 Pet. 3:18–22).

Also, the Spirit summons us to believe in the Gospel of Jesus and follow it faithfully. As soon as Jesus has come out of the desert and from a hidden life to a public one, he has preached the first sermon on the belief in the Gospel. According to his Gospel, the kingdom of victory is sure and within reach. It is also within us. Especially after our baptism, the kingdom established by God within us at our creation has become solid and enterprising. We turn out to be the moving ark built on God's covenant, in which we offer accommodation, shelter, and—if need be—our very life. Thus, we should feel fulfilled and satisfied at every moment of our Christian life. We shouldn't be doubtful of the authenticity of the Gospel we believe in or the ark we stay in. The Gospel of Jesus is the one and only Gospel of fulfillment in human life, and the church of Jesus is the only place which can be called "the ark of fulfillment." It is where we can find our safety and security, plus great strength, to win our battle against evils.

Today's world, where we are led to reside in, is a sort of desert milieu worse than Jesus has been led into by the Spirit. We are shattered by war, poverty, homelessness, violence, unemployment, famine, flood, greed, apathy, crime, global warming, flash mob vandalism, an out-of-touch hierarchy, child abuse, spousal abuse, elder abuse, earthquakes, and more. Undoubtedly, our life is a warfare. It is a never-ending struggle and tension. Simply, we are torn between bad and good spirits. Some of us put the blame for this broken world on "those people" as scapegoats. However, we should keep in mind that just as the sins of a society begin with one individual, so the renewal and transformation of society begins with each individual. Therefore, let us constantly repeat the old cry "Lord, send a revival, and let it begin with me."

5. The Christian Life Is as a "Move-in Settlement"

In him we live and move and have our being
—Acts 17:28a

One of the mind-boggling dimensions of God's mystery, which has been finally revealed in Jesus's coming, is that a life lived with Jesus in this world is a thrilling experience of a "move-in settlement." As we hear from Paul (Eph. 3:2–6), God the Creator has slowly and gradually revealed his identity and nature throughout the ages and generations of mankind. The core of his revelation is that Christianity puts God before us as the complete and total settlement of our human life on the earth. Our life has started from him and will find its end in him also.

God is the biggest dream of our life, toward which we all travel in this world. We are not entirely wanderers or entirely settlers. We have settled in God already, but we also move toward him and with him. We accept fully that we are truly wanderers and pilgrims walking and running toward our eternal settlement, namely, God. All other settlements we have in this world such as tents, religions, homes, societies, and countries are merely temporary ones on the road. They have to be experienced and enjoyed as a "move-in settlement" of mobile homes and trailer houses.

In continuation of Paul's contention, we read in the Bible that God has revealed the stunning climactic dimension of his mystery that while our life must be settled with him, we too must be settled in Jesus of Nazareth, who is the Way, the truth, and the life, plus follow him as the Light as prophesied in OT: "Arise! Shine, for your light has come, the glory of the Lord has dawned upon you . . . Upon you the Lord will dawn, and over you his glory will be seen. Nations shall walk by your light" (Isa. 60:1–3).

The Epiphany story, told by Matthew (Matt. 2:1–12), proclaimed that the three magi were settled in the historical fact of the birth of Immanuel, "God with us," who was none other than Jesus, who was the would-be King of the Jews and the universe. This they found out by their intense reading and interpreting of the available scriptures (Mic. 5:1–3) and traditions. They were sure the promised Messiah should have been born somewhere in Palestine. Being convinced of the amazing event, they began their journey to find him; they traveled through deserts and many obstacles to reach this grand goal.

They too settled well in their faith and conviction they inherited, but they began using the means God bestowed to them to reach Jesus. That was the star. But the story told us that, in between, they missed it; perhaps the Supreme God would not have relished their effort of getting some help from certain criminal-minded persons like Herod. However, being merciful to them, God permitted his star to appear again to them and lead them to the place where the child Jesus was with Mary and Joseph.

Indeed, we notice too many stars moving in the glittering sky. There are too many means at our assistance in searching and finding our eternal goal, God. But we have to choose proper ones and settle with them. They are different religions, authorities, preachers, teachers, and prophets in the media and Internet. We have to choose the appropriate stars for us and take them as our means to realize our big dream.

The star that took the wise men to the baby Jesus is a symbol of his body, the universal church, which we all believe will take us to our settlement. It is the sacrament of love and God. Sometimes we may not fully see its light because of unholy leaders and fellow Christians. But if we are really and sincerely settled in that means, surely, it will come back and lead us to the goal and settle us in the crib of peace, love, joy, and fulfillment.

6. Let's Do Our Best; God Will Do the Rest

Owe nothing to anyone, except to love one another.
—Rom. 13:8

All evil deeds, done by humans, are rooted on what the Bible calls "wickedness." Many of those sins may be committed either unknowingly and ignorantly or deliberately and intentionally. Because of this wickedness, conflicts and maladies—such as wars, infighting, peacelessness, insecurity, dissension, rebellion, and even schisms—have become part of human life. The God of our scriptures and traditions has been doing the task of purifying the sinful and wicked hearts of humans and trying to bring them back to him. In this venture, he expects our cooperation.

The problem with us is we ignore or don't care about his invitation. This is because to be involved in God's redeeming works is so hard, bitter, and painful. Undoubtedly, to make others listen and return to God is the most cringe-making job.

Even Jesus, who was the greatest Miracle Worker, despite his immense power, seemed to fail in this. In his life, he did numerous miracles in which water obeyed and made itself into wine, broken limbs and bones of humans obeyed him and cured, nature resource like wind obeyed him and became still; much more so, when he ordered the dead bodies to rise, they all obeyed. But when he approached humans to correct them, knocking at their doors, they retorted, "Stop, we are free beings. In our own time, we will respond to you."

It is in this sort of bitter-tasting job that God wants us to join him. In the Bible, we read about him reaching out to his prophets and to his other chosen ones and expressing his longing to become partners in redeeming affairs. He persists, commanding us, "You, son of man—I have appointed you as a sentinel for the house of Israel; when you hear a word from my mouth, you must warn them for me" (Ezek. 33:7). Being aware of our resistance to God's demand, Jesus has offered us some advice on how to accomplish this redemptive work fruitfully and with a light burden.

First, Jesus instructs us that we should start and fulfill this duty only in his name, namely, through him, with him, and in him. Since the task is too onerous to be performed by our lithe human strength, Jesus recommends to include him in our team as its center and source. Therefore, he has promised, "For where two or three are gathered together in my name, there am I in the midst of them."

Second, all our efforts of correcting the so-called wicked must be based only on the spirit of love and mercy as God indeed exhorts us through Paul (Rom. 13:8–10) This implies that we should take the first step toward the wicked as a loving icebreaker and not as a tough law binder. Pope Francis deliberates this guideline of love and mercy in his apostolic exhortation "The Joy of Love": "No one can be condemned forever, because that is not the logic of the Gospel! Mercy does not exclude justice and truth, but first and foremost we have to say that mercy is the fullness of justice and the most radiant manifestation of God's truth."

Third, Jesus wants us to proceed in this task very slowly, gradually, little by little with patience and tolerance and do all the possible tactics (Matt.

18:15–20). We should start our correctional effort with one-to-one dialogue; if we fail, Jesus asks us to do it as a group of one mind and one heart. In other words, we should try to be together as one team of God. Let us always give heed to the clarion call of God, which is being repeated in our inner sanctuary, to cooperate in his redemptive plan of correcting our fellow humans as our Master guides us. Let us do the best we can in our own limited way to bring justice and mercy, and God will do the rest.

7. A Faith-Filled Heart Is Always a Restful Heart

You have faith in God; have faith also in me.
—John 14:1b

There are many modern prophets in media and in secular as well as religious circles who conduct many crisis management workshops and write so many books about it. Jesus, our Master, in his own heavenly style, also has offered us a gospel of life management, which includes crisis management.

To teach humans some strategies regarding our crisis management, he came to this world. Not only did Jesus speak about it but he also lived it. As a Good Samaritan and Good Shepherd, throughout his life, Jesus went all the way out of himself to console and strengthen by deeds the people affected and hurt by human life's crises.

In John's Gospel, we heard Jesus telling his disciples, "Let not your hearts be troubled." And he continued to explicate the application of this valuable strategy (John 14:1–12). The Lord said those consoling words to his disciples who were so anxious, dejected, and discouraged at the separation of Jesus from their physical life. They were very much troubled about their present and future; they were worried about the rejection Jesus and they experienced from their enemies. He didn't stop there simply with his encouraging words, but with his eternal wisdom and human experience, he offered them a principle that would make them free of worry. In the light of scriptures, we discovered that this principle is a twofold faith: faith in him and faith in ourselves.

Jesus expects us first to believe in God and himself, God's Son. By these words of advice, he confirms that his disciples' faith in his godly identity— which is powerful and efficacious—will bring peace and needed strength to bear the pain and suffering. In addition to their belief of his divine identity, he suggests they should concretize that faith in following him as "the Way, the Truth, and the Life." That is the way to make their faith most effective and fruitful. He requests his disciples to follow his way of love—forgiving, patiently forbearing and merciful, being consecrated to his wholistic truth, being honest and sincere in all their undertakings. He also prefers that they lead a life of service and sacrifice, helping and supporting the needy even when one's own life is at stake as he has done.

The second dimension of faith, which Jesus has recommended through his disciples, is having faith in ourselves. We, however clay and dust we may be, are born again by his blood and in his spirit. We were once no people, and now we are adopted as children of God and disciples of God's Son. Apostles have been empowered with such faith and hope and have preached about it day in and day out. They state, "You are a chosen race, a royal priesthood, a holy nation, a people of his own; like living stones, let yourselves be built into a spiritual house" (1 Pet. 2:9). We must attentively read this statement of Peter. While he honors Jesus as the living Stone prophesied by the prophet (Isa. 28:16), he too surprisingly qualifies us as the living stones of the edifice Jesus has established.

Upholding firmly this two-dimensional faith, we are assured by Jesus that we will be esteemed and very precious in the sight of God. We will accept the bittersweet life in this world joyfully as Jesus's disciples have been living happily even in their crises. Plus, we will be accomplishing great things, even greater than our Master's, as Jesus has promised, "Amen, amen, I say to you, whoever believes in me will do the works that I do, and will do greater ones than these." It is with the above-mentioned mind-set that our hearts will be settled in peace despite the impending troubles.

8. Be Prepared for Surprises from Jesus

Whoever receives a prophet will receive a prophet's reward.
—Matt. 10:41

Through the Bible, the Spirit teaches us that we, the disciples of Jesus, must always welcome God's messengers in our life and be open to their message. To welcome God's message through these messengers brings so much blessing to us as what has happened to the Shunammite woman as we read in 2 Kings 4:8–17.

It was a very ordinary story about a woman who offered her TLC hospitality to Elisha, whom she esteemed as a man of God. Elisha, as most of God's messengers would do, offered to repay her hospitality with power and security. But she did not want any help in return from the prophet. But Elisha desired, by all means, to do some good deeds for her. With his spiritual intuition, he discovered a secret sadness filling her heart and soul. Something was missing from her life. The woman and her husband were childless. Elisha promised that, despite her barrenness, she would embrace a son.

What we notice in this story is that when the woman has welcomed the messenger of God into her home, she has received much more than she has bargained for. Along the way, she has learned that welcoming God's message and living with it is rarely easy and seldom simple but often surprising and sometimes risky. Nonetheless, ultimately, his Word—which is welcomed and hosted lovingly—performs miraculous deeds in human lives, which even the entire world cannot contain. Unfortunately, most of us do not offer a warm welcome to God's Word because it is very difficult to observe and at times very risky, especially the hard demands of Jesus, the great Messenger of God. For example, he tells us, "Whoever does not take up his cross and follow after me is not worthy of me" (Matt. 10:37–39).

Besides God's Word, the instruments or agents through whom he makes us hear those words are also very hard to be welcomed. They seem to us either cranky, strange, and low to our standard or typically weak and fragile like any humans.

The woman in the story accepted the prophet into her home though, in that region, any prophet of his kind was not well accepted by the public (2 Kings 2:23); we too hear in NT how the public treated Jesus, Paul, and other apostles unjustly and viciously by jeering and stoning. These messengers were rejected by most people, saying they were either strangers or weird, in their proclaiming God's Word.

The same is true today in this modern world. Because of such wrong notions about the vocation to proclaim the Gospel demands of Jesus, as a recent survey shows, society today does not esteem this vocation as an honorable one. The world considers these ministers of God's Word as useless and leading a strange life. The Spirit expects us to examine how we relate to God's Word and his messengers.

The messengers of God's Word today are composed of the ordinary people whom we meet daily but overlook because of their strangeness. Married or single, ordained or lay, every human person finds ultimate fulfillment in answering Jesus's call to "take up the cross," which brings life out of death. Among them are many who—by birth, by formation, or by any accident—carry their crosses temporarily or permanently. They may be the homeless, the poor, the orphans, the widows, the handicapped, the disabled, the socially and physically spoiled ones, and so on. Jesus asks us today to be their hosts and welcome them into our hearts and homes. Let us warmly welcome Jesus's prophets with their divine words because of Jesus's surprising promises (Matt. 10:40–42).

9. Saying Total Yes to God Is the Right Choice in Life

Jesus Christ . . . was not "yes" and "no," but "yes."
—2 Cor. 1:19

Every one of us respects our individuality. To say yes or no to others is our right and prerogative. We choose to say either yes or no absolutely or change them anytime we want. The Spirit of God, through a short parable of Jesus (Matt. 21:28–32), demands from us the right use of our right for the fullness of life.

In our personal lives, whatever be our status, we have repeatedly behaved as the sons in the parable. As the elder son, we may initially say yes and later not do it. As the younger one, we may say no first; but then after reflecting, we may act positively.

Basically, almost all of us, as Christians, have said "I do" to the Lord at our baptism and repeatedly renewed the same answer throughout the year. The tragic fact is we fail in our relationship with God by not adhering to the yes, and consequently, we also fail other humans in our social relationships. Knowing the seriousness of human entitlement of uttering yes or no, our Creator has been continuously reminding every human being to always say yes to him—to his commands and directions. If we don't listen to him, then we have to reap its consequences.

When disasters occur, like hurricane, bomb blast, tornado, cyclone, earthquake, wreaking havoc and claiming lives, usually, humans look for someone to blame. OT Israelites too were blaming God and others for their misfortunes. But through the prophets, God exhorted them; rather than looking for a scapegoat upon whom to heap their guilt or even finding fault with God foolishly, they should look only to themselves and to their own responsibility for conversion. He urged them to say yes to him by turning away from their own wickedness (Ezek. 18:25–28).

Jesus continued the same ministry of coaxing all humans, especially his followers, to say a total yes to God. Through his parable of the two sons, he reminded his disciples how Israelites behaved like the first son, saying yes first but then not following suit, and how the sinners and pagans, though they said no, warmly said yes to God. Besides, he pointed himself out in this regard as a pattern to all his disciples.

As Paul wrote, Jesus's perennial attitude was simply saying yes to God, and that too was total and absolute. However, this absolute yes to God seemed to take its toll on the very life of Jesus. For his every yes to God, Jesus had lost more and more of himself. First, he agreed to surrender his equality with God and then his freedom, "taking the form of a slave"; his dignity as "he humbled himself"; his independence, "becoming obedient"; and his very life, "even death on a cross" (Phil. 2:1–11).

Surely, saying yes to God may appear like a very risky business in our earthly life. But we should never lose sight of the result of this marvelous yes. We know Jesus, for his total yes to God has been exalted as the Lord of glory, by whose saving efforts sinners are saved. Therefore, following Jesus, let us be bold enough to respond yes to God's will totally and consistently. That is the only way to gain his fuller life.

CHAPTER II

CONTINUE THE DAY WAITING AS IF AN ADVENT DAY

10. Waiting for Jesus
Not Speculatively but Realistically

It is the hour now for you to awake from sleep.
—Rom. 13:11b

Our earthly life in this world is built up on the biggest hope, as the prophet Isaiah has once foretold, of Jesus's coming in our midst. While Jesus is alive physically, he has made all possible efforts to potentially establish our dreamed better world. Gospel writers as well as all the apostles, in their letters, confirm their belief in the repeated promises of Jesus, before his death and even after, about his Second Coming. They have heard from Jesus that "the Son of Man will come" (Matt. 24:37–44). In addition to his promise, he too has cautioned them that his coming will be "at an hour they do not expect."

Knowing our human fragility and anxiety, he encouraged us to stay always awake and wait with hope. In this precarious time of waiting, he told us he would "not leave us orphans." He too promised he would stay with us, even after his death, in disguise and in signs and symbols and share with us all resources of truth and fullness of life, peace and love, justice and unity. He said, "The kingdom of God is already in your midst." As he was ready to be lifted to heaven, he emphasized, "And behold, I am with you always, until the end of the age."

Such surprising statements of Jesus make our Christian life an active waiting for Christ's continuing coming. As stewards of Christ, we must always be ready to recognize the Lord's coming by being faithful to the mission in life given to us by Christ. Regrettably, most of his foretelling has not been realized totally. Too many of us don't walk in the light of the Lord. Most of us are still slumbering, sleeping tight in our couches, and brooding over our past or groaning over what we lack in. As Paul exhorts us, we who still lead a life not in daylight but in the dark night "should throw off the works of darkness and put on the armor of light; let us conduct ourselves properly as in the day" (Rom. 13:12–14).

Every human person, young or old, dumb or smart, holds a view of his/her own about human life. Some, like small babies, crave for the possession of everything of the world—our relationships, physical beauty, health, strength, mental and intellectual capacities, material possessions, name and fame, power, influence—which are none other than varieties of colorful balloons, very enchanting and attractive; but unfortunately, one day or the other, they have to "burst" and depart from us.

Jesus expects us to behave like grown-up adults who esteem human life as redeemed by God in Christ Jesus, and every earthly step becomes a trustworthy ladder through which they can climb up and ascend to their climactic destiny. Our Master's advice is worth adhering to. It helps us lead an optimistic life. Plus, we are enlightened by the risen Jesus through his scriptures and the tradition of his church; we will be scheduling our daily life, making it not just waiting for him speculatively but actively and realistically performing certain spiritual and charitable deeds on his behalf ritually and socially. He comes in various disguises, particularly as the needy, the sick, and the downtrodden.

11. Living in the Spirit of the Catchy Word "Watch"

Those who wait for the Lord will inherit the earth.
—Ps. 37:9b

All of us have so much trouble to keep up our interior rest because of fretting over too many worldly matters and consequently being unable to settle down in serenity. Jesus never fails to invite us to go deeply into this perennial problem and try to salvage the genuine rest by his resounding advice: "Watch" (Mark 13:33–37).

By the catchy word "watch," Jesus means that we must not be ignorant, careless, complacent, or cold and indifferent to God, his design for us, and our responsibilities in this world; also, positively, he has advised us to be aware of the significance of this earthly life. It is so important in God's eyes that every moment of life is very precious to him. He has designed it in so much wisdom to accomplish his creative and salvific goals for the entire universe and his creatures.

Also, he has blessed us with abundant gifts. Acknowledging those blessings gratefully, Paul reminds us that in Jesus we were enriched in every way with all discourse and all knowledge, not lacking in any spiritual gift during our lifetime of waiting. And since God is faithful, he will keep us firm to the end, helping us be blameless on the day of the Lord's coming (1 Cor. 1:3–9).

Through such marvelous design, God intended to make the future of his creation good, better, and best. He longed that all his creatures, especially his human children, must live in peace, joy, and fullness of contentment. For this, he relied on his super creation, humanity. He entrusted to the humans certain responsibilities to fulfill his creative goal and vision of restoring the world to its original status.

Sadly, we know that our world will never be such a paradise. Imperfection is the mark of our world and of every human being. Nonetheless, if we let God come into our world to straighten out its system and order and if we let him enter our life, we will find our settlement in him, and then everything will get better.

In fact, we profess God has come already; he is here with us in Jesus. The only thing we have to do is to be fully aware of this redemptive fact. With him, we can make this world not yet a paradise but at least much better if we learn to bear with him the pain of the evil in this world and fight it with all our might. Then it may become a sign of the paradise of heaven.

There are so many among us who have been blessed by God abundantly—being healthy, wealthy, and energetic and with enlightened mind and spirit by Christ. Unfortunately, very few respond to God's eternal call to work with his Son in making our world order just, peaceful, and joyful. Instead, so many don't apply this truth in our lives; we behave like wanderers or, worse, sleepwalkers. This is what Jesus means by his clarion call to watch and pray: Be alert. Get up from couches of self-gratification. Don't behave bullheaded. Be on your knees and pray to the Father, "Let your kingdom come. Let your will be done."

12. Surviving during His Delay

According to his promise, we await new
heavens and a new earth.
—2 Pet. 3:13

While we wait for God's interventions in life, there is one thing that disturbs us. It is his "delay" in coming and interacting. The Good Book, however, tells us that we need not worry about God's delay because "with the Lord one day is like a thousand years and a thousand years like one day." We too are told that the reason for God's delay is that he patiently waits for his children to come back home. He does not wish even a single person of his family to perish. Peter also underlines that, because of our impatience and the so-called instant-craving attitude of postmodern humans, we shouldn't consider that the Almighty delays in fulfilling his promises; rather, we should wait anxiously for our repentance and conversion to him with dignity and appreciation of God's fidelity and goodness (2 Pet. 3:8–16).

Very positively, we are exhorted by the Spirit to pursue getting mature in our personal relationship with the divine despite our material and physical limitations. We know how long it takes for a seed of man to become a developed baby, youth, and adolescent and to reach one's adulthood. The same thing is true for our spiritual development. Our Creator, understanding this human factor, bestows sufficient time for us to gain our spiritual adulthood.

During this waiting period, there are so many marvelous deeds God performs in our life. As OT prophets (Isa. 40:1–11) have foretold, when the risen Lord's Spirit encounters every human in day-to-day life, he tries to comfort our hearts with the assurance of the Shepherd's tender compassion and patient love for us, the cherished sheep of God's flock. He will feed us, console us, educate us, inspire us, and bless us with abundant riches and talents; and especially, he will direct us in right path so that we can escape, as much as we can, from imprisonment and from losing a good name and respect from our family and community. The same Lord is knocking at our doors. He is not sleeping and indifferent to our daily ups and downs. He is always ready and alert more than we are to intervene in our lives. He is indeed waiting to enter into our lives with full power, with his rewards, and with his shining glory.

Unquestionably, the coming of the day of God, as the Bible states, will be like a "big bang" factor, and tremendous power will be unleashed to judge and to transform the human race and the entire creation. "The heavens will be dissolved in flames and the elements melted by fire. But according to his promise we await new heavens and a new earth in which righteousness dwells."

If we desire to meet this powerful, lucky, redemptive, and loving Person at his coming and to get all that he has promised, what we have to do is — as John the Baptist has preached (Mark 1:2–8) — "to prepare the way of the Lord." What he has suggested, as a preparation work for facing the day of the Lord, is first to be baptized in water of repentance as he has done in Jordan; then he too wants us to go to the risen Lord and be baptized in his Spirit of fire, love, justice, faith, hope, and joy. We should make sure that while the first baptism is very ritual, the second is nothing but our actual life. If we comply with John's proposal, we can win at the end of the day, meeting the Lord face-to-face as the sun and moon encounter each other.

13. Waiting for the Lord Calls for A Heavy Weight of Faith, Hope, and Charity

Wait for the Lord, take courage; be stouthearted!
—Ps. 27:14

Once being irritated by my friend's attitude of failing in his reciprocal friendly relationship, I reproached him, pointing out that when he comes to me, he expects what I will give him; and when I go to his home, he says, "What do you bring to me?" This is how we selfishly behave in our dealings with God. While we expect from God numerous benefits and gifts, we behave indifferently and sluggishly toward his demands or try to blame him for our inability. In this regard, the Spirit today desires to offer more insight to us during our reading and meditating of his Word on how to maintain well our reciprocal relationship with God.

Indeed, God has promised us so many blessings and unthinkable benedictions. All his gifts are bundled and packaged in the form of scriptural promises. They are concerned with a fuller life—"quality life" as I love to say—that is filled with true justice, joy, peace, love, and healing. Those numerous promises have been fulfilled among Israelites both individually and socially as they are recorded in OT books.

We interpret most of God's promises made individually to his kings, judges, and prophets and socially to Jewish clans, especially Judah, as proposed to us. We have gotten this insight largely from NT writers. In this vein, we hear the archangel Gabriel reminding Mary that those OT promises of God have very well applied to her baby Jesus. In the second book of Samuel, we read God promising to King David, "I will raise up your offspring after you . . . I will establish his kingdom . . . and I will establish his royal throne forever. I will be a father to him, and he shall be a son to me . . . I will not withdraw my favor from him" (2 Sam. 7:12–16).

Apostles, like Paul, continue to profess that this realization of OT promises has happened in Jesus of Nazareth. He esteems such factor as a unique historical revelation of the mystery kept secret for long ages (Rom. 16:15–27). In addition, he exhorts us to believe and totally place our trust in God with the confirmed thought that all the promises we uphold are according to the Gospel and the proclamation of Jesus Christ; the only intention of God for such manifestation is, as Paul underscores, "to bring about [in us] the obedience of faith."

The cardinal virtues of faith, hope, and charity are intrinsically intertwined; and therefore, if we neglect one of them in our application, the other two lose their identity and vigor. This is why Paul includes all three in his remarkable song about charity (1 Cor. 13); he does the same in his discussions about faith and hope. Hence, when he writes about God's intention of bringing about the obedience of faith, he means we should relate to God's promise about Jesus in faith, hope, and charity.

There are millions of God's children, like Mary, who have lived in history as role models in living the obedience of faith. God asks us today to do the same in our lives. Our life with God should be like that of Mary, who has respected and loved all of God's promises; despite of many hurdles and odds in her personal life and very sadly not even seeing its total fulfillment, she has given gifts to God in the form of rituals, religious practices, and loving services like performing her role in the family and society sincerely and gladly. She has totally surrendered to the Giver of the gifts. Her unceasing heartbeat has been "Behold, I am the handmaid of the Lord. May it be done to me according to your word" (Luke 1:38).

As long as we live in this world, we carry not only all fulfilled promises of the Lord in our lives but also many unfulfilled ones. The Christian act of waiting for God's promises being fulfilled in every one of us demands a heavy weight of faith, hope, and charity. Let's wait with that same weight for joy, peace, and powerful coming of God to take care of our unfair life situation.

14. Wait for Jesus as a Merciful and Just Judge

They will see the Son of Man coming in a
cloud with power and great glory.
—Luke 21:27

Hoping daily in faith and love for the Second Coming of Jesus is the main characteristic of every Christian. This is why we can proudly call ourselves as Adventists, though we may belong to various denominations. Now the valid question should come to our mind: "Who is this Jesus for whom we are eagerly waiting?" And we need to get the right answer for it if we are sincere about our waiting.

In the light of scriptures and Christian tradition, we are inspired to believe that the one for whom we are waiting is not an ordinary leader as the secular world defines, nor is he a prophet (*nabi*), as our Islamic brethren consider, or one of the many incarnations of God, as our Hindu friends uphold. Rather, he is a person who is named Jesus Christ, the Son of God and the Lord of the universe.

In the midst of trials and perils troubling the entire Israel, the prophet Jeremiah was sent by God to encourage and console his people with an oracle about the wonderful days when all his promises would be fulfilled. This is what the prophet said: "In those days, at that time, I will make a just shoot spring up for David; he shall do what is right and just in the land" (Jer. 33:15). This prophecy was later understood by the church, by the inspiration of Jesus's Spirit, as a foretelling of Jesus of Nazareth, who in fact belonged to the clan of David. Plus, the prophet was speaking not only about Israel's future but also about the New Israel, the church of Jesus.

In the Gospels, we observed Jesus referring to himself as the Son of Man, which he took from the prophet Daniel, who had predicted him as the "One who would be coming from heaven in glory and power to judge the entire human family on their performances during their earthly life." As biblical scholars interpreted, the term "Son of Man" that Jesus used was to define his dual identity of both being the "glorious Son of God" and being a "suffering man of God." This might have been shocking to the Israelites of his time. He repeated such flabbergasting statement many times, especially when he was standing for the trial at the Sanhedrin. Answering the question of Caiaphas whether he was the Messiah, the Son of God, "Jesus said to him in reply, 'You have said so. But I tell you: From now on you will see the Son of Man seated at the right hand of the Power and coming on the clouds of heaven'" (Matt. 26:64). Everyone in the Sanhedrin confirmed that he was uttering a blasphemy. But he never flinched from his standpoint, and surely, we know how such a staggering took him to undergo ignominious sufferings and death.

Jesus, for whom we are waiting, is also identified by his followers as the Savior of the world. The name "Jesus" means, in Hebrew, "God saves." Israelites expected a deliverance from bondage of slavery under the Roman Empire; they were longing for his powerful coming as their prophets had foretold. History testified there were many in those days emerging with the name of Jesus and tried to work for their political liberation in violence and hatred, but this Jesus of Nazareth promised a twofold salvation—social and spiritual—that could be attained by forgiveness, love, and truth—a deliverance from sin and death. And his followers were convinced that he gave that salvation by his sacrifice on the cross.

Faith is indeed a leap into darkness but not a leap into ignorance; we should know what our faith is, where it leads us to, and who it projects. It is because of the lack of such knowledge that many among us drift away from Jesus's sheepfold. We not only should be well informed of these truths about Jesus but also put it earnestly in our daily walk of life.

As Paul attests, Jesus's disciples earnestly asked and exhorted others, while they are waiting for their Lord's coming, to follow strenuously the footsteps of Jesus. They should conduct themselves to please God and to be blameless in holiness before our God and Father at the coming of our Lord Jesus with all his holy ones (1 Thess. 3:12–4:2). Let us be enlightened more and more in our faith toward Jesus so that we fervently and meaningfully wait for him, and when he arrives, he may find us awakened, and we may encounter him not as a stringent Judge but more as a Good Shepherd who will take us with him to his chamber to partake in his eternal banquet.

15. Attention! Caution! Roadwork Ahead!

Make straight in the wasteland a highway for our God.
—Isa. 40:3b

"**A**ttention! Caution! Roadwork ahead!" We are familiar with such signboard as we drive on our highways and country roads. Surely, this is the theme of John the Baptist's message.

When I have browsed the Internet to get to know how the modern world uses the term "roadwork," I have found three usages. First, it means repair of roads, road construction, or repair work being carried out on a section of a public road or on the utilities located near it, creating a temporary obstruction for road users. Second, in the sports world, it means a training exercise consisting of long runs on roads, done especially as part of a training program. Third, in the music world, it is used to denote the activity of taking a band, especially a rock band, on a lengthy tour of performances. Through the preaching of John, God invites us to apply this triple dimension of roadwork in our Advent life.

Human life is a journey that starts at conception, but it doesn't end with a dead end. It is rather a lively pilgrimage to glorious Jerusalem. We, the disciples of Jesus, do not join the depressed people who feel very negatively that their life is heading toward its horrible dead end. Our conviction is that our life is a sort of pilgrimage marching onto a decisive goal, namely, to enter into heaven, the holy of holies, as Jews make their pilgrimage to Jerusalem, the Holy City. The prophet Baruch (Bar. 5:1–9) describes that our life in this world is like the pilgrimage toward heaven symbolized by Jerusalem. Baruch makes us realize that, in our human endeavors of enhancing our earthly life, our God accompanies us in the liberation march from the bond of social injustice and conflicts to a spiritual realm of true justice, peace, joy, and unity of the human race.

John the Baptizer, the last prophet of the OT, confirms all prophecies about our life pilgrimage and adds to them a down-to-earth explanation of it (Luke 3:1–6). He calls our pilgrim way, where we and God meet together, as "the way of the Lord." He agrees with our feelings about the rough pilgrim way of human life—a path full of ups and downs; depths, pits, and gorges; and winding roads.

As Luke portrayed, in the times of John and Jesus, people's path of life was perilous and scary in all its dimensions. Politically, people were enslaved citizens of the Roman Empire. Religiously, they were surrounded by corrupted leaders who were desecrating the holy of holies by making it a den of thieves. Socially, John and Jesus were born and bred in a tiny, little province in the eastern part of the empire; this means they were living as members of a minority group of Jews who were very sincere in observing God's commandments because the only hope for them to walk in the pilgrimage peacefully and joyfully was the belief in their Lord, who—as the prophet foretold—was "leading Israel in joy by the light of his glory, with his mercy and justice for company."

Today we encounter the same bitter life situations as Jews of Jesus's time have had, even worse still. God invites us to go on our journey with no fear despite the hurdles and odds we face in our journey. We are fully aware of the Christian path we have taken as our pilgrim way to reach God's hilltop; it is very dangerous, damaged, bloody, evil filled, full of temptations, narrow, and slippery. God tells us today we should never be fainted or frustrated on the way seeing how difficult it is to pass through this life journey because God is the one who has called us and mooted this pilgrimage of life. As Paul writes confidently, "The one who began a good work in us will continue to complete it until the day of Christ Jesus" (Phil. 1:6). We too must uphold in our hearts that our powerful, just and merciful God in Jesus's Spirit walks with us, he is Emmanuel God with us.

As we walk the walk of pilgrimage, let us be vigilant and patient, unceasingly praying and never losing hope. Plus, while we move on traveling, let us do something about the bloody path in society as Jesus have done. But before we do anything in this matter, we should try to level and repair first our own life path, which will have become a path of injustice, the road of disunity, the way of violence and terrorism. As we move on to reach our heavenly goal, we should do our best to clean the disorderly, damaged, and deteriorated path. Through John the Baptist in the Gospel, we are called to take such radical actions while we are journeying toward the coming of Jesus.

CHAPTER III

KEEP YOUR SPIRIT ATTUNED AND RETUNED TO GOD THROUGH THE DAY

16. To Err Is Human; to Repent Is Divine, But to Persist Is Devilish

God may again repent and turn from his blazing wrath.
—Jon. 3:9

I think the most central theme and message of our religion and surely of the entire Bible is that human life in this world is short lived, and therefore, every one of us must repent. This is the theme of the first but most bewildering homily of Jesus (Mark 1:14–20).

In OT, we saw God sending his messengers to his people with the one and only message of repenting as he did in Jonah's life. Jesus knew the mind of his Father, and this was why he started his public ministry with that Gospel message: "This is the time of fulfillment. The kingdom of God is at hand. Repent, and believe in the gospel." Though his first sermon was a very short one, it contained superb and brilliant exhortation. Shockingly, it contained a message perennially hurting all of us; but being the one and only Word that came out of his Father's heart, he knew his Father's mind in this regard.

The verb "repentance" means "change of mind." If we keenly read the scriptures, we will find why Jesus is—from the onset of his public preaching ministry— insisting that we repent. In the OT book of Jonah (3:1–10), we read that when we repent, the Creator God also changes his mind of punishing us. "When God saw by their actions how they turned from their evil way, he 'repented' of the evil he had threatened to do to them; he did not carry it out" (Jon. 3:10). Also, through Jeremiah, God tells us, "If that nation against whom I have decreed turns from its evil, then I will have a change of heart regarding the evil which I have decreed" (Jer. 18:8).

This means, if we positively desire to be filled with the gifts of God in our life, we should get rid of whatever God considers negative in us. Therefore, Jesus expects us to recognize our wrongdoings and be sorry about them, to feel regret about a sin or past actions and change our evil ways or habits. Positively speaking, we should come out not only of sinful behavior but also from living only on the basis of our blindfolded spiritual and religious accomplishments. We need to be growing in our salvation daily. There is no place in this life where we can be content to say, "I have arrived. I'm mature enough." Explicitly, Jesus wants us to repent of our self-satisfaction. In the book of Revelation, Jesus says, "You say, 'I am rich; I have acquired wealth and do not need a thing.' But you do not realize that you are wretched, pitiful, poor, blind and naked'" (Rev. 3:19). We must never be lying satisfied with our status quo.

According to Jesus, our repentance must be from our growing lukewarm and complacent, and we should rise and change our mind-set, either detouring or taking a U-turn to start another new life. Being tepid and self-righteous is perhaps the most dangerous mind-set for a Christian. Let us remember what Jesus is telling us in the book of Revelation (3:15–16): "I know your works; I know that you are neither cold nor hot. I wish you were either cold or hot. So, because you are lukewarm, neither hot nor cold, I will spit you out of my mouth."

Jesus also includes in his first homily one more positive reason to repent: "This is the time of fulfillment." By this, he points out that "you should grow adults; never play your life a childish game; your fulfillment in life depends on some other thing; be matured and think matured and do matured." Plus, Jesus offers us an encouraging good news in his preaching.

The second thought in his preaching is positive thinking about our human life. He says, "The kingdom of God is at hand." In other words, he proclaims to us that "you are not alone; God is with you; He is Emmanuel. So don't be afraid of your own limitations and weaknesses. Join together as a group of my disciples; and I will be with you till the end of the time."

Jesus has never left us with no other tips for what we should do after our repentance. He exhorted us, "Believe in the gospel." That is to say, we should accept all his Gospel values of justice, forgiveness, love, truth, and peace and start living and abiding by them. Then he promises that we will reach our fulfillment as what our human spirit longs for in this world and the world to come. Jesus expects us, as soon as we hear his clarion call to repent, to follow the footsteps of his first disciples, who have responded promptly to his call to follow him; they have even abandoned their nets, their family, and their friends for the sake of the eternal kingdom.

17. Everyone Is Entitled to a Second Chance

We must celebrate and rejoice because your brother was dead and has come to life again.
—Luke 15:32

Our God, being just in his judgment, is also very merciful and compassionate toward us, bestowing us a life-giving second chance whenever we fail him and ourselves in observing his laws. He has demonstrated this truth to mankind in his benevolent dealings with them. Throughout the scriptures, we observe this.

When typical sinners like King David sinned, God—though he was infuriated in his justice—stooped down to him and offered pardon. When David cried out to God for forgiveness, the Lord immediately granted it to him (2 Sam. 12:7–13).

Jesus, the beloved Son of God, never ceased for even a single moment to proclaim about the merciful character of our just God. We read in the Gospels frequently that he attested himself to be "the friend of sinners" like his Father. In one of those happenings (Luke 7:36–50), humans who were born blind were scandalized at his surprising move toward a public sinner in the presence of a very self-righteous elite crowd. They questioned him for such impropriety. He paid no attention to them because he was busy seeing in his heart his Father in heaven, with his angels, rejoicing over this moment as the sinner demonstrated her atonement for her sins. She would travel farther down the road than any of those who were now judging her. By welcoming her as Jesus did and graciously accepting her, Jesus put wind in her sails. Because a sinful woman shed tears of repentance at his feet, Jesus granted her a second chance to live again, and she indeed began to live a new and better life.

Together with this woman, we noticed that in Jesus's life so many daredevil women approaching God in Jesus boldly received forgiveness (Luke 8:2). As a result, their life was renewed, shaped, groomed, strengthened, and filled with joy and contentment. They had never experienced anything like this before. Jesus was the best person they had ever met. Hence, they were not only forgiven but also loved by Jesus. By treating them with kindness, Jesus helped them believe in their own power and goodness. They started following him wherever he went but always serving him in his needs.

All of Jesus's disciples had experienced the same in their lives. Let us remember Paul as number one in this matter. He once had been a sinful and wretched Saul, but in the middle of his life, because of God's compassion, he got forgiveness with no condition.

This is why he loves to emphasize continuously in his letters that all of us are justified not by our good deeds but by our faith in the mercy of God. Once we get forgiveness from God, we will join Paul and dare enough to say, "I have been crucified with Christ; yet I live, no longer I, but Christ lives in me; insofar as I now live in the flesh, I live by faith in the Son of God who has loved me and given himself up for me" (Gal. 2:19–20).

There are many in our midst who won't accept the possibility that people can change. They are not willing to give people a second chance. A culture that doesn't believe in redemption is a culture without hope. Often our guilt feeling and fear prevent us from drawing close to the Lord. Let us humbly turn to the Lord with all our burden of sins, confident that we will find acceptance and forgiveness. Also, with compassion and forgiveness, we have to relate ourselves to the persons whom we consider sinners. Jesus, though he hates sin, does not condemn the sinners. Come, let us go to the forgiving table of the Lord and spread such merciful tables to all our sinful friends and relatives.

18. Repentance Is Change of Biased Views

Let each of us please our neighbor for the good, for building up.
—Rom. 15:2

Before Jesus came to the public, John the Baptizer—the forerunner of the Messiah—already echoed Jesus's primary Gospel requisite to enter into his kingdom: "Repent, for the kingdom of heaven is at hand" (Matt. 3:2). Repentance is the translation of Greek word *metanoia*, meaning "to think differently after." The act of repenting means, therefore, a change of mind accompanied by regret and change of conduct, change of mind and heart, or change of consciousness. It means simply a conversion of attitude and action. By the invitation to repent, John exhorts us to alter the way we deal with our religiosity, to change from twisted old religion to new, from fake to genuine, and from reel to real.

He recommended a transition from performing all religious duties not just as external rituals but also as spiritual ones, interiorly on fire. He referred to his own ritual action of baptism in water, the relevance of which he didn't deny; but he wanted us to go beyond the mere ritual. He said, "I am baptizing you with water, for repentance, but the one who is coming after me is mightier than I. He will baptize you with the Holy Spirit and fire" (Matt. 3:11).

There was another important dimension contained in the conversion John proposed. He forewarned us to be prepared to meet the consequences of such conversion. Quoting Isaiah, saying, "Prepare the way of the Lord," he told us to be prepared for an awesome, groundbreaking, or radical view and conduct of our human life. Consequently, we would be keeping Jesus in our daily life as our way, truth, and life, who in turn would be leading us to a life of justice, peace, and love.

Indeed, through this sincere conversion of heart, our human but wrong view regarding the Messiah would be shattered; his leadership would be seen as more humble than powerful, more merciful than judging, more peaceful than violent, more tolerant than intolerant. In simple terms, as John said of Jesus, "This is the lamb of God who takes away the sins of the world."

This conversion is supposed to be total and wholistic. As we have a change of view about Jesus, we too begin to modify our attitudes about one another and to kill all the biases against our neighbors. Instantly, Paul underlines in his letters that we will be leading a Christian life of harmony and peace (Rom. 15:1–7).

In the light of Christ, we should interpret John's preaching not as a threatening but as a positive tip for managing our life. Let us remember Jesus, who called himself a vine tree, relating us to him as the branches (John 15:1–6). As John reminded, Jesus emphasized, "The Father will throw out the branches into the fire if it does not bear good fruits in proper season; even if we are branches that bear good fruits Father would prune us so that we can bear more and better ones."

The conversion, which Jesus the Messiah expects from us, is not only a change in moral behavior but also an intellectual change; it implies a new way of thinking about God and his religion. We must take seriously the demand of Jesus to see modern life through the spectrum of the fiery Spirit, which never quenches until we change our perverted mentality and our immoral and prejudiced attitudes and ways. This is the only way to make our world a better living place of unity and integrity, of justice and peace.

19. Renewal Demands Bending and Repenting

Repent, for the kingdom of heaven is at hand.
—Matt. 4:17

From the day of its inception, our Christian life revolves in and around the kingdom of God, which Jesus wants us to be immersed in deeply. To succeed in this effort of immersion, Jesus offers us a strategy as the primary action. To possess a renewed life, he advises us continuously to repent, which means not simply brooding over but most importantly rethinking, revisiting, reviewing, and reevaluating our life. It is because, as Jesus has emphasized, the presence of God is within us; God's house in this world is built more in every person's soul than anywhere. Jesus, therefore, has proclaimed that the "kingdom of heaven or God is at hand, in our midst, among us, within us." Therefore, if we desire any change in our lives, Jesus asks us to go inside of us and review our own attitudes, our own customs, our own teachings, our own value systems that we have coveted from our birth, our formation, and our society. We will be free to become the "original of God." Renewal demands both bending and repenting.

There are millions of people who live in sinful darkness in their lives. This situation of groping in darkness can be encountered by most of us while we are being tossed by doubts, worries, sicknesses, mental tortures, Down syndromes, unforgiving and stressful life, discontentment in everything we handle, and inability to discern, to manage ourselves, to make the right choices, and so on. Such a dark road takes a surprise turn when we become spiritually and morally blind. As a consequence, we not only happen to be useless to our family or society but also turn out to be social criminals, harming others in everything we are engaged in.

This adherence to darkness can make us see even the good things very badly. For example, many darkened souls—unfortunately mishandling the marvelous gift of faith—use it as source to be stonehearted, intolerant, very individualistic, totalitarians, cruel leaders, and ready even to destroy others on the basis of their faith judgment that they are the only right persons, while others are too bad to live. It is from this dark dimension or situation of human life that God wants us to be liberated.

Most of us feel very cozy and comfortable in that dark status, but regrettably, we are outside the kingdom of God and in exile, pining for a true home. Undoubtedly, our journey of the salvific liberation from darkness to light is a hard one. However, scriptures encourage that this darkness can be easily overcome. As the prophets have preached, "The people who sit in darkness have seen a great light, on those dwelling in a land overshadowed by death light has arisen" (Isa. 9:1). Gospel writers contend that this prophecy is referring to none other than Jesus of Nazareth. Jesus, who is alive today in our midst, is waiting with his open arms to accept us, though we feel ashamed of our stupidity.

At the same time, he expects us to fulfill certain prerequisites and conditions such as to express our earnestness toward his promised life, living in his bright house, and to unhesitatingly reach out to Jesus, the spiritual doctor, with no fear whatsoever regarding our past sinful life because he has promised that "only a sick person needs a doctor."

20. Celebrate Life with God in an Unbiased Mind-Set

*My son, you are here with me always;
everything I have is yours.*
—Luke 15:31

One of the God-given pleasures that we can legitimately indulge into is eating and drinking. Especially if it is a banquet with sumptuous meals and delicious select drinks, our hearts are enthralled. Such a pleasure trip turns out to be very limited and sometimes very dangerous to our health too. But the banquet to which God invites us daily to enjoy is something unique; it is healthy and ever tasty and never comes to an end. It is nothing but the banquet of God's mercy, love, compassion, and forgiveness.

It is amazing to read in the Bible how God spends not only his timeless time in his heavenly abode but also his "Emmauelic" time among humans. Jesus very well portrays through his parables that God's one and only preoccupation is celebrating joyfully; preparing sumptuous meals of joy, peace, and forgiveness; and inviting and waiting for and on all his human creatures at his table.

That is what Jesus has expounded through his three superb parables that Luke shares in his Gospel (15:4–32).

The only source of enjoyment in God's celebration is, above all, the times when we receive forgiveness and thus a warm welcome ceremony from the Lord. During those moments, our hearts beat with David's hymn: "The Lord is the redeemer of the souls of his servants; and none are condemned who take refuge in him" (Ps. 34:23). Our lips mutter frequently, "My God has forgiven me and accepted into his Banquet Chamber." It is this thought and conviction that makes us rejoice and celebrate our every minute joyfully as the younger prodigal son has done.

Unfortunately, there are too many among us who lose, like the elder son, such noble moments Jesus states in his parable. The only problem with such "elder sons" is they easily forget the fact that they too are still sinners like their younger brothers. Every human being is a sinner. Henri Nouwen has beautifully described it, writing, "We are all handicapped; some are more visibly handicapped than others." Whether our sins are more visible like those of the younger son or more hidden like those of the elder son, the message of Jesus for us is that we all need to repent and return to the Father's house. Just as the younger son does, so the elder son needs to turn back from anger and resentment and learn to share the house with the apparently undeserving younger brother.

The elder son was indeed a very nice young man, always with his beliefs and values. But he could not enjoy as much happiness as his younger brother at the father's banquet. Even though he was grown up physically, he was yet underdeveloped in his emotions and spirit.

There are too many among us who feel like the elder son and who are complacent in what we hold in life today. We are content with what we perform in religious observances, but we never have time to look into our relationship with our God. We may apparently stay inside the house of the Father, but very sadly, like the elder son, they will be far distant from the heart of the Father.

So today God speaks to us: "Are you far away from my heart of forgiving and compassion though you are inside my home? You should celebrate the life I gave you." He too, with his brokenhearted fatherliness, tells us through David, "Oh, that today you would hear his voice; do not harden your hearts . . . your ancestors tested me; they tried me though they had seen my works. Forty years I loathed that generation; I said: 'This people's heart goes astray; they do not know my ways.' Therefore I swore in my anger: 'They shall never enter my rest'" (Ps. 95:7–11).

21. The Sweet Agony of Surrendering to the Divine

You seduced me, Lord, and I let myself be seduced.
—Jer. 20:7a

In the OT scriptural passages, prophets like Jeremiah, Isaiah, and Ezekiel proclaimed to their people the one and only message from God who told, "Return to Yahweh." Before they began sharing this message of God with people, they personally listened from the same God who compelled them to obey his message and then preached about it. We heard from Jeremiah

(Jer. 20:7–9), for instance, that he truly returned to his God; but seemingly and surprisingly, the One whom he returned to didn't offer him a lot of hope and consolation.

Being duped by God, as the prophet confessed, he was compelled to preach about the reform at the time of the destruction of Jerusalem and subsequent exile; very sadly, obedience to God's call brought him great misery and abuse. He too added that his relationship with God seemed to destroy his youthful life. Not only did it force him to remain unmarried but it also created situations in which his fellow Jews regarded him as a traitor to them and their country. This was why biblical scholars named him as "a man of constant sorrow." Delivering God's Word brought the prophet tremendous pain and woe; worst still, not delivering it brought him even greater pain and woe. However, Jeremiah survived many ordeals to compose the majestic verses of both lamentation and consolation that encompassed Israel's exile and restoration. His fidelity, through trial to triumph, made him one of the great voices in the Bible.

Being seduced and overpowered by Almighty God is not an experience of Jeremiah. Anyone who has been and is fully committed to God the Supreme has been undergoing such ordeals in their lives.

Jesus, our Master, was the embodiment of that costly and bleeding encounter with God in his life. God created within him certain insatiable hunger and unquenchable thirst for fulfilling God's will. Throughout his life, he was fully aware of what God wanted him to accomplish, even though sometimes he could spell out his inability to carry on. We can remember what he experienced while he was in prayer at the Garden of Gethsemane: "Father, if you are willing, take this cup away from me; still, not my will but yours be done." During the time of his crucifixion, he had the same agonizing moment: "My God! My God! Why have you forsaken me?"

Jesus esteemed God's possessive and compulsive deal with him as the most burdensome cross in his life. But knowing the benefits thereof, he carried it willingly and freely because that was the only way to attain the ultimate destiny. Indeed, he considered it as sweet agony. Hence, he advised his disciples to follow him strenuously in taking up our crosses. Before he underwent his final agony of that cross, he advised them not to be afraid of this cross of life and resurrection, even if it demanded from them denial of one's self, relatives, and even very life (Matt. 16:21–27).

True discipleship happens only after we hear and accept this challenge. Jesus's statement helps us understand that carrying one's cross originally hasn't referred to patiently enduring some dramatic moment of suffering. It has described an ongoing, generous, open, and honest relationship with God, a daily quest to discover what God wishes of us during this specific day. Such a quest involves a real death to self and real sacrifice.

We should uphold a mysterious truth that every cross is an altar where, as Paul points out (Rom. 12:1–2), we should offer our bodies (the total earthly life) as a living sacrifice, holy and pleasing to God, our spiritual worship. I always love to assert that the cross is, after all, the "crisscrossing of God's seducing vertically and humans' surrendering horizontally."

CHAPTER IV

NEVER LOSE INNER JOY IN THE DAY'S DRUDGERIES

22. A Blissful Life Is Possible in This World, If . . .

Be glad in the Lord and rejoice, you righteous.
—Ps. 32:11a

Joining all religions of the world, Christianity accepts the experience of unending joy as its ultimate goal. Justice, peace, love, and any other virtues spoken in scriptures and by spiritual authors are simply the components of that sparkling spectrum of a joyous life. The eternal life that the Lord speaks about and promises to his disciples is simply a blissful life forever. "Bliss" is another way of saying "complete joy." We also profess that this blissful life starts already here on the earth. What makes even our earthly life blissful is the one important factor that differentiates Christianity from all other religions. That is a person, Jesus, born in Bethlehem two thousand years ago.

God has created us to be as he is, namely, as he is joyful. Therefore, our human life is totally a celebration of joy in this world to be continued in heaven. It is for this reason, we believe, that Jesus of Nazareth has been born, lived, died, and risen. The core of our Christian faith is that Jesus Christ is the true source of our complete joy. The prophet Isaiah fittingly acknowledges the right reason for Jesus's coming into this world: "The spirit of the Lord God is upon me, because the Lord has anointed me; he has sent me to bring glad tidings to the poor, to heal the brokenhearted, to proclaim liberty to the captives and release to the prisoners" (Isa. 61:1–2).

We should never forget that merely knowing and accepting Jesus as the source of joy will, in no way, offer us complete joy. True, when we accept Jesus as our Lord and Savior, the joy begins to dwell in us. However, that joy can fade away or dwindle by our carelessness in the course of our life. The only way to keep this joy getting its completeness is by allowing Jesus to interact with us, and we should develop an intimate relationship with him; in other words, it is not by simply adhering to certain doctrines and practices but more by an experiential life with God in Jesus.

Isaiah wrote how he was leading a joyful life: "I rejoice heartily in the Lord, in my God is the joy of my soul; for he has clothed me with a robe of salvation and wrapped me in a mantle of justice, like a bridegroom adorned with a diadem" (Isa. 61:10–11). The same thing was true in Mary's life: "My spirit rejoices in God my Savior," she sang. "For, he has looked upon his lowly servant."

There is one more way to preserve our joy growing: we should try our best to make others joyful. We are very grateful to Jesus proclaiming in his Sermon on the Mount that we are "the light of the world." Each one of us, by our baptism, has been sent to be the light in the world but with difference— obviously not the original Light, who is Jesus, but only the ones to give witness to this Light as John the Baptizer. Stressing vehemently about John's genuine role before Christ, the Gospel writer portrays, "John was sent from God. He came for testimony, to testify to the light, so that all might believe through him. He was not the light, but came to testify to the light. And this is the testimony of John."

Obviously, we are supposed to be the light of Christ in the same way as the moon is a reflection of the sun.

There are so many people out there who live in darkness, feeling lonely, rejected, and marginalized. They are sincerely waiting for the light of Christ to shine on them and to turn their lives into experiences of joy. Jesus has entrusted that work to us so that our joy may be complete. Our dream of this blissful joy will wither away or never become complete unless and until we share that joy with others who need it as our Master expects.

Let us remember the great apostle Paul who has lived according to our Master's demand. This is why, even while he is persecuted, imprisoned, and waiting for his final end, he could encourage his fellow Christians, "Rejoice always. Pray without ceasing. In all circumstances give thanks, for this is the will of God for you in Christ Jesus . . . The one who calls you is faithful, and he will also accomplish it" (1 Thess. 5:16–24).

23. Never-Ending Joy through a Rare-Blend life

Rejoice in the Lord always. I shall say it again: rejoice!
—Phil. 4:4

Prophets of OT, while they have foretold about the coming of a redeeming Messiah, have prophesied also the inevitable results of his coming. One among them is a joy-filled life. We read Isaiah prophesying that at the arrival of Immanuel, God with us, the entire nature will be rejoicing with joyful song (Isa. 35:1–2); and he too says, "Here is your God, he comes with vindication; with divine recompense he comes to save you. Then the eyes of the blind shall see, and the ears of the deaf be opened; then the lame shall leap like a stag, and the mute tongue sing for joy" (Isa. 35:4b–6).

In this connection, we would remember Jesus acknowledging that all the prophecies of Isaiah had been fulfilled in his coming (Luke 4:16–21). And Jesus too confirmed through John the Baptizer's disciples, "Go and tell John what you hear and see: the blind regain their sight, the lame walk, lepers are cleansed, the deaf hear, the dead are raised, and the poor have the good news proclaimed to them" (Matt. 11:4–5).

From the beginning of Jesus's Messianic mission, he was firm that his followers would be filled with joy, which would be complete if they not only talk his talk but also walk his walk of enduring love and compassion. Accordingly, he blended both our hope-filled dreaming of, and waiting patiently for, rejoicing at his Second Coming—as James wrote, "The coming of the Lord is at hand; and he is standing before the gates" (James 5:7–9)—and our daily chores of love-based performance to make others more rejoicing as *in persona Christi*.

For such a rare-blended life, John the Baptizer had been among many role models and messengers of God. John was praised by Jesus for his remarkable life of this "rare blend": he was firm and unshaken, *not a reed that is swayed by the wind* in his enduring waiting for the Messiah; he lived a simple and humble life, *not dressed royally in fine clothing*; he was more than a prophet and teacher; and he repaired and renewed and turned the hearts of people to fully comply with God's justice and compassion. When people asked him what they should do in their day-to-day life, he insisted they should lead a just and compassionate life (Luke 3:10–14).

We, disciples of Jesus, who profess our faith and love in our Master are asked by him to keenly observe the evidence of his words and deeds and to make a free and right decision in our discipleship. He expects us never to be tired of proclaiming his Gospel of mercy and compassion day in and day out; it should not be merely by words but much more so in activities. In his physical absence, we must act as Jesus by making others, especially the needy, joyful.

We may try our best to move and work within the enlightened territory of God; however, we should never think that there will be no problems and hurdles. They are part and parcel of our discipleship. At those moments, as one leader has said, "We better have our own vision, and we better have our own will and our own passion and determination; holding always in mind that now the life requires work and sacrifice and sometimes it's painful, but there is a lot of joy and there is a lot of hope and possibility."

24. God-Favored Humans of Goodwill Are Ever Joy Filled

You have brought them abundant joy and great rejoicing.
—Isa. 9:2a

A recent research study of "culturometrics" (a fancy term to describe quantitative data analysis applied to individuals in society) demonstrates that among the top one hundred historical celebrities, Jesus is number one. Very frankly, this is not the only reason why we are proud to be called Jesus's followers. There is something more to it.

Whenever we read and celebrate the birth of Jesus, we hear from God a twofold important good news to the world: "Glory to God in the highest" and "Peace and joy to those on whom God's favor rests—the people of goodwill." God, as a benevolent Father, because of his uncontrollable love for us, performs an unthinkable, curious, remarkable but weird act for the sake of his adopted children and the entire human race. That is what we hear from the scriptures.

Our Father in heaven, out of his recklessness of immense love, not only emptied his only begotten Son but also made him take the form of a tiny, little boy—vulnerable, weak, and fragile, like all humans who are born like bundles of flesh and bones. In a way, the Father ordered his Son to live like a slave of love and a sacrificial Lamb. At the same time, he also did a marvelous deed to his Son. He made his Son resurrected and take up all the works of his Father in his hand.

This is why we all fully agree with the prophet Isaiah to honor Jesus of Nazareth with words like "He is Wonder-Counselor, God-Hero, Father-Forever, and Prince of Peace" (Isa. 9:5–6). By appropriating God's gratuitous favor through this Jesus, we who begin to live obedient and committed to God's will, that is, human goodwill, are filled with true joy and genuine peace. Scriptures abound in spelling out these results. "The people who walked in darkness have seen a great light; upon those who dwelt in the land of gloom a light has shone. You have brought them abundant joy and great rejoicing" (Isa. 9:1–2).

Historically, we observe these proven characteristics and qualities in every person who has been committed to God's goodwill. The friends of the joy filled Jesus have always been lovers of peace. As they stand and walk erect with goodwill long to see true peace settled in the hearts and minds of the whole humanity. It is true today more than ever before; in front of the cross and crib, they may cry aloud as the psalmist mourns in Psalm 120, "Long enough have I been dwelling with those who hate peace! I am for peace, but when I speak, they are for fighting." However, we can observe an internal peace settling inside their minds and hearts. They are always smiling sunshine to people around them.

These humans of goodwill never flinch from what Paul exhorts about love. "Owe nothing to anyone, except to love one another; for the one who loves another has fulfilled the law" (Rom. 13:8–10). Their love always seeks the good of others, forgives everything others do out of malice and weakness, and never sells and buys other people for the sake of their personal profit. They have developed a personality that can both adopt and adapt—I have taken these two words from a wise saying: "Adopt your own views and adapt to others' views too." This is 100 percent true policy of any humans of goodwill. Adopting means approving, embracing, and surely and firmly implementing their values, being enlightened from the wisdom of their God; but at the same, they too must adapt, which refers to amicably adjusting and even bending to the views and teachings of others for the sake of the common good, according to the signs and situations of time and place.

25. What Should We Do to Seize the Christian Joy?

The just will be glad; they will rejoice before God.
—Psa. 68:4a

A genuinely committed Christian life is a life of joy. It cannot be anything else. According to scripture and our church tradition, the entire Christian life is a joyful time and definitely not a gloomy one.

Prophets, like Zephaniah (Zeph. 3:14–18), and apostles, like Paul (Phil. 4:4–7), were genuinely committed to God and intimately connected to his love. They were true to their religion. Therefore, they could be full of joy and express that joy in their poems, writings, and letters and inspiring their fellow men to have the same feelings of joy. They even made their God sing with them the song of joy. They enlisted so many reasons for such joyful feelings. But one thing was very clear: this joyful attitude was simply the result of their uninterrupted religious commitment to the God they worshipped.

We too, as committed disciples of Jesus and members of his religion, are supposed to be filled with this complete joy because of the kind of God we have, the kind of God Jesus has revealed to us right from the very first Christmas. He is called Immanuel, that is, God with us, God for us, and God on our side. He is a God in whom we can believe and trust as absolutely and entirely and only good, and we believe in this kind of God even in the midst of seemingly insuperable trials and sufferings. He is a God who is kind, merciful, understanding, considerate, constantly loving, and caring. This is the beautiful, wonderful kind of God who has come to us some two thousand years back, continues to come to us, and will come to us even at the very end of ages. And because we know that this is the kind of God we have, we are at ease, at peace, and therefore able to be full of joy in all of life, without any gloom, fear, guilt, or anxiety, notwithstanding our faults, failures, weaknesses, and blindness, notwithstanding even our sins.

Very sadly, we observe that so little among us are joyful people and that many are riddled with fear, guilt, and anxiety. If we desire to be liberated from these sources of sadness to get back our original joy-filled life bestowed at our baptism, we should ask ourselves, "What is wrong with us?" And we also should ask the Lord as the Jewish crowd asked John the Baptizer, "What then should we do?"

The right answer comes from God in the words of John: First, he says, "Whoever has two tunics should share with the person who has none. And whoever has food should do likewise." It means that accepting the Gospel demands a change in one's personal conduct. We need a radical change from a self-centered personality to a self-sharing one. We must become persons who love to share, rather than persons who are avaricious to accumulate the good things in life.

Next is finger-pointing, an unjust habit of tax collectors of his time. He emphasizes, "Stop collecting more than what is prescribed." John proposes another kind of radical change from unjust behavior to a justice-oriented life.

Tax collectors, in Jesus's time, had a bad reputation of paying a lump sum to the empire and were then left to their own devices to get back that money and make a profit. Such a dishonest and unjust system led to a good deal of extortion, which hurt the welfare of the people, particularly of the poor citizens.

In addition, John said, "Do not practice extortion, do not falsely accuse anyone, and be satisfied with your wages." It was his answer to the question raised by soldiers who were burdened with anxieties in balancing their life. Thus, John recommended to people a radical change from arrogant power play to compassionate service.

While he preached through his words all the above-listed messages, he preached also another very important one by his own life. It was about the need of a radical change from a proud mind to a humble melting heart. He was very straightforward and humble in performing his duties as the forerunner of Christ. One example to this was included in the Gospel of Luke (3:10–18). When he was asked whether he was the Messiah, he never bluffed or gave any confusing answer. Rather, he was plain in saying that he was not the Messiah, whose sandals he was even unworthy to untie.

To sum up all the advice of John, to be eternally joyful is simply to lead a life of commitment to the Lord and live a godly life. And as Fr. Tony de Mello says in his book *Awareness*, "We have everything we need here and now to be happy. The problem is that we identify our happiness with people or things we don't have and often can't have."

26. Becoming the Cheeriest Groomsman for Jesus

Even if I am poured out as a libation,
I rejoice and share my joy with all of you.
—Phil. 2:17

Many of us confuse the term "happiness" with "joy." For example, at certain days, certain moments, or even seasons, we tend to feel like floating in the air with euphoria. We think and say that we are joyful. No, we aren't. We are merely happy because our zest stays only for a while and then fades away once the gala time comes to an end. The reason the feelings fade is that we are created not just for happiness but also for joy. There is a vast difference between the two.

Happiness comes from happenings. But joy is a distinctively holy and religious experience that springs up from deep within a faith-filled heart. Joy remains untouched by outward circumstances, and it is not extinguished even by suffering, struggle, or sorrow.

It was this joy that Jesus came to give to us. He affirmed to his disciples, "I have said these things to you so that my Joy may be in you, and that your joy may be complete." Jesus came on the earth to give not mere earthly happiness but also joy, which is eternal happiness.

Throughout his life, he behaved as a "jolly good fellow." He had shown this character already while he was in his mother's womb. Luke pointed out in his Gospel (1:39–44) two pregnant women greeting each other and the baby Jesus from inside Mary psychically and spiritually, in a way, sharing his joy with baby John, who was in the womb of Elizabeth, who then burst out, saying, "For at the moment the sound of your greeting reached my ears, the infant in my womb leaped for joy." This joyful mind-set stayed with Jesus till his last breath. Nothing would deter him from coming out of his genuine inner joy.

In addition to his promise of bestowing us complete joy, he has demonstrated the way to covet this wonderful gift. First, he testifies that this is possible only when we totally surrender to our God, the Creator. The letter to the Hebrews spells out this truth of how Jesus has begun his life in this world. "When Christ came into the world, he said: 'Sacrifice and offering you did not desire but a body you prepared for me; in holocausts and sin offerings you took no delight. Then I said, "As is written of me in the scroll, behold, I come to do your will, O God"'" (Heb. 10:5–10). Jesus wants us to hold a similar attitude in our lives when he has said yes to his Father when he has come to this world. For that yes, he had to pay a tremendous price by sacrificing his very self, his life, and all his glory and identity.

His sacrifice is indescribable. His identity and nature, as we strongly uphold, is divine. The prophet Micah has already proclaimed (5:1–4) that Jesus is the ruler in Israel. His origin is from of old. He will rule with power; his rule will reach to the ends of the world. He is also called "peace," not just a peacemaker or prince of peace but the source of peace. Despite all these highest qualities, Jesus has said yes to God's will and emptied himself, detached himself from his true identity, and accepted to be born as a slave. And Paul won't stop writing about his admiration for this humble and sacrificial attitude of Jesus in all his letters.

Following his footsteps and messages of joy, we witnessed in human history millions of people who gained complete joy. Mary, the mother of Jesus—first bowing down to her Creator—said, "Behold the handmaid of the Lord, be it done unto me according to your word." And for such humble gesture, she experienced this joy as she sang, "My spirit rejoices in God my savior."

Along with so many disciples of Jesus, John the Baptizer—with humble surrender to his God—was daring enough to bow down to a new preacher and teacher in the person of Jesus and point out Jesus as the Lamb of God, smilingly admitting, "The one who has the bride is the bridegroom; the best man, who stands and listens for him, rejoices greatly at the bridegroom's voice. So this joy of mine has been made complete. He must increase; I must decrease" (John 3:29–30).

The apostle Paul was always joyful in his ministry. He learned how to live and rejoice in every circumstance. While he was in prison, he would write with exuberance, "Rejoice in the Lord always! I say it again. Rejoice!"

Every one of us crave for true joy. But true joy can't be defined in words, nor can it be measured or tested in any scientific lab. It can only be experienced. Most of it exists in the spiritual realm. We know by our past lives that we, by ourselves, cannot experience such true and complete joy, nor can any other human being, pet, or thing supplement it. This is why Jesus expects us to always approach God, who is the source and storage of that joy. Joy becomes possible only after we lend ourselves to his Spirit; finding out how selfish we are and how we live our daily life filled with injustice and hatred, we should start working on those imperfections.

27. Complete Joy Is the Result of Total Love

My joy may be in you and your joy may be complete.
—John 15:11

Most of the disciples of Jesus find it hard to listen and practice many of the Master's demands, specifically his new command "Love one another." The world knows our Master has led a paradoxical life on the earth that spells out a bewildering fact: he has lived to die but died to live as a grain of wheat that dies and disappears so that, from it, a newer life can sprout. He wants the same order of life to be lived by his followers.

In the history of Christianity, we noticed that all disciples—committed to Jesus's paradoxical way of life—lived a life of death but finally died a victorious death that led them to eternal joy and bliss. The more they died in life to sin and to other imbalanced ways of humanness, the happier they were in the midst of trials and persecutions.

As a matter of fact, such a paradoxical life is not that easy to lead in this world. Therefore, Jesus has offered us a strategy that is very close to our hearts. "As the Father loves me, so I also love you. Remain in my love . . . This is my commandment: love one another as I love you" (John 15:9–17).

He wants us to remain in the way he loves us, in the way he has died to live in love, in the manner he has lived to die in and for love. He has emphasized this fact when he has said, "No one has greater love than this, to lay down one's life for one's friends." Inhaling Jesus's breath of love, the apostle John writes, "Beloved, let us love one another, because love is of God . . . Whoever is without love does not know God, for God is love . . . not that we have loved God, but that he loved us and sent his Son as expiation for our sins" (1 John 4:7–10).

When Jesus asks us to remain in his love, there are two criteria that will help us distinguish true love from a fake one. The first criterion of true Christian love is one that always proceeds from and ends with the recognition of our privilege to have been chosen by Jesus, who has categorically stated, "It was not you who chose me, but I who chose you and appointed you to go and bear fruit that will remain." True love does not remain isolated, being puffed up with proud individualism that forgets Jesus, our Master, who has been remaining with us as Immanuel. Jesus cannot bear any spiritual form of egoism, staying closed up in oneself and searching for one's own advantage. Therefore, to remain in Jesus's love means to be able to communicate and dialogue uninterruptedly both with God and our neighbors.

The second criterion is that love is more in deeds than in words. It is not a saga of love, a fantasy. True love is not soap-opera love, a whim, or something that makes our heart beat a little faster and then nothing more. Rather, it is found in concrete actions, which we discover from the apostles' love in action.

Peter, though he was aware of the biased attitude and the unlawful custom of early Christians' relationship with the Gentiles, went to pay a friendly visit to Cornelius and his friends (Acts 10:25–48). The main reason was, as he stated, that the "God of love has shown him that he should not call any person profane or unclean." The astounding result of such love in action was, while Peter was still speaking these things, the Holy Spirit fell even on all the Gentiles who were listening to the Word.

True love is not simple enthusiasm; many times, it can be a painful act that must be borne as Jesus has carried the cross. Unquestionably, only by remaining in Christ's love and keeping his commandment of love in attitude and in action will the disciples find the remarkable and unending joy that our Master has promised.

CHAPTER V

STAY PUT ALL DAY CARRYING THE CROSS OF LOVE

28. The Mind-Blowing Triune Love Is Our God

Whoever is without love does not know God, for God is love.
—1 John 4:8

God can be called various beautiful names according to the ages, cultures, and experiences of human beings around the globe. However, the most striking and the closest one to our hearts and minds is the name that NT authors have used in their writings. And that is "God is love." Every other explanation about him is centered on and swirling around the name "Love." Our uninterrupted Christian faith is that God is love not only in relation to us or to the created universe but also in himself, in his intimacy, essentially, infinitely, eternally. And Augustine rightly insists, "If we see love, we see the Trinity."

Love in God is his origin, basis, process, and total life. Love is his personality. "Love" means a spirit of relating, a sense of togetherness, a reality of bending and binding with the other. Therefore, God the Love is not solitude but communion; the ocean of his being vibrates with an infinite movement of love, reciprocity, exchange, encounter, family, and celebration. This is the background of our identification of God as the Triune God, about whom let us meditate and pray this weekend.

From scriptures and traditions, we discover the "creative love of God" as the Father who has formed the universe out of chaos and nothingness. But the deeper truth is he has created this world out of love for human beings. Moses, writing about one of his encounters with God at Mount Sinai, says, "The Lord passed before him and cried out, The Lord, the Lord, a merciful and gracious God, slow to anger and rich in kindness and fidelity" (Exod. 34:4–9).

We too are instructed by our faith resources about the "redemptive love" of the Son of God, who has reformed the world through his passion, death, and resurrection. This redemptive love is meant for all but especially for those who have strayed away from the divine love. "God so loved the world that he gave his only Son, so that everyone who believes in him might not perish but might have eternal life" (John 3:16–18).

God's Son, Jesus, therefore went in search of the least, the lost, and the last in society. His love broke the barriers of division and built the bridges of love among people, social groups, and religious compartments. His love embraced all the spheres of human life: tax collectors, lepers, sinners, prostitutes, prodigals, the abandoned, and the unwanted. He still continues to redeem people from all these bondages through his representatives.

From the biblical and church history, we too learn that the unchangeable "sanctifying love" of the Spirit of God from the beginning of creation continues through the centuries, sanctifying the kings, the priests, and the prophets, apostles, and disciples of Jesus, who have been chosen to lead the people of God. The same Spirit performs the same work of sanctifying love in our midst. The Spirit immerses us in the rhythm of the divine life, which is a life of love, making us have personal relations with the Father and the Son. When the Spirit dwells in us, the Word—the Son of God, who bestows the Spirit—is in us too, and the Father is present in the Word.

When we hold strongly that God is the Triune Love, then we begin to understand God much more easily and appreciate what he has done for us. We discover that he keeps loving us as a forgiving and merciful Father who cares and is as tender as a mother, as the Son who has become one of us and made us free at the cost of his life, and as a Spirit of love, unity, and strength who keeps guiding and inspiring us. This is why Paul never misses, in his greetings to Christians, an emphasis on the Trinitarian nature of God: "The grace of the Lord Jesus Christ and the love of God and the fellowship of the Holy Spirit be with all of you" (2 Cor. 13:13).

29. Jesus's Love Command Is Three in One

Love God . . . love neighbors as yourself.
—Matt. 22:3–39

Containing all the laws and regulations written by OT writers as God has proposed to humanity, Jesus, our grand Teacher, has offered us a small package of how to maintain our life. Though it may seem twofold, interpreting this law package, theologians and preachers ascertain that God in Jesus has placed before us three lovers to be loved, of whom two are mentioned directly and the third indirectly. He wants us first "to love him," second "to love our neighbors," and third "to love ourselves." Love your neighbor as yourself.

By experience, we know it is very hard to love our neighbors in the same way we love ourselves. To love oneself is the norm of survival for every human being. Loving our neighbors becomes an extra fitting into our lives. As long as others feed our self-love, it is okay to love them. But it is something beyond our self to love anyone who is different from us, who are a pain in our neck, who are strangers, who are useless to us, to our family, and to society such as widows, orphans, refugees, enemies, and older people. Yet God expects us to love our neighbors as ourselves. This is what God has been commanding from the beginning. "You shall not oppress or afflict a resident alien . . . you shall not wrong any widow or orphan." Besides, he too—as a champion for these vulnerable and needy people—has threatened his people with curse and death if they violate his order of neighborly love (Exod. 22:20–26).

Since God knows our inability to love ourselves and others in an integrated way according to his will, he—out of compassion and mercy—has designed his law in such a way that he places himself as the Lover who grabs our "first love" for him; and by such divine love, he makes it easier for us to integrate both loves. He insists, "Love yourself for my sake and love your neighbors too for my sake." This sounds like a mother directing her child to love his siblings for her sake, even though he does not like them. If that boy possesses true love for his mother, surely, he will forget his prejudices against his brothers and start loving them for the love of his mother.

This is why God points out that loving him should be our priority in life and that it should be total. Once it is well set on that foundation, we can build up our home of love for others and ourselves. When God is worshipped and loved in the right perspective and at his terms, we begin to love our body, our soul, and our very life; and added to it, we will include our neighbors with the right motivation and sincere concern. An Indian proverb sums up the above: "The narrow minded ask, 'Are these people strangers, or are they members of our tribe?' But to those in whom love dwells, the whole world is but one family." What will happen is we start seeing God in everyone we meet.

Once, a journalist visiting Saint Teresa in Calcutta watched her dressing the wounds on a man with gangrene in his leg. He was appalled by the wound but was full of admiration for the mother who seemed to show no disgust as she was cleaning the suppurating wound. "I wouldn't do that for a million dollars," said the journalist.

"Neither would I," said Mother Teresa. "I do it for love of God."

Certainly, saints like Mother Teresa who have tried their best to follow the three-in-one love command of God have testified that they have not reached its total success. The Christian life is not a done deal. It is an ongoing process of becoming. Every day we take steps to becoming a full-fledged Christian. It is very true in the case of fulfilling the three-in-one love command of God in Jesus.

30. Keep the Inner Light of Love Burning to Meet the Lover

Stay awake, for you know neither the day nor the hour.
—Matt. 25:3

When we read in the Gospel Jesus's exhortations about our final hours, many may think, *Does Jesus ask us to be prepared for the worst?* This is how they misinterpret Jesus and get themselves ready to face any casualties as people have done preparing at the eve of the year 2000 to face Y2K or Millennium Bug.

But if we look deeper into Jesus's sayings (Matt. 25:1–13), in the light of his Spirit, it is indeed a very salutary one; it reminds us to be on our guard, to have our priorities right, and to expect to be called to face God at any time. Jesus invites us to be prepared for the best. This positive consideration emerges when we see him comparing our final hour with the wedding. Any wedding invitation makes us feel joyful as it summons us to join in one of the happiest celebrations in human life. Jesus invites us to a heavenly wedding reception, which will be a feast beyond our wildest dreams.

Jesus's parables about the reign of God are simply his admonishing words to prepare us well for that great day when we shall see him face-to-face. Our Christian faith and its practices are the means by which we anticipate that day without fear. Only the authentic Christians who have been gifted with the fullness of truth can face that most terrible of day without trepidation. The fullness of truth that comes from Jesus exhorts us to be responsible, in the first place, for our own salvation.

The ten bridesmaids in the parable, equipped with their lit torches and waiting for the bridegroom, told us a lesson by which we should examine our own lives. The five foolish virgins did not prepare adequately; they did not bring oil along with them. They could not predict how long the waiting period might be. This was why Jesus ended his parable by saying, "Stay awake." When Jesus urged us to be awake and be prepared for "that day," he meant we needed to daily live our Christian faith fully and consciously.

Unfortunately, our worry is always about our human sleep of death, which may be either the effect of our own sinfulness or that of our neighbors. We too are anxious about how all of us will be withstanding and scoring on that day.

Nonetheless, the Spirit—through Paul—encourages all of us about the happenings of that day: "Then we who are alive, who are left, will be caught up together with them in the clouds to meet the Lord in the air. Thus we shall always be with the Lord" (1 Thess. 4:13–18). One thing is certain: those of us who, as the wise virgins, love, seek, and watch diligently and prudently for the arrival of Jesus—who has been metaphorically named in scriptures as the Eternal Wisdom—and busy ourselves in our daily tasks of loving and merciful deeds will meet the wise Bridegroom on that day and will be taken into the wedding feast with him. It is biblical truth: "One who watches for her [Jesus, the Wisdom] at dawn will not be disappointed, for . . . seeking those worthy of her, she graciously appears to them on the way, and goes to meet them with full attention" (Wis. 6:14–16).

31. Let Us Love Our Life as It Is Now

The Lord bless you and keep you!
—Num. 6:24

It is said that when a young man has asked, "What should I do to be happy for life?" a sage has told him, "Just love your life as it is." Though it sounds good, the answer seems unsatisfactory for many of us. When we reflect over our life over the past years, especially last year, though it might have been somewhat productive and creative, perhaps more sentimental and pleasurable as well as a little bit exciting, for most of us, life has seemed very vulnerable, demanding, risky, unfair, and unpredictable. Hence, our mind bubbles with the question Have I to love such a life, which is a blending of ups and downs, negative and positive, a life that is transient and temporary? However, the Spirit asks us today to fathom the deep truth contained in the answer of the wise man and meditate on it.

Let us go back to the sage's answer: to make ourselves happy, we have to love life not as it looks like but as it is. Many a time, human life is misinterpreted and misunderstood by all of us. This is why we do not truly love it. We pretend to love it. But as Christians, through the revelation we have gotten from God through Jesus Christ, human life is not as it appears. Our life in this world is a gift from God. We are his creatures, created in the likeness and image of the Word, which has existed already in the beginning. We have been predestined by the Triune God to enter into a relationship with him and stay with him eternally. We, as his special creations, possess abundant gifts and resources to live in this world for us to know, to love, and to serve him.

To safeguard us, nourish us, and make us move forward fearlessly and happily at every step of our life, he offered us abundant and powerful promises of blessings. He even delegated his power of blessing to his elders: "The Lord let his face shine upon you, and be gracious to you! The Lord look upon you kindly and give you peace! So shall they invoke my name upon the Israelites, and I will bless them" (Num. 6:25–27).

Unfortunately, such a beautiful, gratified, and blessed life has been utterly damaged by our frequent and stupid disobedience. Sin has spoiled the amazing image in us. So God has sent his beloved Son to us to heal that image of God in us and redeem it to its original status of beauty, power, wisdom, and godliness. Our life has been renovated by our covenant with the Son of God, Jesus. Paul gratefully testifies (Gal. 4:4–7) to the immeasurable grace we have received through the Son's coming: "When the fullness of time had come, God sent his Son, born of a woman, born under the law, to ransom those under the law, so that we might receive adoption. He too sent the spirit of his Son into our hearts, crying out, 'Abba, Father!' So we are no longer a slave but a child, and if a child then also an heir, through God."

In the same spirit, the church prays in one of its morning prayers, "Lord God, you restore our human nature to a dignity higher than you gave it at creation." The life we live today is truly face-lifted and supported by so many sources of grace in the church—from the scriptures, traditions, sacraments, and the entire body of Christ.

Given the factual truths listed above, God expects us to start anything, any day, and any enterprise of earthly life with strong hope and start again dreaming the dreams of heaven. We are not to be depressed discovering in life the fact that I am not okay, or you are not okay. We should rather be fully convinced that our life is worth living because Jesus is okay. Also, in our journey of life, we have around us God as a Father, Jesus as a Brother, the Spirit as a Lover, Mary as our heavenly mother, and all the holy ones who have already gone to heaven as our brothers and sisters. "When all of them are with us who will be against us?" So let us love our life as it is as of today.

32. Love Makes All the Difference

*No one has greater love than this to lay
down one's life for one's friends.*
—John 15:13

Every human being born in this world has got the bucket list of dreams as this lady has had. Every disciple of Jesus surely is expected by God to hold such a bucket list of dreams for our human survival and satisfaction. However, to win the race of life, to fight the good fight in life, and finally to covet the crown of victory at the end of life, the same God wants us to add one more important dream into the bucket list. That should be both the first and the last dream to be accomplished in each one's life. And that dream is to become a prophet, namely, to be a man/woman of God.

Prophets had written in their OT books that they were born for greater things. They were called to be prophets, namely, to be men and women of God dedicated only to him as his messengers or liaisons. Actually, when the prophet Jeremiah wrote such affirmations (Jer. 1:4–5, 17–19) about his prophetic identity, he was living in a moment of great suffering, during which he had realized the failure of his mission. Suddenly, he felt divinely inspired to recall the original grace and draw strength from it against disappointment.

What we noticed in the lives of prophets in the Bible was when they were dedicated to their God, they also dedicated themselves to God's sons and daughters. Preserving the high self-esteem God instilled within them, the prophets plunged themselves into the troubled waters of earthly life, however dirty it could be.

In this regard, Jesus—the greatest of all the prophets—showed an example to us. As soon as he enthusiastically proclaimed to the public the manifesto of his ministry, the opposition started rising against him (Luke 4:22–29). Unlike many leaders who enjoyed what had been called a honeymoon period after taking on the burden of authority, Jesus seemed to have gone straight from the proverbial frying pan into the fire. No sooner had he amazed his listeners with his stated agenda of good news, healing, and liberation than his detractors began to attack him, criticizing him for his all-too-familiar origins and for his willingness to offer his gifts to the heavily non-Jewish population of Capernaum before he did so for his hometown friends and neighbors. As a matter of fact, Jesus accepted all the inimical oppositions smilingly and sportively. This sort of chivalrous behavior had been generated out of his heart burning with love for God, whom he fondly called Abba, and for his human brothers and sisters, to whom he related intimately as friends.

As Jesus and other prophets, those of us who commit our life as discipled leaders of Jesus will encounter different whimsical reactions from our people. Sometimes they will speak highly of us and will be amazed at the gracious words that come from our mouth. Many times, they might suspect and underestimate our identity. And several times, they will be filled with fury to hurl us down headlong. If as real prophets we are filled with the love for God and for our neighbors, we can take the challenges come what may; we will take with audacity all the rejections, oppositions, and hostilities against our prophetic efforts.

We usually love to hear and hold very warmly all the positive things told by God about our identity and take pride in it, calling ourselves the chosen race, royal priesthood, and people set apart; and precisely, we are called to be prophets whom God esteems as his beloved, as his love partner, and as his children. However, when God expects us to wear agape love as our main boot to walk in life, it surely hurts us because love always disciplines and curtails our freedom and independence, and it always kills our self-centered gratification. Love is indeed a dreadful task.

The Russian writer Fyodor Dostoevsky describes love this way: "Love in action is a harsh and dreadful thing." Jesus and other prophets are fully aware of this. As modern-day prophets, let us grasp this: in small things as in great ones, love makes all the difference.

33. Make Life
A Perfect Sacrifice of Covenant with God

Offer your bodies as a living sacrifice,
holy and pleasing to God.
—Rom. 12:1b

Our entire life as a human is fully based and centered on promises; this is 100 percent true in our dealings with other human beings. It includes also our dealings with God. In the scriptures, our Christian life is described as a covenantal journey to reach our destiny of glory. It depends solely on the covenant God has made with us and mutually on how we freely respond and commit to it in our daily life.

This historical covenant is of three dimensions. The first dimension is the fact that it is the Creator who has taken the initiative in making the covenant with his human creatures and substantiated it through his mighty deeds in their midst. In OT, we read God confirming, "You have seen how I treated the Egyptians and how I bore you up on eagles' wings and brought you to myself . . . I am the Lord your God, who brought you out of the land of Egypt, out of the house of slavery . . . You shall be my people and I will be your God."

Second, through the gift of commandments, God gave to humans directions to govern the relationship between him and humans (Exod. 20:3–23:33). And as the third dimension of the remarkable covenant, we were told that covenants between God and Israel were often confirmed as a seal by the sacrifice of an animal, whose blood was offered to expiate sin and whose flesh was cooked and shared as a sign of communion between him and his people (24:9–11).

We know the sad fact that several such covenants were made and broken throughout Israel's history. However, God's prophets continued to dream and proclaim of the covenant of God as unconditional and everlasting. Unlike the stipulations of previous covenants, which were carved in stone, the terms of the covenant—envisioned by the prophet Jeremiah— "would be recorded in the human heart," and all, from least to greatest, would be privileged to know God. This covenant would also bring the forgiveness of sins. Humankind would be forever free of guilt, for God would remember their sins no more.

Those promises remained only as mere dreams until Jesus came. It was only through Jesus and through his embrace of the cross that this covenant was realized. Jesus, seen in the Gospels, had been emphatic in confirming the fact that his entire life, together with its challenges, had only one raison d'être, namely, to establish, solidify, and ratify the new and eternal covenant that the prophets had dreamed and promised centuries before. Jesus made this amazing covenant come true by revealing God in human flesh and blood and by enunciating, in his every word and deed, the love God has for sinners. Love of God and love for one another became the law by which this covenant would stand. To guarantee this unending love relationship, Jesus used his bleeding and death as a grain of wheat falling to the earth and dying to sprout new life. He offered himself to be lifted on the cross so that sinners would be forgiven (John 12:20–33).

Attesting to the historical contribution of Jesus toward the renewal of God's covenant with humans, the letter to the Hebrews announced that it was not just the moment and act of death of Jesus that had a great effect on God's covenant with us but also his entire life, in which he obeyed God's will in every moment. He was conceived in obedience, he was born poor in obedience, he was tempted in obedience, he earned his daily bread by sweat and blood in obedience, he encountered trouble after trouble daily in obedience. Thus, he made himself as the perfect sacrifice and the most fitting seal for the covenant made between God and humans (Heb. 5:7–9).

Like Jesus, we have to become a fitting sacrifice in the covenantal life with God. This is the goal of us Christians as we travel this earthly journey of the covenant. Like him, we have to grow in wisdom and grace; we should grow in obedience by suffering the flings and arrows of our unpredictable life. We gradually grow in grace by traveling the dusty road of everyday events. That is the way to make our filthy, vulnerable, fragile life a perfect sacrifice for our covenant with God.

34. The Cross Is Not a Sign of a Death Wish But of a Life Spring

I will give the right to eat from the tree of
life that is in the garden of God.
—Rev. 2:7b

In our churches and in most of our homes, the cross or crucifix is given a place of honor. Does that mean that we have to love our sufferings? No, but it suggests that we love the love it points out, we love the Lover who is hanging there for us, we love the One who so loves us that he has sent us his own beloved Son and made him die on the cross. He has saved us by his cross and resurrection. He is the sign that God loves us so much that he has given us his only Son to bring us forgiveness, life, and love. And more than all this, the cross has become a tree of life as Paul explicates (1 Cor. 1:18–31).

In the Gospel (John 3:14–21), we hear Jesus explaining splendidly to Nicodemus the unfathomable goal of his life: "For God so loved the world that he gave his only Son, so that everyone who believes in him might not perish but might have eternal life."

Though the God of wisdom is fully aware of our sinful condition, surmounted by so many transgressions and blunders against God's love, he proves his identity and worth as a great lover. Paul, in his letter, elaborates this unfathomable mystery of God's love: "God, who is rich in mercy, because of the great love he had for us, even when we were dead in our transgressions, brought us to life with Christ by grace you have been saved" (Eph. 2:4–7). We are indeed surprised when Jesus affirms that we are loved—unconditionally, everlastingly—by God.

If we browse our daily life schedule, we will discover how terribly we hurt God by our sins. The Hebrew root word for "sin" means "to miss." In sacred scriptures, therefore, sin is described as "missing the mark" and "turning away from God." It also refers to moral blunder, rebellion, evil intent and actions, and debt. Our act of sinning, more than anything else, is an event or action of missing God and his love through our misconduct, misbehavior, and mistake. It makes the bond of love existing between the divine and humans broken and a few times null and void. Sin is something like death that we bring to ourselves. Surprisingly, we are bestowed the good news by Jesus that our God, because of his condescending love, brings us always back from the results of our sins. It is an uninterrupted human history that while, on one side, humans slap the face of a loving God, he on the other side continues to reach out to them, trying to liberate them from all the evil repercussions of sin.

In OT, we heard about the good Lord's covenant of love with his people and how easily they ignored it and lived careless about it. As they were reaping the bad consequences of their blunders, he came again to their rescue. God's love was far reaching. He proved his greatness and power even by the help of a foreign pagan king, Cyrus. He freed his people from their exile, and he also arranged for the rebuilding of the temple in Jerusalem (2 Chron. 36:14–23). However, humans never yielded to his love demands. Hence, this was what God ultimately did when the fullness of his time arrived. He sent his beloved Son to save us.

Unquestionably, we are torn between the two factors of our humanness: we have been called to be holy, but we are susceptible to fall low to be sinful. As one modern spiritual leader has stated, most of our sins are both personal and social, namely, against the love family of God. We are used to making eight blunders: "wealth without work, pleasure without conscience, knowledge without character, commerce without morality, science without humanity, worship without sacrifice, politics without principles, and rights without responsibility."

Despite these blunders of modern generation, God loves humankind and graces us with the immeasurable riches of salvation. For this reason, blundering sinners need not fear approaching God for forgiveness. In the forgiveness we experience from God, we learn the love that enables us to also forgive one another. Forgiveness calls forth forgiveness, just as love calls forth love. This is the history and story retold time and time again as we face the cross on which the crucified Lord hangs. The Spirit constantly injects in us more appreciation and gratitude toward the crucified Lord, the symbol of God's love, plus responsibility and accountability on our part to reciprocate God's love.

35. No Pain, No Gain

*If a grain of wheat falls to the ground
and dies, it produces much fruit.*
—John 12:24

As we experience the wear and tear and struggles of daily living, we are bound to pick up some scars along the way. Some of these are physical and of little consequence as in the little bumps and scrapes of childhood's rough-and-tumble play. Others are more severe as in the bruises of the abused or the wounds suffered by victims of war, injustice, and illness. There are other scars that go more than skin deep. Emotional and psychological and even spiritual traumas can create lasting mementos of suffering that are difficult to heal. These experiences are written on the faces and on the souls of those who suffer them and often come back to haunt them with uncanny freshness. In this regard, we—as disciples and prophets of Jesus— are not exempted at all. Jesus has borne ignominious sufferings and finally experienced horrible death for the sake of the Gospel.

Despite the wonders he had done and all the healings and the conversions he had effected, we noticed that the people, who thought they knew him best, rejected Jesus. While "they were astonished at his wise teachings and miraculous charitable deeds, they took offense at him." Indeed, his people were astounded at his doctrine, yet they were offended at his person, namely, they were prejudiced against him and looked on him with contempt; and for that reason, they would not receive his proposal that they should accept him, sent by God, as their way, truth, and life (Mark 6:1–6).

Undoubtedly, Jesus found it hard to cope with such blind and arrogant rejection from his own people. But from the onset of his earthly life, he was fully aware of his call to act as God's prophet. He was convinced that the Spirit of the Lord anointed him and sent him to preach God's kingdom values. He too cherished a vivid memory of what he read about the deplorable lives of prophets like Jeremiah, whom God already warned about the horrible things he would face in his prophetic ministry: "I am sending you to the Israelites, a nation of rebels who have rebelled against me; they and their ancestors have been in revolt against me to this very day. Their children are bold of face and stubborn of heart—to them I am sending you" (Ezek. 2:3–4).

Hence, Jesus faced all his life's odds and obstacles triumphantly, putting up with his people's denunciation not only as a "human thing" but also mainly belonging to any prophet's territory. It was not surprising. As the Gospels stated, he performed some healings among them; setting aside the snubs they put on him, he exhibited his graciousness even to the evil and those with an unthankful attitude. Also, being smarty, he didn't permit himself to brood, groan, and mourn on his failure in the town; rather, he went round the villages and continued his teaching.

As Christians, being baptized and anointed by God's Spirit to live as the disciples of Jesus and to carry on in this clumsy but good world the prophetic role delegated by our Master. "Prophet" means to be a person for God. As one spiritual author puts it very well, it is a ministry of reaching out to the world in, through, with, and for God in Jesus. In whatever duty we perform in society—be it homemaking, nursing, teaching, caregiving, pastoring, or serving the community as a journalist, artist, or politician—we are demanded by Jesus to carry it out as a prophetic ministry responsibly and steelheartedly.

Imitating our Master, as Paul has done (2 Cor. 12:7–10), we should boldly endure insults, persecution, rejection, and a certain personal suffering as Paul's "thorn in the flesh." We must also take positively and endure willingly the scars and bruises we will wear, because of our prophetic ministry, on our body and even our inner spirit. As a matter of fact, let us remember that those who reach out to others by witnessing always to the goodness and truth cannot travel through this life unscathed. Only then can they covet the imperishable crown. "The way to victory is through hardship, the way to rest is through toil, and the way to life is through death."

36. Anyone who Suffers Is Great in God's Kingdom

But it was the Lord's will to crush him with pain.
—Isa. 53:10a

Some of our nonreligious friends always make a cynical comment about the Christian assertion that human sufferings play an important role in every person's life. They mistakenly criticize us, saying we worship a God who is bloodthirsty and seemingly a sadist who always enjoys the sufferings of humans. Perhaps some of us may be tempted to join their club. This is because we don't open wide our inner eyes and ears to the valuable scriptural teachings on human sufferings.

In faith, we uphold that our God is, in his essence, all good. He has produced in his creation period every creature that is good and not evil. He therefore cannot be the source of any evil, of which human sufferings are a part. Prophets and messengers of our God have continuously declared this truth. At the same time, they have emphasized that all evils have entered into God's creation by the willful disobedience of human beings. This being said, it is crystal clear that every human being undergoes sufferings. And it also is interpreted by biblical writers that death and sufferings are the wages of sins or the inevitable results of each human's blunders. At this point, a valid question arises: while sinful people are permitted to suffer as punishment, why do the just and righteous also suffer? There are very good reasons as proposed by Jesus.

Our Master Jesus, from the onset of his life, recognized the importance of his sufferings and accepted willingly the title "the Suffering Messiah" as prophesied in OT: "It was the Lord's will to crush him with pain." He endured them victoriously with certain inner convictions. Besides resigning to his Father's design for his life, he endured all hardships and his ignominious death for the sake of his friends—you and me. "No one has greater love than this, to lay down one's life for one's friends" (John 15:13). He dreamed that his patient enduring of all his sufferings would be the enriching source for his followers to enjoy a fuller life in this world and the world to come.

Undoubtedly, he proclaimed to us an "eternal prosperity Gospel" but with difference, that is, achieving such an amazing prosperity only by sufferings. He was very clear in his demand for discipleship to him. "Whoever wishes to come after me must deny himself, take up his cross, and follow me. For whoever wishes to save his life will lose it, but whoever loses his life for my sake will find it" (Matt. 16:24–25).

Yes, his uniqueness consists in his proclamation of the Gospel of death and resurrection. This is why countless crowds of his friends over the centuries, like Paul, have claimed and proclaimed through their preaching and sufferings, "We proclaim Christ crucified."

Jesus was never tired of instructing his disciples to follow his footsteps in carrying their own crosses. But we observed his disciples, as most of us did, wrongly considering a fuller life in God's kingdom as earthly glory, appreciation, recognition, higher position, and an environment where all—except themselves—felt low, bowed to them, and served them. And they too were very much preoccupied with how to covet it. That was why, as we read in the Gospel of Mark (10:35–45), James and John—the sons of Zebedee—approached Jesus to clarify which position or portfolio they would be granted by their Master in the future. Jesus never denied their eternal ambition for a fuller life. But he pointed out that such a dream can be realized only by sufferings and death. He asked them, "Can you drink the cup that I drink or be baptized with the baptism with which I am baptized?" Jesus expected his disciples to undergo daily death exactly like he did. What he meant was that they should die of the self as the center of its own concern and should die to the world as the center of security and identity.

To put it realistically, the deaths every disciple faces in daily life are totally surrendering to a God who always seems to be invisible, staying in eternal absence, eternal distance, and eternal silence; patiently living our human life, which is unfair, unpredictable, vulnerable, and slowly disintegrating; enduring the blunders our neighbors done out of their ignorance, arrogance, and weakness; and above all persevering in our charitable services to the needy, sacrificing our peace, our identity, our glory, and our self-esteem and even losing our grip of life. All these are ultimately to please God by our sin offerings for the world as our Master demands. This is the only way of proclaiming and witnessing to Jesus's eternal Gospel of the cross.

37. Simplify Ritualistic Extravagance, But Amplify Love in Action

You have neglected the weightier things of the law:
Judgment and mercy and fidelity.
—Matt. 23:23b

When God has created human life, he has said "good" because of its simplicity. Regrettably, human life today has become so much complicated. We are torn to pieces by our own getups, setups, dreams, ambitions, opportunities, ideas, philosophies, theologies, worldviews, cultures, and so on. Many times in history, some enthusiastic religious teachers and leaders have tried to add some more complications to human life in the form of too many dos and don'ts, commandments, rituals, rites, and rubrics in religion. But the Spirit of God always wants us to not be bugged down to such complexity of religious performances.

Normally, we prefer to take a simplistic way of leading life. We want our teachers to help us simplify our religious obligations and requirements, or we ourselves will try to find ways and means to accomplish it. "Let us simplify religion" is not just the cry of the modern generation but this has been the outcry of the Israelites at the time of the Lord as well.

There were too many interpretations and subtle details on the commandments of God. People were burdened with thousands of secondary laws and regulations to be observed as religious people. God, in OT, did offer to his people only the Ten Commandments, through which he wanted them to realize their longer life of more prosperity, joy, and peace (Deut. 5 and 6). Very sadly, the religious teachers who came after Moses had a tendency to endlessly multiply the commandments and precepts of the law, creating norms and obligations for every minimal detail of life.

In Jesus's time, the religious elders and teachers behaved hypocritically in their brainy formulation of precepts and neglected to observe the divine law of God. When Jesus noticed this awkward situation, he even cursed them, saying, "Blind guides, who strain out the gnat and swallow the camel" (Matt. 23:24). Besides, he tried to simplify all the precepts of God into two, using verses from the OT books. The first is this: "Hear, O Israel! The Lord our God is Lord alone! You shall love the Lord your God with all your heart, with all your soul, with all your mind, and with all your strength" (Deut. 6:4–5). The second is this: "You shall love your neighbor as yourself." He too asserted this twofold command's greatness: "There is no other commandment greater than these" (Lev. 19:18).

Jesus's simplistic form of religion sounds so good and pleasing to our ears. However, when we dig into it and live by it in our daily lives, we go through nightmares.

Loving God is okay. A very simple and cozy life it will be if we choose to be out of the family, out of the street, out of town, and out of the country and select a desert to live a monastic, isolated life and die. There is nothing we will perform but solely and undistractedly expressing our total love for God. But that is not the complete summary of Jesus's religion. He adds to it a second one: "Love our neighbors as ourselves." Surprisingly, if we go to another version of his discussion of his proposal of a simplified dual command (Matt. 22:34–40), Jesus includes in between the two commandments a tiny, little statement that takes our breath away: "The second is like it," meaning the second commandment of loving our neighbors has the same validity and totality as the first commandment.

This means we should love our neighbors with all our heart, with all our soul, with all our mind, and with all our strength as we love our God. In no way should we leave our neighbors and our relationships with them. After living in the midst of our neighbors—namely, parents, spouses, children, friends, relatives, and other strange neighbors—we should be, by now, well aware of the hard truth about our neighbors. A French philosopher, Jean-Paul Sartre, has exclaimed, "Hell is nothing but our own neighbor." That is the reality. Nonetheless, it is with them, through them, and in them that we have to lead a life of love for God. Loving them as ourselves is a hard thing to do. What Jesus has described about this command is that we should wholeheartedly accept our neighbors with all their weaknesses, strengths, good and bad smells, sickness, health, inabilities, sinfulness, wrong and good choices, and prejudices and hypocrisies as we condone our own.

This at least was tolerable, but Jesus, before he went back to heaven, demanded us further a step to go and love these unbearable neighbors as he had loved us. He wanted us to love even our enemies, to forgive them as he forgave, and to be ready to share everything of ourselves, including our very lives for them.

I always divide these two commandments. The first one is directed to the irreligious people who have developed a tendency to stop with their love for human beings, and the second one is focused on the religious people who already find God as their only sovereign Lord and love him totally. The first group forgets God but concentrates on neighbors, and the second group, while focusing their attention on God, totally forgets their neighbors. We need to simplify our religion but never obliterate our love for God and neighbors but rather amplify and enlarge it as big as our heart.

38. Help the Needy
On Their Bloody Path to Heaven

Bear one another's burdens, and so you will fulfill the law of Christ.
—Gal. 6:2

Any lover of the love command of Jesus gets the name of "Good Samaritan" from the parable of Jesus. The Samaritan in the story is there to help the man at the time and place of his need. The word "neighbor" means in the dictionary of Jesus "one who is in need" and not "one who is in proximity" or "one who is close to us."

Among the three in the parable who happen to meet the person suffering and bleeding on the roadside was a Samaritan who seemed to be a good one, upholding love and mercy as the only norms for his life. There were no strings attached on his life schedule unlike those other two so-called holy people, the temple priest and the Levi. There was no any prejudice on which he based his relationships or help. He had no busy schedule of accomplishments or enterprises that distracted or diverted him from doing this love deed. He had no better or bigger priorities than volunteering to help the needy. He helped the needy in whatever way he could and afforded to do. He too went out of the way to carry him to the inn and pay his board and lodging.

Jesus was a typical Good Samaritan. He had proved it and witnessed to it many times. This was why, while he exhorted his disciples about his new command of love, he told them at his farewell discussion, "Love one another as I have loved you" (John 13:34). He too had stated how he loved us: as a good friend and Good Shepherd, he laid down his life for us, his neighbors. All this spirit of love—combined with justice, service, and sacrifice—was inherited by him from his heavenly Father, the God of love. Jesus professed and wanted us also to believe that "God so loved the world that He sent his only begotten Son, so that everyone who believes in him might not perish but might have eternal life" (John 3:16).

God's eternal love has no partiality. That is God's love of perfection.

After his heavenly Father, Jesus lived a perfect life of love as a Good Samaritan. He started his life in love for his Father and continued it with the same love till the end. In many surprising ways, he demonstrated that love through his neighborly love. He knew that his Father gave to humanity the one and only command for their prosperous and fuller life, namely, "love God with your whole heart and your whole being" (Deut. 30:6). At the same time, Jesus too believed unhesitatingly what his Father declared through Moses about observing his love command, with which he added, "Love your neighbors as yourselves." In other words, Jesus understood that his Father expected humans to demonstrate their love for him by loving their neighbors around them.

This was why Jesus was found anywhere and anytime the humans were in need. He taught love to the crowd. He took his cross, hung on it, and died on it. He candidly and repeatedly stated that the requirement to attain eternal life is to love our neighbors and emphasized it by the parable of the Good Samaritan. He too was quoted saying that he would judge us according to our love deeds and not according to any other religious or even spiritual deeds. The Good Samaritan's love deeds were the ladders that would take us to heaven. The apostles fully grasped Jesus's vision of love and preached about it as we read in the First Letter of John: "Whoever does not love a brother whom he has seen cannot love God, whom he has not seen" (4:20b). The evil force is roaring like a lion to devour us and tries to make our life dangerous and risky and recreate us, as John has written, as the worst liars.

Jesus has used relevantly as the place of event in his parable of the Good Samaritan a road that runs between Jerusalem to Jericho that is called Bloody Pass, a dangerous road where journey is so risky, so dangerous, and so unsafe. Human life too is a precarious path to heaven. To make life safe and to free and heal people from their wounds and dangers, Jesus longs for all his disciples to act like him. He expects us to act as his hands, his feet, his heart, and his body. He demands that we should get down from our donkeys (as the Samaritan in the parable has done) of indifference, complacence, pride, coldness, and ignorance. It is all for nothing but to prove that we love our Father in heaven wholeheartedly.

CHAPTER VI

KEEP EYES FIXED ON "WHOABOUTS" AND "WHATABOUTS" OF JESUS

39. The "Search and Find" Game
In the Disciples' Life

Rise up in splendor; the glory of the Lord shines upon you.
—Isa. 60:1

All disciples of Jesus are born as God's creation and reborn in baptism and must show their worth as Jesus has dreamed: They must be convinced of their status as the children of God, calling God "Abba, Father." They too are established as the light of the world and the salt of the earth, and as his delegates, they must manifest his divinity, his glory, his power, and his priesthood. Along with this, they should acknowledge that they are mere humans with limited physicality that can be rotten, dust and unto dust. Every Christian, therefore, is built in three dimensions: powerful and godly but breakable clay vessel.

Accepting this triple dimension of our true self as a whole and manifest it in our daily life, by playing with it or plying with it, is very hard for ordinary humans. Sadly, we always try to show one and hide the other two. Thus, we fail Jesus and ourselves. The Spirit informs us that we can overcome such failures through the light appearing in human history. As Isaiah has proclaimed, such light is closer to our door (60:1–6).

However, this "enlightening manifestation of God" takes place in a slow but steady process. Every revelation God makes in history of mankind as his values, teachings, events, and so on is an occasion and channel to see his true self. We humans possess very little brain, and that too often does not cooperate with us. God, therefore, slowly but gently reveals his truths to us. We are reminded by Paul that God's revelation, unlike the past, "has now been revealed to his holy apostles and prophets by the Spirit" (Eph. 3:5).

In the Epiphany story (Matt. 2:1–12), we read about the sincere and enduring human efforts of such searching for God's light and how finally they were endowed with God's joy and peace. All the persons who were involved in this magi event were searching for God's manifestation. While Mary and Joseph and the shepherds had already sought and found God's Epiphany, still, they were seeking him more. Mary kept everything in her heart and pondered over it. Joseph was always thinking about God, and even in his sleep, he had encounters of God. The magi, in particular, were searching God very intensively. With the help of available media, they started studying the stars and all possible scriptures accessible to them. Their quest for meeting God, born man, might have blended with curiosity and spirituality. But once they saw the star that guided them on their journey of searching, they were so glad. They finally reached their destiny. They found whom they were searching for.

40. Come, Let Us See His Whereabouts and "Howabouts"

"Rabbi where are you staying?"
"Come, you will see."
—John 1:38–39

Whenever I read the inviting words of Jesus to "come and see" in the Gospel of John (1:35–42), I am reminded of the invitations we hear and read in many TV or social media ad jingles to allure us to go and buy their products or their values and thoughts. Unquestionably, Jesus doesn't intend that way of promoting his project or any of his product with consumeristic promotional tactics.

When he invited the seekers with these words, he was very faithful to the references that God had used whenever he invited humans in different ways to have home with him. For example, when God invited Samuel for his purpose, though he was not mature enough to understand that it was God's calling, at the advice of his mentor, Eli, he responded to the Lord in surrender and obedience, "Speak, for your servant is listening" (1 Sam. 3:3–19).

In the New Testament books, we are told this was the customary way for Jesus. From the moment of his coming into the world up to his death, he continuously responded to God the Father's invitation: "Sacrifice and offering you did not desire, but a body you prepared for me; holocausts and sin offerings you took no delight in. Then I said, 'As is written of me in the scroll. Behold, I come to do your will, O God'" (Heb. 10:5–7). He behaved like an obedient and innocent lamb, even ready to be taken to a slaughterhouse. Surprisingly, John the Baptizer introduced Jesus to his would-be disciples at the start of his public ministry by saying, "Behold, the Lamb of God."

This outstanding Lamb of God was fully aware of God's appreciation of his childlike obedience by hearing God's attestation from heaven: "This is my beloved Son, with whom I am well pleased." Therefore, he demanded the same kind of obedient, lamblike attitude from his disciples. When he invited his new disciples with the words "come and see," that was what he intended: "I am sent by the Father to fill you with the same blessings I am filled. For that, first and foremost you have to come out of your selfish darkened tombs of sins, getting out of your slumbers; don't remain lying there as couch-potatoes. Come to me."

In addition, he used the word "see" to point out very clearly that those who seek his values and blessings must see through his very life. His heart was intently proclaiming to them, "Watch keenly, probe intelligently and absorb and uphold truth, nothing but the truth. This is because I am the way, the truth and the life. Everything you seek for is found in me."

Jesus goes on inviting all humans, especially the true seekers of genuine life, proposing to them, "Come and see." It is a factual truth that most of us are willing to go to him, sit with him at his feet, or even walk with him wherever he goes; but very sadly, not all of us find it easy to see the truthful facts of his life. When we closely watch him and his life, we can see what the true reality of life is, what it means to be a child of God, how a man or woman can rise from the dunghill and downhill of human life, where and when we can encounter him very intimately, what is our Creator's intention when he has created us in our mother's womb, and surely what an admirable body we possess. We too get in touch with the new stature we have been bestowed with by the grace of God in Jesus.

Paul never misses in his letters to expound this unfathomable status that we, as Christians, are settled in: "Do you not know that your bodies are members of Christ? . . . But whoever is joined to the Lord becomes one spirit with him . . . Do you not know that your body is a temple of the Holy Spirit within you, whom

you have from God, and that you are not your own?
For you have been purchased at a price. Therefore,
glorify God in your body" (1 Cor. 6:15–20). When we
ardently accept Jesus's invitation to follow him, let us
be ready to go wherever he takes us and to intuitively
watch and observe the where, who, why, when, and
what of his daily life's words and deeds.

41. Only Faith in Jesus Is Our Lifesaver

Take courage, it is I; do not be afraid.
—Matt. 14:27

From all we have been told by Jesus and his disciples
in spirit and in truth, we know well that all our
religious practices are not ends in themselves; rather,
they are performed to realize the biggest goal in life,
namely, to encounter the glorious and powerful God
not just during our prayer times but also in everyday
chores, especially in life's critical situations. In many
life's events where the disciples have encountered such
crisis, Jesus has exhorted them and, through them, told
us how to handle those critical moments.

In one such event, as we read in Matthew 14:22–33,
the disciples were hitting upon a natural disorder as
wind and waves tossed their boat about. Their fear of
capsizing was aggravated by wrongly thinking about
Jesus, who came to join them, as a ghost approaching
them. In that dangerous situation, though they showed
their weak faith, Jesus insisted that they should have
courage, asking them, "Do not be afraid." Even though

Jesus had demonstrated at some other time his power to calm the roaring sea, in this event, he didn't do anything about it but compelled his disciples to hold on to their faith in his continuous mighty presence. Even when Peter was daring enough to ask Jesus to prove his worth, Jesus asked him to walk by his own faith on the water. Since Peter did not possess a strong faith at that moment, he failed in walking on the water; but using this event as a grace-filling occasion, Jesus strengthened Peter's faith.

Through this miraculous event, Jesus tells us that the mighty encounter from heaven is always open to every human, but it requires a strong and sincere faith in him. We discover this truth from many of our forebears. For example, read about the prophet Elijah's encounter with God, especially during one of his worse life situations (1 Kings 19:9–13).

Elijah earned the wrath of Jezebel, wife of Ahab, because he spoke on behalf of his true God. As a result, the prophet had to flee into the desert. There, he was in despair and frustration. He sat under a broom tree and prayed for God to take his life. While he felt lonely and helpless, he would have expected God to encounter him. The compassionate Lord indeed heard his inner mourning. He sent an angel providing the prophet food for his journey.

But Elijah wanted more, namely, an intimate experience of God's divine presence. God certainly tried to satisfy his desire of his messenger's heart but in his own unique way. Like most humans, the prophet expected God's powerful presence in wild natural forces like strong, heavy wind or earthquake or in burning fire. But God had "his own way as the high way." He made the prophet experience the divine presence in a tiny whispering sound of breeze.

This is to say to us that God will meet us surely in our trials and tribulations but at his own time and in his own way. Our only faith-filled job is to vigilantly wait for God's timely move. God has been behaving the same way in human history. Very sadly, as his Son, Jesus, God has lamented many times over his adopted children's stubbornness and unfaithfulness. It continues till this day. We are told by Jesus that the reason for the absence of such miraculous deeds of God in our midst is the lack of faith among us.

Today more than ever before, as we are thwarted and tossed in every aspect of life, God does want us to encounter him. We are in the midst of a roiling sea. Can he still be found in the perils of our time? Yes, he is there, but it is hard to recognize him because we don't hold the true faith, even the mustard seed size as he expects. If we really encounter him in faith, friendship, and deep love, then he will make every bit of our life's perils become quiet when the stormy wind keeps blowing; even we will be empowered by his presence to walk coolly on the troubled waters.

42. Jesus Is the Only Safety Gate to Heaven

No one comes to the Father except through me.
—John 14:6

One tourist visiting a sheepfold in a Middle East country asked the shepherd, "There is no door to close and shut out the wild animals. How are they protected from danger?"

The shepherd replied, "I am the door. When the light has gone and all the sheep are inside, I lie in that open space. No sheep can go out without crossing my body, and no predator can enter without stepping on me." A good shepherd is supposed to be the gate of his sheepfold.

In the Gospel, we read Jesus stating that he is the gate through which those of us who choose to enter will be saved (John 10:7–10). What does he mean by this unprecedented claim? We should remember his astounding claim that he is the Good Shepherd. When he says he is the gate of the sheepfold, he emphasizes that he is so good a Shepherd that he doesn't hesitate to fight against the evil intruders, like wolves, trying to enter into the sheepfold and planning to devour his sheep. He has said, "I came so that they may have life." And he has fulfilled it by dying on the cross.

This amazing "gate" is not only the right entrance into the divinely designed sheepfold but also the proper exit to the green pasture and the living waters of God. Nonetheless, there are millions of sheep among us who feel unsafe, insecure, and deprived of proper nourishment of spiritual food and water. The main reason for such deplorable condition is nothing but being unaware of the worth of this "gate," not listening to his voice that repeatedly cries out, "Come to me all who labor and are burdened; I will give you rest" (Matt. 11:28). And he too has exclaimed, "I stand at the door and knock. If anyone hears my voice and opens the door, then I will enter his house and dine with him, and he with me" (Rev. 3:20). He supports us as our Leader, Guide, and Provider.

It is this faith in Jesus that opens our minds and hearts to him to drink deeply from the inexhaustible riches of life and forgiveness. He invites us every day, "Come to me, I will satisfy and feed you . . . I will quench all your thirst . . . I will fill all your emptiness and powerlessness . . . I will heal and strengthen you in your sickness and sorrow . . . I will teach you and enlighten you in your ignorance and darkness . . . and I will give life eternal when you die."

Jesus also expects us to be fully aware of the difference existing between us, his sheep, and those who are outside his fold. We hear a constant exhortation from the apostles: "Save yourselves from this corrupt generation" (Acts 2:40). Jesus is the one who has insisted this awareness of difference existing between his disciples and others. We are in the light; they are in darkness. We are chosen, but they are not. We are sheep, but they are only goats. We follow the Good Shepherd; they are led by the thieves and robbers. We follow the Spirit; they follow the flesh.

Very sadly, some of us are still hesitating to honor and choose our present state in Jesus's fold. We are like the contestants in the game show *Let's Make a Deal*, who are invited to choose among three doors. Prizes hidden behind the doors could be as valuable as a new car or a great vacation or as worthless as a pile of straw. After choosing a door, the contestant will be tempted with another offer in exchange for the first choice. In the end, because of their indecisiveness or desire for more, some contestants are left with little or nothing at all. Jesus offers us today a choice; he assures, "I am the only door that can offer more abundant life. Check 'yes' or 'no.'"

43. The Radical Life Lived and Proposed by Jesus

For to me life is Christ, and death is gain.
—Phil. 1:21

Practically all radicals are ridden down in life but always end up in glory. This is a historical and perennial truth that is not just narrated in classics and novels but also can be traced out through the centuries in the real lives of chivalrous men and women who have been the causes of ushering historical paradigm shifts in human civilizations. We can say boldly that Jesus of Nazareth is number one of that kind who has become an eternal icon for spiritual and religious radicals who have ever lived.

The word "radical"—coming from the Latin *radix*, meaning "root"—has been historically used (quite distinct from the modern usage to denote political extremes of right or left) to designate individuals, parties, and movements that wish to alter drastically any existing cultural, social, and religious practice, institution, or system. In this historical sense, Jesus of Nazareth seems to be a typical radical.

From the day of his youth, Jesus was so anxious to fulfill his Father's will of bringing radical changes in all his children. In Luke, we read Jesus saying to his parents, "I must be in my Father's house" (Luke 2:49). This saying, according to biblical scholars, can also be translated as "I must be about my Father's work." Referring it as the fire of purifying and refining the twisted and distorted conducts of humans, he was quoted saying, "I have come to set the earth on fire, and how I wish it were already blazing!" (Luke 12:49–50). In his program of bringing about radical changes in human society, he chalked out through his life and sayings the list of those changes.

First, Jesus's radicalism proposed that humans should choose God and his covenantal love as their life's priority. He has preached, "Seek first the kingdom [of God] and his righteousness, and all these things will be given you besides" (Matt. 6:33). Righteousness, he has recommended, is nothing but a change of heart and conduct, a turning of one's life from rebellion to obedience toward God. Undoubtedly, he has first lived up to this attitude of righteousness.

The second radical change Jesus endorsed was that we should lead not self-centered but a self-sharing life. He wanted us to become mature persons who love to share rather than to accumulate the good things of earthly life. In his own life, he upheld this radicalism. From womb to tomb, as Paul explained, Jesus was living a life of emptiness (Phil. 6–8).

At the same time, Jesus also kept on proclaiming the most challenging historical paradigm shift to be encountered in every human. He envisioned that there should be a radical change in us from arrogant power play to merciful and compassionate serviceability, from a proud mind-set to a humble melting heart. "I came to serve and not to be served," he said. In addition, he exhorted his followers, "If anyone wants to be first let him be last."

It is very hard to do such radical changes within ourselves, and even just hearing them seems madness. However, thousands of saints have tried to imitate Jesus in his radical and controversial ways. Come, let us follow their footsteps. The paradigm shift, lived and proposed by the radical Jesus, is worth following.

44. Jesus Coveted His Kingship
By Sacrificial Obedience to Truth

I came into the world, to testify to the truth.
—John 18:37b

Jesus Christ is King of the universe. That is our belief because the scriptures and the church say so. Unless we understand the intricacies of this entitlement well, we cannot profit anything from that ignorant faith. Let us get into a clearer portrayal of the kingship of Christ and into a greater knowledge about the genuine quality of our franchise in his kingdom.

In the Gospel, we read Jesus accepting that he is King, even knowing that he was standing in front of Pilate, who was a great dignitary in that society as a Roman governor, as powerful as any king. And Pilate himself ascertained that he had power to release or to crucify Jesus. In spite of it, Jesus firmly claimed he is the King. To the governor's question "Then you are a king?" Jesus answered, "You say I am a king. For this I was born and for this I came into the world, to testify to the truth. Everyone who belongs to the truth listens to my voice" (John 18:37).

Jesus's claim is well based on the scriptures. We read Daniel prophesying on the kingship of the Messiah: "When he reached the Ancient One and was presented before him, the one like a Son of man received dominion, glory, and kingship; all peoples, nations, and languages serve him. His dominion is an everlasting dominion that shall not be taken away his kingship shall not be destroyed" (Dan. 7:13–14). In the book of Revelation, John has seen in his vision Jesus as the ruler of the kings of the earth. "Jesus Christ," John writes, "the faithful witness, the firstborn of the dead and ruler of the kings of the earth" (Rev. 1:5a).

Indeed, it was a surprising historical story that Jesus—a man of Nazareth, son of a carpenter—became king, and that too was not by political maneuvering, lobbying, shrewd diplomacy, or purchasing people with unethical and undoable promises; rather, as Paul wrote in his letter, "God instituted Jesus so high above all principalities that at his name every knee should bend, of those in heaven and on earth and under the earth. The only ladder through which Jesus climbed up to this august position was made of humility, total surrender to God, and truthful and faithful behavior with integrity to God and to people" (Phil. 2:6–10). In seizing his supreme status, Jesus considered "testifying to the truth" as his primary job.

His second purpose in his kingship life was to establish and run only a spiritual kingdom and not a worldly or earthly one. "My kingdom does not belong to this world. If my kingdom did belong to this world, my attendants would be fighting to keep me from being handed over to the Jews. But as it is, my kingdom is not here" (John 18:36).

And his third engagement was to witness the truth by death. The ultimate goal of his life was to free us from our sins and make all of us "supernaturalized" as his citizens. He freed us from our sins by his blood, and he made us into a kingdom, priests for his God and Father (Rev. 1:5b).

All that Jesus accomplished willingly in his life, as he was pursuing his life's remarkable goals, were not wasted. All were resourceful and very productive.

He gave his very life, but we got his life back. He gave out his breath, but we were filled with his Spirit. And he was buried, but we, with him, rise. He was a slave before God for our sake, but then we, with him, became kings and queens in his kingdom.

Humans traditionally greet their kings or queens by exclaiming whenever they appear in front of the public, "Long live the king/queen!" We too certainly can greet Jesus today, "Long live the King of kings!" It is not because he has left behind him kingship through his posterity as humans do; rather, with John, we firmly believe the words of Jesus: "I am the Alpha and Omega, the one who is and who was and who is to come, the almighty" (Rev. 1:8).

45. Jesus Claims Leadership in His Unique Style

My kingdom does not belong to this world.
—John 18:36a

Usually, a leader of a nation or a community emerges from the people, sometimes elected and chosen by the people but always for the people. We can observe this in both past and present histories of humanity. In scriptures, we notice one more striking thing in "from, by, and for the people"—every step of making leaders, if they are genuine, includes God's hands upon him or her.

For example, in the election of David as king of Israel, we were told God was there in the human process as they crowned him king because he was of their own flesh and blood; plus, he proved his worth by his chivalrous deeds, and they were certain that their Lord had anointed him and abided with him (2 Sam. 5:1–3). In the same track, followers of Jesus accepted him as their leader and king because, surely, he was of their flesh and blood, a person of the human crowd; because he did show his worth and power in their midst with miraculous deeds; and, above all, because they were certain that he had been anointed by God.

Yet the wonder of wonder was while the whole universe, including the Father in heaven, recognized his worth and identity, Jesus never claimed himself a king as the humans perceived. In his lifetime, people tried to make him king, but he denied it and disappeared from their midst. To the wonderstruck people like us, he denied ruthlessly that those three elements that we esteemed as yardsticks to make somebody a king did not make him king at all. Rather, he had his own way of making himself a king and leader. He became a winner, victor, and ever-conquering king not as our human leaders, kings, and queens did and do.

His deliberation has been demonstrated while he is hanging on the cross. We see a man being executed in shame and ignominy, bleeding and battered on a cross, one of the cruelest and degrading punishments ever devised. Over his head are the mocking words "This is the king of the Jews." Jesus preferred such throne of the cross and the crown of thorns and be called a king. It is a place of execution for the very worst of criminals. He hangs shamefully in his nakedness. No disciples are to be seen. Gospels mention no friends, not even women, at the foot of the cross. His only companions are two gangsters, also crucified, and a jeering crowd. "If you are the king of the Jews, save yourself!" It is not exactly what we imagine about him. We rather prefer those triumphant pictures where Jesus wears a crown and an expensively embroidered cloak with a scepter. Yet here precisely, Jesus is at his kingliest (Luke 23:35–43).

In the light of Jesus's life background, starting from heaven to Calvary, and of his sayings, we can conclude that his concept of becoming a king or queen or any sort of leader to rule and guide others includes the following things: emptying oneself; being born poor; relating oneself as friends to the poor, the downtrodden, the sick, the needy, and surely the sinful; vesting a strong willpower to defeat the evil of sufferings traveling into them; scoring the highest mark in forgiving one's enemies; leading a role-model life, unflinching in witnessing the truth and nothing but the truth; and above all—in breathing, eating, walking, relating, praying, and anything—preoccupying oneself with the one and only concern of bringing salvific renewal in the hearts of the humans, one's brothers and sisters.

This is the same attitude Jesus wants all of us to uphold in our discipleship with him. We should fully believe that we are not merely subjects of our King and his kingdom. Unquestionably, we are also his partners in the making, in the bringing about of his kingdom. We are reminded by Paul that, while Jesus is the head, we are his body. We should be kings and queens because we are his people, kith, and kin, because we are chosen and anointed by him. The only thing left to our ability is to prove our worth to be victorious kings and queens in his kingdom. That is possible not by our wealth, IQ, glamour, power, or other human abilities but only by following Jesus's footsteps of humble and simple life but always very rich in merciful deeds.

46. The Unquestionable Glory of the Risen Lord

Everyone who calls on the name of the Lord will be saved.
—Rom. 10:13

All our preachers and evangelists are never tired of proclaiming about our exciting relationship with the risen Lord, Jesus Christ. Many times, our intentional relationship with the risen Lord is at stake, especially when our life stands at its edge.

The same crisis was experienced by the disciples of Jesus as they were exposed to so much disappointment and deception at the demise of their Master. As Luke ascertained, Jesus did and taught until the day he was taken after giving instructions through the Holy Spirit to the apostles, whom he had chosen. But they couldn't grasp fully all his teachings and sayings about his identity. That was why when he met them after his resurrection, he scolded them, saying, "Oh, how foolish you are! How slow of heart to believe all that the prophets spoke!" (Luke 24:25).

Even after Jesus presented himself alive to them by many proofs after his death, appearing to them for forty days and speaking about the kingdom of God, they still showed their ignorance and foolishness about the risen Lord's identity and mission. However, gradually and slowly, they got enlightened in Jesus's mysteries as the risen Lord encountered them, most importantly at the time of his ascension. Through the Spirit's anointing, the whole enlightenment process was complete in them. They became fully aware of the most central truth about Jesus and his mission through two symbolic factors Jesus chose for the event of ascension.

First, Jesus selected a location for his ascension, proving the mighty, powerful identity of his lordship. Luke stated it as Mount of Olives. Such a mountain locale signifies the biblical reference to God Almighty. According to all religions, especially Judaism, mountains are symbols of Almighty God's dwelling place.

The second symbol Jesus used on this occasion to demonstrate that he is God and Savior was a gesture. Luke picturized it in his Gospel (24:50–52), saying, "Jesus raised his hands, and blessed them." Lifting the hands suggests a priestly blessing. The reaction of the disciples was to worship him. Only here did we learn that the disciples had responded appropriately, paying homage to Jesus. Their worship of Jesus signified that they had recognized Jesus for who he was.

This ascension factor was the starting point for the disciples' strong faith in Jesus as their Lord and Savior. Their whole mind and heart were filled with only one faith element: Jesus Christ is the Lord and Savior. We knew well how then all the disciples of Jesus, receiving power from on high, began speaking about this creed; in every sermon and worship, they proclaimed this unique belief and asked others do so to be saved. The core of Paul's teachings and preaching was this truth about Jesus Christ. "In accord with the exercise of God's great might he worked in Christ, raising him from the dead and seating him at his right hand in the heavens, far above every principality, authority, power, and dominion, and every name that is named not only in this age but also in the one to come" (Eph. 1:17–23).

"Human salvation is possible only by the proclamation of the faith that Jesus Christ is Lord and Savior." This has been the one and only message all disciples have preached. This belief in Jesus and in our mission of life continues intact in the spirit of today's church. To this, there is no exception in status or whatever role each one of us takes in daily life. All of us—as members of the church, while we are waiting to join our Head, who has already entered into heaven—hold a very important role.

47. The Passionate Passion of the Master

You must have the same attitude that Christ Jesus had.
—Phil. 2:5, NLT

During his final days, when Jesus was entering into Jerusalem to meet the climactic end of his physical life, he got a warm and glorious welcome from his followers, beneficiaries, and onlookers. With pride and joy, all the Gospel writers added this event as the introduction to their passion narratives. Spreading their cloaks and strewing leafy branches on the road where Jesus was riding, waving palm branches as a sign of jubilation and victory, a large crowd of disciples and common people in Jerusalem preceding him and those following kept crying out and saying, "Hosanna to the Son of David; blessed is he who comes in the name of the Lord."

Undoubtedly, while Jesus accepted this warm welcome, he never put his heart into it. First, it was because he knew the faltering nature of humans. "Jesus would not trust himself to them because he knew them all" (John 2:24). Second, he was fully aware of where his Father, together with this crowd, was taking him—to the slaughterhouse. His only preoccupation was how to surrender himself willingly, humbly, patiently, and joyfully to the passion and

death he would be enduring. He certainly didn't want the
passion he possessed throughout his life, from conception to
the final days, to ever be extinguished. He was filled with
emotions of longing and craving to fulfill the will of his
Father and a passion for performing an eternal sacrifice for
the future of humanity, his brothers and sisters.

We humans are aware of our own humanness.
When we are entangled with an immense passion for
some earthly things, for some living creatures, or for
some worldly ambitions, we forget everything about
ourselves. We go ahead with full will and emotions to
accomplish or covet what we desire.

This was what we encountered in Jesus regarding
his commitment to his Father, to whom he promised as
he entered into this world, "Behold, I come to do your
Will, O God." Hence, this sort of journey of passion
had started as he came into the world from heaven.
Paul, quoting an early Christian hymn (Phil. 2:3–11),
confirmed how the Son of God emptied himself, came
down to the earth, was stripped of his glory, took the
form of a slave, and was ready to undergo any death,
even that on a cross. Jesus's passion to fulfill totally the
desire of his Father was urging him to move forward.

In this journey of passion, besides fulfilling his
Father's will, Jesus's main focus was to bring spiritual
liberation and renewal to humans. When he was greeted
by the people, he felt sorry for them because not all of
them were well aware of what exactly he was engaged
in. Surely, they expected a Messiah as a big warrior
who would support them in their political, social, and
other earthly needs. Unfortunately, he did not possess
any of such identity while he was traveling through
Palestine for three years. His teachings were always
centered on love, forgiveness, peace, patience, and spirit

and truth. When they tried once to make him a king, he drifted away. They were waiting for an opportune time.

Pitiably, they believed that—as Jesus entered Jerusalem visibly—he would demonstrate his real identity of his worldly power, glory, and tenacity. But everything happened opposite to their dreams. They were disappointed completely with him by observing what happened during his final hours. Their hearts were very fickle, so they turned against him and shouted while he was before Pilate, "Away with him!" However, the passion in Jesus never faded away. He stood by his guns and went through the passion events.

This is how we have got Jesus as a world leader and Savior. Let us appreciate him and accept him. Let us also feel proud of being his discipled leaders. Let us follow him wherever he takes us. Let us be bold enough to say to our other discipled friends, as Thomas, called Didymus, has said, "Let us also go to die with him" (John 11:16). Let us be passionate about the passion of the Lord so that we too can be immerged into that bleeding passion to walk the walk of obedience and to lift the world around us as God's kingdom.

48. The Triple-S Yardstick of Jesus

The measure with which you measure
will be measured out to you.
—Matt. 7:2b

Unquestionably, one of the greatest blessings Jesus has promised and continues to shower till this day is that those of us who have been chosen by him as his discipled leaders share his power and authority. In the martyrology as well as in the ecclesiology of the church, we find innumerable events and accomplishments accounted in the lives of Jesus's discipled leaders.

All his true believers certainly have gotten a glimpse of him; they have seen him, spoken with him, touched him, and walked with him as a living and loving friend. These are not fairy tales, like Hollywood movies; rather, they are real and authentic life experiences of millions of Jesus's disciples over the centuries. This is why so many peculiar and sometimes unthinkable things have been spoken and performed by them with unique authority and power. And they have claimed that this exceptional authority has been derived from the risen Jesus, who is alive.

The Gospels prove that Jesus, while in his physical body, has revealed very peculiar authority and power in his words and deeds. This is why the people and higher authorities in his time have been wondering about the authority with which he has spoken and the marvelous deeds he has done. Thus, his disciples have witnessed—within his three years of public life—his marvelous power and authority. Besides, we too read from the Gospels how the first group of Jesus's disciples has encountered his power and authority with his risen body during the forty days soon after his resurrection. For example, we hear from John (21:1–14) that while the human disciples have been frustrated with their limitations and inabilities in their labor of fishing, we see—with the power of the risen Lord—they have succeeded not just in what they want but more than what they have expected.

This was why, even when he was out of their physical sight, they continued to proclaim publicly and proudly that their teacher was a superman with all power and authority. Though he seemed like a voiceless lamb easily mistreated by society, they—like John—never stopped shouting out, "To the One seated on the throne, and to the Lamb, be praise and honor, glory and might, forever and ever!" (Rev. 5:13).

The same is true today; the risen Lord—besides demanding from us, his followers, many duties to be fulfilled—shares with us certain authority and power as our discipleship rights. For this, he fills our soul with his Spirit, who will be empowering us as he has predicted before he has left to heaven, "You will receive power when the Holy Spirit comes upon you, and you will be my witnesses in Jerusalem, throughout Judea and Samaria, and to the ends of the earth" (Acts 1:8a). He is not shy to confirm that, with the Spirit's power and authority, we will do all things as he has done, even greater ones (John 14:12).

It is a historical and factual truth that when Jesus, alive, befriends us and when his Spirit starts integrating with our human spirit, our whole life perspective, worldview, and attitudes change. We begin to live in a totally different realm of life. People around us watch and find out certain strangeness about our behavior: our way of going through life's ordinary and extraordinary events with certain tenacious authority.

While we feel very happy and proud about such an amazing dealing of the risen Lord with us, there are times when almost all of us begin to misuse or abuse the delegated power bestowed by our Master. History and each one's conscience testifies to it. We forget to be very careful in discerning that authority formed in us, truly and genuinely generated from the risen Lord. Lacking such discernment, as we climb up the ladder of power and authority, as many religious leaders do, many of us perpetuate bloody terrorism with crazy religious convictions. Now the question we ask ourselves is how to find out that the power and authority we hold and cherish is truly from the risen Lord or merely out of our IQ, shrewd diplomacy, and political manipulation and maneuver.

Good Peter and his other companions were typical humans, natural-born-connivers like us. Hence, the risen Lord pointed out to us the right yardstick we should judge the genuineness of our "empowerment." We read about this remarkable benchmark in an incident that happened at the seashore of Tiberias when the risen Lord and Peter encountered each other (John 21:15–19). By asking Peter three times whether he loved him more than others, Jesus wanted not only to confirm that Peter did love him before handing over to Peter his personal and functional authority but also mainly to emphasize to Peter and to all his followers that our authority must start with love and end with service.

I love to label Jesus's yardstick as a triple-S gauge: sharing, serving, and sacrificing. This is the only yardstick with which we can measure the legitimate source of the power and authority we own, especially in the kingdom of God. Sadly, according to that criteria, most of our words and actions fall short in their credibility. Subsequently, we fail ourselves and others in our journey toward eternal rest. To make sure our inner power is that of the risen Lord, let us be attentive, namely, to fight the good fight, to love Jesus, to hunger for him, and from time to time check whether our own authority-based actions are emerging out of the triple-S measurement.

49. The Jesus Effect of Startling Creation of the New Order

Behold, I make all things new.
—Rev. 21:1–5

The dream of a new order in our personal and social life is the perennial quest of the human race. In every age, leaders and gurus promise such new order. In their enlightenment and intelligence, they have listed many strategies, tricks, norms, and mantras to realize it; but most of their tips have turned out to be either unproductive or completely wrong and perverted, in some cases pharisaical, diplomatic, and self-centered. Jesus too has preached about this new order but with a difference. He, naming this order as the kingdom of God, has proposed the strategy to achieve it, which is totally different from others.

Before Jesus was born, God promised through his prophets that this human dream of a new order would be realized. Asking people to shout for joy and be glad forever in what he was creating, God declared, "See, I am creating new heavens and a new earth; the former things shall not be remembered nor come to mind" (Isa. 65:17–18).

When Jesus came, lived, died, and rose from the dead, all his disciples believed and proclaimed loudly that the promise of God—as predicted by Isaiah—had been realized in their Master. Paul exclaimed, writing about the Jesus effect, "Whoever is in Christ is a new creation: the old things have passed away; behold, new things have come" (2 Cor. 5:17). And John, whom Jesus exclusively loved, saw a vision about this new order. He not only heard but also saw how the Lamb, Jesus, created a new heaven and a new earth where the former had passed away.

Jesus proposed the one and only means to achieve his and our dream of a new order. In the light of the Spirit and the scriptures, we can very well underscore that this order is nothing but letting our human life be led, renewed, and wheeled around by love. When he arrived on the earth, so many versions about the idea of love were floating in the globe. He compiled all of them but added not a twist but an eternally graded nuance to them. This is what we meditate this weekend.

At his Last Supper, he stated it very loudly: "As I have loved you so you also should love one another" (John 13:34b). The love Jesus demanded from his followers is one that would get the source and energy from the awesome love that had been demonstrated by God the Father and significantly by his Son, Jesus. The characteristics of the love he proposed were three.

First, our love should be agape. The word "agape" means the unlimited, pure love of God. Jesus's human love is fully centered on God and his love. As his Father God, Jesus expects us to be gracious and merciful, slow to anger, of great kindness, good to all, and compassionate.

Second, Jesus wants us to love others only for God and others and not for any reciprocation or recognition; it should be a purely other-centered love. There must be no strings attached to it. In our love for others, Jesus expects us to recognize and accept one another as he recognizes each one of us. This implies we should not draw any boundary, color, measurement, or criterion for reaching out to others. We must consider every human being as the child of God, as the sheep in his sheepfold. We need to love others with a forgiving, serving, and sharing love as Jesus has done and admonished.

Third, Jesus's command is to love like him. Each of us has to discover the best way to express our love in our own small ways, such as by choosing a kind word rather than a critical one, offering a smile or a helping hand, sending a letter to a friend, remembering someone's birthday, listening to the lonely, being patient with the impatient, and showing interest in someone else's plans. Saint Therese of the Child Jesus, who is fondly called the Little Flower, points out this truth in her autobiography, writing, "Only performing little things for my beloved Jesus I gain his love."

Church history testifies clearly how exemplary so many disciples and holy men and women were in fulfilling the love commandment of Jesus. Once they were caught up by the fire of Jesus's true love, they were on their way to proclaim that new love, that new faith, that new order, and that new life in Jesus.

Jesus's teaching about love is very inventive. And it is that inventive love that makes the heart of our faith and our life. If we only had a bit of love like that, we could make ourselves and our world all new.

50. Christ Set Us Free from the Yoke of Slavery

Go, sell what you have . . . then come, follow me.
—Matt. 19:21

We know well how almost all of us, with our good and splendid brain, use certain goals and targets in achieving success. They may be small as short-term goals or sometimes long-term ones that take so much of our time and energy and our sweat and blood. It is our experience that such successes seem to be very temporary and short lived. In the light of Jesus, we know that to lead a self-fulfilling and soul-enriching life of happiness till our last breath that is extended even after our death, we indeed need a lifelong goal. Jesus called it eternal life.

This eternal life, according to Jesus, is an uninterrupted life of bliss, true freedom, peace, and full contentment. To attain this lifelong goal, God's Spirit offers us some practical and radical ways. These ways can be summed up under two categories: attachment to the goal and detachment from anything that obstructs, deviates, and distracts us from achieving it. Any goal-achieving effort demands us to discover our goal and fix it to our mind and heart. Once we find eternal life as our goal, then we need to put our heart into it.

In the Gospel of Luke, the Spirit underscored it by a metaphorical way of pointing out how Jesus was heading toward the final destiny of Jerusalem (9:51). Jesus determinately journeyed to Jerusalem to undergo whatever was necessary for his work to be completed. In this resolute journey of life, he followed the footsteps of his forebears like the prophet Elisha, who—to signal his commitment to the prophetic ministry of Elijah—left all his properties and his likings, which he demonstrated by burning his plow and roasting his oxen to feed his people (1 Kings 19:16–21). Elisha vividly proved his conviction that he would no longer be leaning on his fields and flocks to secure his future as any well-to-do farmer did, but once he had accepted to walk the walk of Elijah, he would be completely dependent on God from then onward.

Jesus did live that detached lifestyle from the onset of his journey to the earth. He emptied himself and left all his glory and blissful life with his Father and angels in heaven. He took the form of a slave, literally meaning that he had very little worldly possessions; not even he had a place of his own to rest, depending largely on God and his people.

Jesus commands those who desire to follow him to do the same. Almost all his disciples, starting from those twelve till this day, leave everything behind once and for all and follow the Master. We know why Jesus sets before us such hard ways to be followed. We carry lots of monkeys on our back willingly or unwillingly to survive in this earthly life. They are nuisance many a time, a kind of large yoke to be borne. Many times, we feel we need them. But Jesus wants us to get rid of those monkeys completely and follow him. Thus, he expects his disciples to solely depend on God and his providence.

When we start following Jesus resolutely in the way he has sketched out, sometimes we may seem hardheaded or freaky; we should not give in to such criticism. However, we shouldn't behave like the brothers James and John (Luke 9:54–55), short tempered and quick fixing. We should never get overwhelmed by our own puny wisdom and perfection model; rather, we should converse with Jesus, our life companion. Let us not lose heart but get going in the path of Jesus, fixing our mind and heart to the final goal—eternal life. Consequently, even in this world, our life will be permeated with the true freedom and joy that Jesus has promised. Even in the midst of trials and tribulations, we will be daring enough to proclaim with Habakkuk, "Yet I will rejoice in the Lord and exult in my saving God" (3:18). Besides, the rest of our life till death, we will hilariously announce the good news with Paul: "For freedom Christ set me free; so I stand firm and I do not submit again to the yoke of slavery" (Gal. 5:1).

51. Jesus Seeks Personal and Friendly Disciples

Circumcision is of the heart, in the spirit, not in the letter.
—Rom. 2:29

Most of us who take pride in naming ourselves as the discipled leaders of Jesus don't possess a clear knowledge about the basic and intrinsic dimension of discipleship that comes with the followers' close connections with Jesus. While he is alive, he has tried his best to explain this fact through his sayings and life events. But his disciples couldn't catch even a glimpse of it. Thanks to the descending of the Spirit, they have clearly understood what he has been driving at. That is the way all the church members learn about the true meaning of being a disciple of Jesus, which we perceive when we read the scriptural passages with the Spirit.

One of the Gospel events of that kind was the miraculous healing of the ten lepers (Luke 17:11–19). Usually, the lepers in Palestine were treated as outcasts; and therefore, they had to hide and live in dark caves and shelters. In this event, they seemed to be bold enough to break that shelter and come out of it to connect themselves to Christ. Also, as they came out of their hidden places, they cried out not "unclean,

unclean" (which they were supposed to shout when they appeared in public so that anyone who walked by would run away from them) but "Jesus, Son of David, have pity on us!" Doing such abnormal things, these lepers showed their faith in Jesus's power and, above all, his compassion.

Indeed, Jesus liked them for their audacious, impudent, and prayerful gestures. However, he did not heal them immediately. As God's usual deed, he put their faith to the test. He commanded them to go and show themselves to their priests. He wanted them to continue their rituals and other religious and social practices even when they noticed their prayer had not been answered yet.

This was what we observed in the healing story of Naaman, the leper in OT (2 Kings 5:14–17). The prophet listened to the prayers of Naaman for healing. Yet not healing him, he ordered him to go and sink ten times into the water. Naaman unhesitatingly obeyed. And he was healed.

In the same way, the lepers in the Gospel hurried to fulfill the command of Jesus; on their way, they were healed. Surely, they were overwhelmed with wonder, surprise, and joy. They surely headed along to the temple to show themselves to the priests. One of them left their company and started running back to Jesus. The other nine were attentive maybe to socialize and enter into the mainstream of society, and therefore, they decided to fulfill the social and religious rituals and not to please Jesus, their healer. They would have surely forgotten the real source of their healing. This was well expressed by Jesus when he asked, "Where are the other nine?"

Jesus too praises the grateful gesture of the returning leper. In other words, Jesus expects every one of his disciples who are called and healed by him to be intimately connected to him. There is no doubt he endorses all our external practices and rituals to show and increase our faith in God. But it is not at all sufficient to be a discipled leader of Jesus.

When we plan to become Jesus's disciples, we must go the extra mile, namely, we should fully relate ourselves personally to Jesus as his intimate friend and lover and connect ourselves to him as branches to a vine. This personal love approach to the Master will make us keep Jesus as our first priority in life. This will make us start everything, proceed in everything, and end everything in him, through him, and with him. Such intimacy with Christ should be the base and core of all that a discipled leader does in the name of religious and social rituals and practices. As the Samaritan leper has done, in every effort we take to perform rituals and charitable practices, we should express our sentiments of love and gratitude to our Master.

The true disciples of Jesus must possess a grateful and mellow heart as the Samaritan leper. Let everything flow out of that heart—everything we perform and accomplish both in our social and religious lives, whether they are targeted to families, communities, or the entire world. Therefore, if we decide to be closely related disciples of Jesus, we must make sure all our performances are generated from our "consecrated and circumcised hearts" as Paul deliberates: with grateful and friendly hearts, "if we live, we live for the Lord and if we die, we die for the Lord" (Rom. 14:8).

CHAPTER VII

NEVER LOSE SIGHT OF YOUR PERSONAL "WHO IS WHO" DETAILS

52. Every Christian Is a Little Lamb of God

God gathers, leads us as lambs and ewes.
—Isa. 40:11

Every human being's name is so precious because it identifies someone in a multibillion population. In many cultures, it also signifies the nominee's personality and quality. In Jewish culture, this is 100 percent true. Every human name in the Bible is an emblem or symbol of what one is predicted to be or one is capable of accomplishing. For example, our Master is named "Jesus," which has been told by angels both to Mary and Joseph before his birth. In Hebrew, the name "Joshua"—meaning "Yahweh helps"—has been interpreted as "Yahweh saves."

"Jesus" was a powerful name bestowed by his heavenly Father. On the basis of such identity and seeing his powerful deeds and accomplishments, his followers gave him many names such as Messiah, Immanuel, Lord, Teacher, Master, Shepherd, and so on. While Jesus accepted all these names and acknowledged them as true, he loved to be called "the servant of God." He preferred this name because he was fully convinced that his Father sent him to this world as Joshua of Nazareth to be the Almighty's servant. As Isaiah predicted (49:36), Jesus heard from his heavenly Dad not only "You are my beloved Son" but also "You are my servant." He was fully aware of the fact that God formed him as his servant from the womb. Jesus's one and only duty in this world was to be his Father's messenger, and as God's voice, he announced God's love, mercy, justice, and righteousness in the vast assembly. Being aware of Jesus's indescribable obedience, humility, simplicity, and innocence, John the Baptist named him "the Lamb of God."

We are prone to covet honorable names such as leader, guardian, protector, priest, prophet, king, queen, and so on. We are eligible to be called so since we have been sanctified in baptism and started our life of righteousness and justice with Jesus Christ. We are proud to be identified as such, proclaiming, "We are indeed a chosen race, a royal priesthood, a holy nation, a people set apart to proclaim your mighty works" (1 Pet. 2:9). But is that all we are to be?

Like Jesus Christ, our Christian name includes servants of God, apostles of God, messengers of God, and surely lambs of God. Let us remember here what Jesus has done and said in front of his disciples at the Last Supper. "I have given you a model to follow, so that as I have done for you, you should also do" (John 13:12–17). Honoring the remarkable name "Christian," we who call upon the name of Jesus must lead a life worthy of that name. In other words, as the prophet has prophesied, we should behave like the little lambs of God. "Like a shepherd God feeds his flock; in his arms he gathers the lambs, carrying them in his bosom, leading the ewes with care."

We are indeed blessed to be called the little lambs of God. At this critical moment when religious conflicts are spawned globally mainly by hostilities ignited by the arrogant supremacy attitudes of certain religious persons, we need to take a pledge before God that we will be faithfully following Jesus as innocent, meek, and peaceful lambs.

53. We Are Light but Always Seasoned with Salt

You are the salt of the earth and light of the world.
—Matt. 5:13–14

The metaphor "light" is frequently used in scriptures in describing the identity and action of God and his Son: "God is light and in him there is no darkness" (1 John 1:5). Jesus proclaims himself as "the true light of the world come to light every man" (John 1:5, 8:12). Very surprisingly, Jesus adds that all his followers are also the light. When he has identified himself as the light of the world coming from heaven, his enemies have been scandalized that he has equalized himself with God; worse still, when he has publicly admitted that his followers were also the light like himself, we can imagine how much their hearts have been pulsating.

At the same time, we should know he never missed the chance to add some more facts about this role of light he transmitted to us. He differentiated our role of light from his own. While he proclaimed in John 8:12 that "he is the light of the world," we also hear him say, "While I am in the world, I am the light of the world" (John 9:5).

In other words, as long as he is physically present in the world, he has been the light of the world. But when he is no longer physically present, his followers are to assume the role of being the light of the world. This role is not something naturally inherited by their birth; rather, it is purely a gratuitous gift from God.

Besides, Jesus has emphasized that this light entrusted to us, his disciples, has to be nurtured and preserved, safely burning within us. To underscore this truthful fact, he has added another dimension of the Christian identity, saying, "You are the salt of the earth." From the early days of humanity, salt has been used both for social and religious purposes. In ancient Near East, there has been a covenant of salt, a synonym for an inviolable covenant as Jesus himself has stated that it is the source of human love and peace (Mark 9:50). In our daily life, we know salt has been the ultimate seasoning that gives taste to food. Plus, it has the power to keep food safe and intact.

In saying "we are the salt of the earth," Jesus suggests that all human nature corrupted by sin has become tasteless; but through our ministry of testimony, the grace of the Holy Spirit will regenerate and preserve the world, if only we melt like salt in the spiritual fire and living waters of God, like Jesus.

He considers the light shared by God within us to be like salt. "If salt loses its taste, what is the use of it?" So light first must shine within the hearts and minds of the followers, and then it will shine outside and will do its accomplishment. He too has given a doable strategy to increase and keep the inner light burning and the inner spirit of salt tasteful. To abide in such light, Jesus has said, "He who loves his brother abides in the light" (1 John 2:8–11).

This is why whenever we hear OT prophets proclaiming that people of God can be light shining in darkness, they have never missed adding the source of such role of lighting others, namely, love deeds (Isa. 58:9–10). Joining hands with our Master, let us declare and try to live up to the concrete way of being light and salt in this world as God's proxies through our orderly, effective, and concrete charity that bends toward the needy, the poor, and the suffering. We are indeed light but always seasoned with salt.

54. We Are an Easter People

If Christ has not been raised, your faith is vain.
—1 Cor. 15:17

Our indomitable Christian creed is "I believe in the resurrection of the body and life everlasting." However, according to the scriptures, such heavenly resurrection will not come to us as a magical sudden touch of any heavenly angel. The apostle Paul and other NT writers and church fathers teach firmly that it is a lifelong journey of continuous deaths and resurrections. There are many deaths we are prone to undergo. Paul profusely speaks in all his letters about two of those deaths: death in sin and death to sin.

Scriptural tradition testifies that we humans, born of Adam and Eve, are originally enslaved by the snare of evil, and Christianity names it as "original sin." The Bible refers to this human state as "spiritual death." When God has warned about this death resulting from human disobedience, he has said, "In the day that you eat of it [forbidden fruit] you shall surely die" (Gen. 3:6). The phrase "you shall surely die" is interpreted as a continuous state of death that begins with spiritual death.

We daily face many deaths, such as the nonstop deaths of acute suffering and pain by chronic and terminal diseases; the daily dying of marginalized people out of hunger, thirst, emotional imbalance, unjust rejection, discrimination, and exploitation; and deaths of going downhill by material and physical deprivation. Plus, knowingly or unknowingly, every person hurts each other by their sinful and silly words and actions. Thus, they bring deaths to each other.

As a matter of fact, we are so blessed to see and hear from Jesus and his disciples that we—who are naturally born dead in sin—are bestowed with a power to rise from those deaths by the amazing grace of God through Jesus's death and resurrection. Christian tradition insists that human salvation depends on both the death and resurrection of Jesus. Yes, by Jesus's death, we are saved. By his blood, we are saved. By his breathing out last, his Spirit is ready to possess us. However, Jesus's redemptive work is not over. By his resurrection, his Spirit has entered into humanity and started his saving work subtly and effectively.

First, his resurrected Spirit makes us die to original sin and daily sins; and second, he raises from the dark pits of ignorance, indifference, faithlessness, hopelessness, and above all selfishness. God is never tired of promising to us, "I will give you a new heart and place a new spirit within you . . . I will put my spirit within you . . . you shall be my people, and I will be your God" (Ezek. 36:26–28).

Raising the valid question "How can we who died to sin yet live in it?" Paul brings home to us (Rom. 6:1–11) that, through baptism, we who have once died in sin have risen from our spiritual death. At the same time, we too have begun a daily life of death to sin; and being purified constantly by his blood, we should encounter spiritual resurrection at every moment of life. Indeed, through his continuous compassionate actions, we receive the resurrection of forgiveness, mercy, enlightenment, healing, power, and heavenly support. By that belief, those who hurt others rise from their death of losing joy and friendship by getting forgiveness from those whom they have hurt by sincere apologies; those who die and go to their blue or dark moments of isolation and depression rise from their daily deaths by truly forgiving those who hurt them and getting a life of joy. Such moments are, as I boldly name them, our "earthly resurrections." Thanks to the risen Jesus, "we are indeed an Easter people."

55. The Awesome Treasure We Are Entitled To

Store up treasures in heaven . . . Where your treasure is, there also will your heart be.
—Matt. 6:20–21

People often dream of finding a treasure, winning the first prize in the state lottery, or getting the big jackpot in the bingo games in casinos. According to scriptures, there is a treasure greater than what humans dream of. Every disciple of Christ, born and reborn, possesses this treasure of fine pearls, such as God's established kingdom, Jesus's Gospel values, and the Holy Spirit's gifts of faith, wisdom, hope, and love.

Jesus points out in the Gospel that this awesome treasure is nothing but the kingdom of God or heaven, and it is among us and within us (Luke 17:21b; the Greek preposition translated as "among" can also be translated as "within"). Moreover, in one of his parables, he metaphorically compares it to the mustard seed, which is buried already in the field of human soul (Matt. 13:31); he is correct in his statement. From Creation, God's image and likeness is within us, which is like the mustard seed, smallest but full of potentials to become large and rich. As the smarty man in the Gospel's parable, we have to discover it as soon as possible. This is possible by reading, listening, and experiencing the words and actions of God in various ways. In another parable (Matt. 13:44–47), Jesus also suggests to us that when we find God's treasure buried within us, we should start doing some prudent and wise actions about it. We must safeguard them, protect them, and secure them from God's enemies as the person in the Gospel parable has hidden the treasure that he has found in his field.

Our Master Jesus is famous for taking risks in life, and so he wants us to do the same in detaching ourselves from all worldly treasures for the sake of seizing the otherworldly one. As we grow older, we begin collecting so many riches, positions, qualifications, and properties and hoarding them as our earned treasures through talents, power, IQ, and luck. Now we have on one side this treasure of worldly and material possessions and on the other God's treasure. As faithful disciples of Jesus, we should judge wisely which treasure is more beneficial and richer. Certainly, for such prudent decision-making, we need the gift of wisdom from God. This is why, as we read in OT, when God has appeared to King Solomon and promised him, "Whatever you ask I shall give you," the king has pleaded to offer him only wisdom and not worldly treasures: "Lord! Give your servant, therefore, an understanding heart to judge your people and to distinguish right from wrong" (1 Kings 3:5–12).

Jesus's main advice to us in our dealing with the awesome treasure is that once we wisely prefer the heavenly treasure to temporary ones, we should dispose of all material goods that we have and cling to God's treasures. Let us remind ourselves here what Jesus has told the youth who wants to inherit the heavenly treasure: "There is still one thing left for you: sell all that you have and distribute it to the poor, and you will have a treasure in heaven" (Luke 18:21–13).

Our earthly life is worth living, in spite of all its ups and downs, because it is a precious gift from God. One can make one's life beautiful or miserable depending on one's attitude toward life God has offered us. We should appreciate every bit, every moment of this life and make the best use of it with all its hidden treasures. We too must try to behave like Paul, who has treasured his faith in the love for Jesus and realized that all things work for good for those who love God (Rom. 8:28–30).

56. We Are Heaven Sent Rather Than Hell Bent

What does "he ascended" mean except that
he also "descended" into the lower regions?
—Eph. 4:9

Just as Jesus himself was the greatest mystery ever lived, so all the events that occurred in his life were exhibiting many riddles. Among those events was Jesus's ascension to heaven, which had become a paradoxical event historically, consisting at the same time in an ending and a beginning: the abrupt ending of the thirty-three years of life of Jesus on the earth and the startling beginning of the final era of salvation history, in which we still live—the period of the church.

If we go deeper into this mystery of ascension, we discover an unthinkable factor occurring inside this event. Very surprisingly, it contains a rare blend of both acts of Jesus—descending and ascending. Referring to Psalm 68, Paul writes, "What does 'he ascended' mean except that he also descended into the lower regions of the earth? The one who descended is also the one who ascended far above all the heavens" (Eph. 4:7–13). Paul surely has meant that as God has been triumphantly leading Israel to salvation in Jerusalem, Jesus too is ascending to a status of mystical presence, becoming the head of the church and the source of our spiritual gifts through his incarnation and descending to the earthly life, consisting in poverty, pain, suffering, death, and burial (Phil. 2:6–8).

Such an awesome mystery of Jesus's descending and ascending is the base and core of our Christian life. It is completely built on certain paradoxical factors from which Jesus's disciples cannot escape even a single moment. The faith we uphold is paradoxical, a blending of "already and not yet" and of "ascending and descending."

We are already saved but not yet fully; already, we enjoy God's peace and joy but not yet completely. The higher we ascend with Jesus through prayer, meditation, and a disciplined life, the deeper we are urged to be involved in earthly affairs. A true and genuine disciple of Jesus cannot remain looking up to heaven all the time as the disciples have done. If we are truly praying and intensively connecting ourselves to the heavenly Lord, we will be asked—as the angel has told the disciples—to go down to our own family, our business, our community, and our life situation to be his witnesses (Acts 1:9–11).

With firm faith in the heaven-focused earthly life and with persistent hope of reaching it at Jesus's Second Coming as angels have reminded, "This Jesus who has been taken up from you into heaven will return in the same way as you have seen him going into heaven," we live together as Jesus's team of disciples at the present age on the basis of his command of love. As he has promised us, we will be bestowed with powerful and authoritative gifts to eradicate and cast out all social and spiritual evils from humanity. This miraculous enlargement of the team of Jesus is nothing but his own ascension, in which we too have the privilege of being ascended with him. Paul proclaims about this remarkable goal of our Christian ascension with Jesus in this world: "That Jesus might fill all things for building up the body of Christ, until we all attain to the unity of faith and knowledge of the Son of God, to mature manhood, to the extent of the full stature of Christ."

As the famous theologian Karl Rahner explains, Jesus, in ascending to God, has taken us with him. He has ascended to heaven with the human body and the human nature, and this means with the entire humanity. Because he wants to come close to us, definitively, he has gone away and taken us with him. Because he has been lifted on the cross, in his resurrection and in his ascension, he and everything in him have become near. The reason for this is that Jesus's Spirit is already in us now. Since something of our humanness already dwells in glory with Jesus, he summons the rest of ourselves to a greater, deeper holiness here and now, not only at liturgy but in the course of our daily existence.

To put it more bluntly, we are to live in accord with the gift that we are heaven sent rather than hell bent.

This is the enigmatic but majestic life of every disciple of Jesus.

57. We Are God's Glad Tidings Today

How beautiful are the feet of those who bring good news!
—Rom. 10:15b

"**M**ay you live long, live strong, and live happy." This is the wish of all promoters of various medicines and diet programs in their weblogs. It is a traditional belief of almost all world religions that the scriptures they have received from their founders or forebears are sacred, generated by God's Spirit, and effective manuals or guides for humans to reach out to the Supreme Being. The Judeo-Christian is not exempted from this. Every book in the Bible bases all its proposals, strategies, and exhortations on the singular faith that—as we read in the Psalms—"they are spirit and life to us."

Surely, we as humans need spirit and life to live long, live strong, and live happy. When Ezra, the priest-scribe, has read the words from the Jewish scriptures (Neh. 8:3–6) to the gathered assembly so that those words will become the source of their life, the cause of their union, and the bond that will forever unite them with God, they have bowed and accepted every bit of those words.

This event reminded us of the first appearance of Jesus in a synagogue. As Luke narrated, Jesus took the OT scroll of the prophet Isaiah and combined two texts to deliver the words that would outline his life agenda. At the end, he added that all that were prophesied by Isaiah in the OT scriptures were fulfilled in him (Luke 4:18–21). In other words, through the NT books we were made to believe, besides the amazing power of God's Word, that Jesus of Nazareth had come down as the Word of God, in whom all that had been proclaimed by God in the past were fulfilled. Unmistakably, Jesus's words about the Word became more powerful by the fact that he spent his life and went to his death to fulfill them. Through Jesus's words and works, the good news was heard by the poor, captives were liberated, the blind began to see, and the oppressed went free.

The amazing achievements, realized for the past twenty centuries by Jesus's disciples, were possible only because they possessed and preserved God's Word, contained both in OT books and mainly in Jesus, the Word himself. Those words were burning in their hearts unceasingly. Plus, they were all transformed into being, moving, and doing as the true replica of God's Word as Jesus did. This was possible not just by reading, memorizing, and repeating God's Word as a litany and ejaculatory prayers. The disciples in the past tried their best digesting them spiritually through meditation and prayer in solitude.

What we notice in those disciples is very unthinkable to us. They have read or heard the words of God as a group of one heart and accepted them with no dissension among themselves. Actually, they haven't played politics in this spiritual matter. Anyone who has watched an American president addressing the Congress knows the leader will get a varied reception. Members of that political party will be quick to applaud, while those of a different persuasion will be silent, refusing to show their approval. No such partisanship should be present among those who gather to listen to God's words. Look at the Israelites; when Ezra has read God's words, all have been attentive, and all have agreed to accept the word of the law with a wholehearted double amen. Without such unity, first, the Word of God will never be effective within us; and then when we utter our words of advice, suggestion, warning, or appeal, they will never have a fruitful and long-standing effect in our listeners.

Moreover, these disciples never stopped by merely preaching and proclaiming God's words by lips. Like the Master, they were able to establish a relationship with the least ones of society such that they were given the desire and the strength to try to break the chains that robbed them of their freedom. This was how the words of Jesus of Nazareth became "glad tidings to the poor."

We who live in the interim, between Jesus's first impact on the earth and the coming of his ultimate impact, are charged with carrying out his agenda. We are to be good news, as he has been, in the very manner of our being and living.

58. We're the Witnesses of God's Abundance

Rejoice that your names are written in heaven.
—Luke 10:20b

Through the revelation of God in Jesus, we are made to understand that our God is the God of abundance, an unlimited stock of all goodness. We can observe this fact in all his abundant creations. He too is plentiful in his redemptive works. He has identified himself as "a God gracious and merciful, slow to anger and abounding in love and fidelity" (Exod. 34:6). We notice in his every movement and interaction with human beings all his richness, especially his mercy, love, compassion, wisdom, and power. He deliberately desires to make us understand and enjoy such remarkable abundance. In addition, through the prophets, as a rejoicing and loving mother, he proudly invites every human being to enjoy in him his copious blessings and gifts (Isa. 66:10–14).

To enlighten us about such incredible truths, God sent his beloved Son, Jesus, to us as an eyewitness and spokesperson. Jesus faithfully obeyed his Father and lived up to his expectation. However, as a human being, Jesus's life was short and very limited. He witnessed to his Father's abundance through his preaching and healing in and around Palestine as much and as long as he could. As the Gospels verified, there were many places Jesus intended to go but could not to fulfill his ministry. Hence, he appointed many apostles and disciples not to replace him but to represent him and his ministry to those people whom he could not reach (Luke 10:1).

Jesus too underscored there are already plentiful blessings ready to be harvested. He longed for many of us to cooperate with him in harvesting them. He wanted his disciples to go and bear witness to his cause and bring many humans into his fellowship. He categorically told them the only weapon, ammunition, or resource they can have with them for their power and strength was sole dependence on their God of abundance and not money, politics, diplomacy, or human intelligence. Rather, the unimaginable power to win or persuade humans successfully in their ministry entirely depended on one single principle or strategy, namely, total dependence on his God of abundance. This was why he asked them not to take with them anything more than the basic necessities (Luke 10:4).

For more than two millennia, Jesus continues his ministry of witnessing to his Father's abundance of love, compassion, wisdom, and power through his selected discipled leaders. He has appointed us and sent us to our life situations to continue his witnessing ministry as his appointees. From his abundance, he has endowed us with limitless faith, hope, and charity. Above all, he has graced us with an attitude of dependence on the God of abundance. We are bearing on us, as Paul writes, the marks of Jesus the Crucified (Gal. 6:14–18). This means all his discipled leaders are marked with the mind-set of Jesus to depend only on God for all our abundance.

We know what we are and how limited the material and intellectual resources we possess. But we are rich and abundant in our faith, hope, and charity. Thus, we testify to a God who has chosen the weak, like us, to defeat the strong. While two-thirds of Christians in this world behave smart in being indifferent to church witnessing and feel they are wise enough to withdraw their involvement in God's ministries, the other third are selected and chosen by Jesus to show the world how our God of abundance has recreated our personal, family, and community life inside his church of abundance. So many development projects in this world have been accomplished over the centuries not by those who esteem themselves as too smart to enjoy independence and self-gratification and fattened by possessions of riches and properties but by spiritual abundance of widows, widowers, the old, the weak, the poor, and the sick, who are indeed the small group of Jesus's committed disciples.

This makes us rejoice, singing praises and the glory of God today and every day, not because we have fully accomplished it in life as designed by God in Jesus but because we are included in his team of witnesses at present. Many times, it may seem as a thankless task to continue Jesus's ministry in this world of darkness and blindness; however, let us be assured by the promises of Jesus about our ultimate rewards, which are abundant and eternal.

59. We Are Wounded Healers And Resurrected Persons

He is not the God of the dead but of the living.
—Matt. 22:32b

The horrible events of suffering and death are part and parcel of human life. When they happen in our own lives, God expects us to think of his life-giving goodness and compassion. We may hold various perspectives and views about them. The most prevalent among them is "God is angry with us because we have sinned against him. Therefore, he punishes us or chastises us." It is a common assumption that suffering and sin are interconnected. Certainly, there are too many references of it in all the scriptures and in various religious traditions. Many times, we who are born after the age of enlightenment are tempted to retort to our religious mentors who visit us at our sickbed, saying like the widow of Zarephath, "Why have you done this to me, O man of God? Have you come to me to call attention to my guilt and to kill my son?" (1 Kings 17:18). However, God thinks in a different way.

In the book of Job, God overturned the thinking of Job's friends who had concluded that either Job or his children might have sinned that was why he was suffering. Like his Father, Jesus too reacted when his disciples jumped to the conclusion that a man's blindness was the result of his sin (John 9:1–3). Rejecting the logic of his disciples, he proposed a wonderful and very positive conclusion: "Neither he nor his parents sinned; it is so that the works of God might be made visible through him." God was not just talking about the good results of our sufferings; rather, in one way or another, he did wonders in the lives of sufferers.

As OT prophets acted on behalf of God as healing and life-giving agents toward sufferers, we come to understand through the Gospels the remarkable good deeds of Jesus performed in his earthly life for alleviating the afflictions of humans. Through many miracles like raising the dead (Luke 7:11–17), Jesus splendidly testifies to the eternal truth that our God is not a God of death but of life and resurrection; our God is full of compassion and goodness. He never wants us to suffer or even die.

Jesus was a staunch protector of life. He healed those whose lives were burdened by sickness and pain. He forgave sinners whose lives were sad and lonely because their sin alienated them from God and others. He reached out repeatedly to the poor, whose lives were broken by their needs. While others avoided the dead so as not to risk ritual impurity, Jesus touched the dead and restored them to life. In the end, he would give his own life and submit to a torturous death to save sinners from death and assure them of a life everlasting. Strikingly, by his death, he offered salvific life to humanity.

In our times of tribulations and trials, after we personally are strengthened and healed by our Master, we are advised by him to act as "wounded healers" and "resurrected persons" toward those who are burdened with such sufferings. We, the disciples of Jesus, are called to continue the prophetic ministry of caregiving and healing among our fellow men. Undoubtedly, it is a great burden thrust on each and every one of us. Actually, we do many things for the needy, the suffering, and the dying as spouses, as parents, as elders, as children, as doctors, as nurses, and as priests. Many times, this ministry doesn't offer any life and contentment to the beneficiaries as Jesus intends. This is because we always do this in a very natural and earthly way: out of emotions, feelings, pity, sympathy, even out of personal agenda.

This caregiving service, according to God's Spirit, must not be merely a natural humanistic service to others in need. Every serviceable or caregiving action we perform must start with the goal of bringing out the glory of our God and not our own; we should continuously connect closely with the risen Lord in prayer and discipline. We should conduct ourselves in this matter as Paul has behaved: "I want you to know, brothers and sisters, that the gospel preached by me is not of human origin. For I did not receive it from a human being, nor was I taught it, but it came through a revelation of Jesus Christ."

Once we rise and walk from the times of troubles
and trials through our prayer and faith, our Master
invites us to testify to it, shouting loud to our friends
who are still in agony as the psalmist sings, "The Lord
brought me up from the nether world; He preserved
me from among those going to the pit; He changed my
mourning into dancing. Yes, certainly He will do it
to you also. Come let us praise the Lord Most High!"
That is the most influential strategy in our caregiving
ministries.

60. Humans, Created Good but Saved to Be Better

Son of Man has come to seek and to save what was lost.
—Luke 19:10

The Bible is fondly called "the Good Book"; I love to add
to the title, making it "the Good Book for Bad People
and Sinners." I have coined this name out of me being
overinfluenced by the millions of verses found in the
Bible. To sum up all those verses, let me quote Jesus:
"I have not come to call the righteous to repentance
but sinners" (Luke 5:32). The Christian scriptures
and traditions have been overwhelmed with the single
proclamation to humanity for centuries, namely, our
God in Jesus relates himself kindheartedly to any kind
sinner on the earth. In the book of Wisdom, we are told
about God, "He is merciful to all, he does overlook men's
sins that they may repent. He loves them because his
immortal spirit is in all of them. Therefore he corrects
little by little those who trespass, and reminds and warns

them of the things wherein they sin, that they may be freed from wickedness and put their trust in him" (12:1). And the psalmist, several times in his hymns, repeats his favorite litany: "The Lord is kind and full of compassion, slow to anger, abounding in love" (Ps. 144).

Therefore, being the God-sent Son, the one and only message that Jesus has lived and preached and for which he has established his church is the same one of God's mercy his forebears have experienced. In the same strain, we find Jesus knowing wisely all of what the humans are; he has thoroughly perceived how we play the gimmicks with the merciful God. As John underlines, Jesus knows what is in man (John 2:24–25). To enlighten and liberate us from such grim make-up situations, he inserted into his life's performances and sayings. One is his encounter with a rich tax collector (Luke 19:1–10).

That tax collector's name was Zacchaeus, who was scorned as a public sinner. He seemed to be a dishonest person at his job of tax collecting. People looked at him with contempt mainly because, in their eyes, he was a traitor to his religious and national heritage. The unanimous verdict by the public on Zacchaeus was guilty. Inevitably, a rich man like Zacchaeus would be privately disturbed about his dishonest life, in which case he was intimidated to appear in the crowd as he wanted to be acquainted with Jesus. This was why he climbed up the tree to look for him.

This is a typical behavior of any sinner. When we commit any sin against God and others, we try to hide from the public, sometimes like what our first parents have done (Gen. 3:8). We try to hide ourselves from God by becoming very busy in our development. Many of us put on a smile or behave as champions of morality by joining extreme positions and ideologies like terrorism, fanaticism, fundamentalism, and so on. This is what Zacchaeus has done in the Gospel event.

However, while most of us—to appease our guilty conscience—chose drug addiction, alcoholism, or any other perversions, Zacchaeus was searching for Jesus and his acquaintance to get relief. According to the Gospels, there exist a perennially high "psychic vibration" between Jesus and his disciples, whom he would be recruiting for his cause. Immediately finding the contrite heartbeat of the sinful "would-be disciple," he looked up and said to him, "Zacchaeus! Make haste and come down; for I must stay at your house today."

That was the heart of Jesus. Jesus pardoned Zacchaeus's sins not just because he offered him a sumptuous dinner. As the Gospel said, the sinner showed his repentance by the loving gesture of penitential reparation in front of the public. He decided to share most of his riches with the poor and with those he hurt by his injustice as retribution. This made Jesus say, "Today salvation has come to this house, since he also is a son of Abraham."

Not only those who were planning to become discipled leaders in Jesus's gang but also those of us already recruited yet had not been reconciled with God's mercy should do something about our burden of guilt by taking positive steps, like Zacchaeus, to liberate ourselves from guilt feelings. The Creator made us humans out of clay to be good, to be godly, and to live and enjoy God's favor and peace. But like Zacchaeus, many times, we failed to be so and fell into the pit of desolation. But out of his mercy, God sent his Son, Jesus, through whom we were given salvation to become better and greater as our Creator intended.

61. The Right Scale
For the Right Judgment about Us

He is the one appointed by God as judge
of the living and the dead.
—Acts 10:42

Very frequently, people around us judge us either rightly or wrongly; but most of the times, we know their judgment is wrong because they don't use the proper yardstick or criterion in their half-baked judicial enterprise. The same is true about our own judgments of our life. It is true, we too are incorrect in our judgments because we use improper yardsticks, and even in a pharisaical way, we interpret those yardsticks according to our convenience.

We often say to ourselves, *Am I leading a proper life pleasing to God?* The question arises from the way we have been brought up, formed, groomed, nourished, and developed by society, which is disorderly, unjust, and dishonest in so many ways, especially making every human and every nature's creations as mere commodities for buying and selling and worth nothing more, even the name of God, his religion, his scriptures, his traditions, and all that have been erected as his house of prayer and divine interactions. A sample of such millions of commercial brutalities is seen in the Gospel event (John 2:13–25) of Jesus cleaning up God's temple by whips of anger and zeal. We hear him shouting out to those sellers, "Take these out of here, and stop making my Father's house a marketplace."

As God is good and holy, he expects his creation to be so too. Anything that goes beyond or below his will must be either riveted or punished by him. God knows what is human and what is inhuman: "Jesus would not trust himself to them because he knew them all, and did not need anyone to testify about human nature. He himself understood it well." Hence, to safeguard the holiness and goodness of his creations, especially human creatures, God has proposed his laws as our best touchstones for assessing our handling of life. Those are the Ten Commandments, which he has handed down through Moses to his chosen ones and those who have come after (Exod. 20:1–17). These laws are to govern humans' attitudes and actions toward God and one another as the terms of their covenantal relationship with God. These precepts challenge our efforts at honesty, uprightness, justice, and fairness. They safeguard us and our communities.

This was why Jesus applied those ten yardsticks very faithfully, and by the same, he judged his own life as well as those of his disciples. He emphasized, "Do not think that I have come to abolish the law or the prophets. I have come not to abolish but to fulfill. Amen, I say to you, until heaven and earth pass away, not the smallest letter or the smallest part of a letter will pass from the law, until all things have taken place." He too, following his Father, highlighted the efficacy of those laws, bringing either blessings or curses: "Therefore, whoever breaks one of the least of these commandments and teaches others to do so will be called least in the kingdom of heaven. But whoever obeys and teaches these commandments will be called greatest in the kingdom of heaven" (Matt. 5:17–19).

While he was totally in alliance with God's commandments, he observed how badly God's people desecrated and damaged those commandments and heavenly values. Hence, taking his own revelatory whip of wisdom and power, he enhanced those laws. We noticed this in all his sayings, in particular in the Sermon on the Mount and in his newly packaged and synthesized law of love, and he ordered us to love God totally and to love our neighbor as he did.

This means that our love for God should be the zeal that has consumed Jesus and that our love for neighbors must be the sign of the cross and the only medium to proclaim to the world, "Christ crucified as the power and wisdom of God" (1 Cor. 22–25). Our Master has averred that this is the only way to get into the heavenly mansions: "I tell you, unless your righteousness surpasses that of the scribes and Pharisees, you will not enter into the kingdom of heaven" (Matt. 5:20). Today his Spirit calls us to revisit our way of judging ourselves and to apply some appropriate benchmarks, through which we can honestly reach the right conclusion about our life.

62. The Christian's God Is Two in One

God is a just judge, powerful and patient,
not exercising anger every day.
—Ps. 7:12

Kindly don't misunderstand that I am disowning my faith in the dogma of Trinity. I firmly uphold my Christian creed of "God in three persons." Here, I want to throw some light on another dimension of our God spelled out throughout the Bible, which reiterates that

God is both just and compassionate. This fact is plainly brought out by Jesus's tiny parable about a fig tree (Luke 13:6–9).

In the story, besides the fig tree representing humans, there are the two persons debating with each other about the fate of the fig tree that has not yielded any fruit as it is designed. These two persons symbolize vividly the two characters of God. The owner of the orchard symbolizes the justice side of God, and the gardener epitomizes his second side of being compassionate and patient. Ultimately, the winner is the compassionate character of God.

Jesus, as we know throughout his life, has never been exhausted in emphasizing the compassionate dimension of God's character. He has so many sayings and parables to portray this truth. In his story of the fig tree, he expresses the eternal patience of God with humans, waiting and waiting in their pathway of life for their conversion from sinfulness. The merciful God is patient and gives everyone a chance. At the same time, Jesus has never missed to remind his contemporaries the just side of God's nature by explaining the historical accidents and calamities that have occurred at his time as well as in biblical history (Luke 13:1–5). As matter of fact, Jesus insists how God's compassion and mercy can wear out because he is just, and he will punish the sinners.

Though Gospel writers list many conditions to follow Jesus as his disciples, they underscore the effective strategy of maintaining our discipleship with Jesus to claim our rewards from God. This strategy is nothing but "to be just as the heavenly Father is just" and "to be merciful as the Almighty is merciful." There is no alternate way to attain the heavenly crown for all that we accomplish as Jesus's disciples.

In this regard, Paul is our role model. From his letters, we perceive how awesomely he intertwines God's resolute justice and his enduring. He points out how God could not tolerate the disobedience and indifference of human beings, especially his chosen ones. He writes that our merciful God—though he has done so many miraculous deeds for the life, freedom, and happiness of his people—has not been pleased with most of them and therefore has struck them down in the desert; he has even destroyed them all because of their evil deeds. God thus has showed his nature of being just. At the same time, Paul adds that the same God, out of compassion, has led his people through the saving waters and given them manna to eat, despite many who have failed to respond to his love and perished (1 Cor. 10:1–12).

Our God whom we worship is both compassionate and just. As a holy and heavenly Father, his only dream is that all his human children should attain their destiny. An entire lifetime is given to each one of us to bear fruits to carry with us to the eternal life. At the same time, God knows we—on our way to eternity—fail, stumble, fall, faint, detour, and deviate because of our human weakness, sinfulness, ignorance, perverted freedom, and pride. With deep concern for us, God waits for our complete winning.

In compassion, God is patiently waiting for our conversion and sanctification. He gives us freedom to choose to rise and to return to him; he too gives a long rope and allows us to prolong our indifference, coldness, and carelessness and even permits us to hit the bottom. We are left to decide whether to catch the same rope and climb up from the pit or to use the same rope to hang and ruin ourselves. He uses the signs of the times to bring us back to our right senses and to view our life as it is. These signs are natural calamities, disasters, other people's sickness, death, and especially all the evil things that occur to us in our private and family life. God waits for our conversion. This is God's justice-oriented compassion. The justice of God always makes itself felt, but regrettably, to us, it sometimes appears unjust.

63. Our God Is Life, Love, and Communion

In the name of the Father, and of the
Son, and of the Holy Spirit.
—Matt. 28:19

One of the most controversial terms perennially debated in humanity is "God." It has become not only a contentious issue but also a source of fight, terrorism, war, and murder around the globe. Because of so many versions, teachings, and convictions about this name, millions of human beings are drifting away from that name, which a large portion of humanity esteems as the only life-giving force. From the beginning of human race, people have felt an inner and intrinsic connection between themselves and this God.

While they experienced him and his presence, they could not explain him totally and fully. When their children asked them to explain about their God, they tried to offer some explanations, but it was always incomplete such as "He is wisdom, power, force, nature, and even pleasure in itself." There are others who consider God as a judge, destroyer, policeman, or sleeping beauty. Many fell so short of words that either most of them failed or were incomplete or they even spoiled the integrity of God. Therefore, many religions advise us to approach God as a mystery and behold his power and support through contemplation and meditation.

Christianity, through its scriptures and tradition, has tried to describe this mystery as clearly as possible. So we believe God as Father, Son, and Spirit—three in one. They, though different from one another, are united in equality. As St. Augustine acknowledges, this description is still limited; though Jesus has delivered his revelation as complete and total, still, we humans have to struggle to understand it. Hence, in every age, solid attempts are made to know this mystery a little more clearly. In this postmodern age, possessing all kinds of research studies of different religions and their description of God and combining our own as Trinity, we can understand and meditate about our God in the following way, which is more relevant to our daily life.

Our God is the Father, meaning he is the Source of Life. The Hebrew term for father, "Abba," denotes the creativeness of God. He is the Source of all things in the universe. He maintains it, protects it, and destroys it. Everything is functioning according to his will. This is what Moses tells his people about their God, who has been interacting with them as they have made their journey to the Promised Land.

Our God is the Son, denoting he is the Source of Love. "God is love" is a theme of our religion and scriptures. Jesus has shown in his incarnation that, by being the Son of God, he has suffered and died for love of God and love of people. God becomes a victim of love, a sacrifice of love. He has loved us first. He expects an intimacy of love in him and around him. In the second reading, Paul speaks about that intimacy of love that exists between God and Jesus and us.

And our God is the Holy Spirit, pointing out he is the Source of Communion. God is a communion floating in love. The Spirit Jesus has introduced us to is the symbol of God's communion. He connected the Father with the Son, Jesus, and he is connecting them with each and every one of us. This is what the Gospel of Jesus is all about. "Go to all nations and bring everyone to this communion. I shall be there among you until the end of ages." It is the Father and Jesus's Spirit of communion that remains forever with us. God is a family, a community, and a relationship.

This is what we believe in. This is what we participate in. Through baptism, together with our children and children's children, we have entered into the Christian faith in the name of the Triune God as our life, our love, and our communion.

If we go to a psychologist and ask him to help you find out who you are, he will answer you, "First, you tell me who your friend is, and then I will tell you who you are." But if you come to a religious, spiritual counselor with the same question, he/she will surely reply, "First, you tell me what kind of God you profess and worship. Then I will surely tell you who you are." It is a truthful fact of human behavior that its large portion is being influenced by each person's approach to the God figure.

64. The Christian Life Is
A Beatified Kingdom of God

Let the same attitude be in you that also Christ Jesus had.
—Phil. 2:5

We read in the Gospels Jesus preaching about the kingdom of heaven. In the past and even now, many of us hold a misunderstanding or misinterpretation about the term "the kingdom of God." Some say that Jesus has congratulated the weaklings for their disabled status, neediness, and homelessness. Many consider the kingdom of God as the heaven we are supposed to go after our death. Some others explain it as the political and social territory of our religion, Christianity.

Unfortunately, all those descriptions and definitions are not what the Lord intends to tell us. In the textual context, the word "kingdom" denotes our human life. Every one of us, as we grow older, begins to establish or build our own life with self-respect, freedom, and responsibility. Therefore, each one of us forms our own life as our kingdom with its boundaries, walls, rules, formulas, and codes; it includes first our individuality with its body and soul and then our family and so on.

However, as human experience shows, almost all the time, the kingdom we build turns to be full of sadness, discontentment, and peacelessness and many times very destructive. Let us look at the human history where we observe nonstop family feuds, infighting in communities, wars with destructive ammunitions, and even problems existing perennially in the kingdom of our own body and spirit. As the scriptures state, the whole human race—in their own kingdoms—live and move in darkness and gloom.

This was why God sent his Son as the Lamb, the Light, the Way for humans to restructure once again their personal kingdoms as realms of joyful and peaceful living. Jesus's entire life ministry concentrated on this matter and taught us how to keep our kingdom, our earthly realm of life, as God's. He firmly convinced us that we humans are the children of God and created in God's image and likeness and that, therefore, we possess the capacity to rebuild our kingdom into God's.

The kingdom that Jesus points out is a godly realm, and it is a life full of justice, love, contentment, joy, and peace. In that kingdom, there is always blessing, fraternity, balanced mind-set, and level-ground walking. He longs that, in all steps of life, his disciples should be joyful. To understand the tips Jesus has offered for possessing this unique "beatified" life situation, as Paul advises, we have to look at Jesus himself, "who became for us wisdom from God, as well as righteousness, sanctification, and redemption" (1 Cor. 1:30).

As Jesus preached in the Sermon on the Mount about the nine steps to achieve our beatified life (Matt. 5:1–12), he was more concerned about our present life than what would come after this life. Undeniably, he emphasized that there is heaven beyond this earthly life but only as its extension or continuity. To enter fully the heavenly kingdom, we should start it here before we die. The Gospel slogans of the beatitudes of Christ, therefore, challenge us to accept the kingdom of God, live accordingly, and try to make our lives as truly the kingdoms of God. The Christian life is nothing but a beatified kingdom of God.

65. The Christian Life Is a Risky But Very Rewarding Business

Well done, my good and faithful servant . . .
Come, share your master's joy.
—Matt. 25:21

Jesus never hesitated to expose his desire to see his followers being aware of the big bang event happening after our death. It is going to be a kind of ultimate tax-return day, with all its payments back and forth, when we are supposed to submit to our Creator and Proprietor regarding how we have made use of his talents, gifts, and blessings according to his will. This means every use of every talent God has provided us with should most likely have or be near to the desired outcome.

Through the parable of the talents (Matt. 25:14–30), our Master stated that our heavenly Father bestowed to every one of us plentiful gifts to trade with in his kingdom. We should know that, in Jesus's time, a talent was a large sum of money, the equivalent of six thousand denarii or the equivalent of the wages of a day laborer for fifteen years. One denarius was the wage of a common daily laborer.

God distributes such enormous gifts according to his plan of action. We have no say in it, or we can murmur and be frustrated over the matter and do nothing about the gifts being offered to us. Jesus expects us to use whatever gifts we are endowed with as best as we can.

There are also people among us who find excuses for their laziness as the third person in the parable by saying, "Master, I knew you were a demanding person; so out of fear I went off and buried your talent in the ground. Here it is back." In other words, some of us think that—since our God is very good and kind and therefore will surely save us, no matter what we do— we do nothing to improve, to multiply, or to apply the available gifts for better use. We too hold another wrong notion about the "fear of God," by which we think the merciful Father will waive his punishment against us.

On the other hand, God instructs us in the book of Proverb (chapter 31), pointing out an industrious lady whom he praises highly and presents to us as a role model in handling the fear of the Lord in a wise way. Her fear is not merely a fright but rather reverential awe and respect for God. It is her human consciousness about the existence and intervention of a Supreme God who is, for her, the sole giver of the talents and blessings she possesses, and she tries to use every bit of her talents as an opportunity for acknowledging God and serving others.

God's revelation also instructs us that we must be conscious of our risky but only available present moment. "As children of light, you are not in darkness," insists Paul (1 Thess. 5:1–6), who uses verbs in the present tense, suggesting that the life of the future, for which we wait, begins here and now. Jesus will indeed come again, but let us not lose sight of the fact that he has already come and moved among us, showing in his words and works the loving mercies of God. The life that we long to live forever has already begun in us at baptism.

Therefore, our belonging to Christ and to God should be evident in words, deeds, thoughts, and motivations so transparent that they reflect the goodness and grace of God. We should uphold this daily in our relationships and dealings with others: all of us are the children of light and children of the day.

66. The Rare Blend of the Christian Life

You are thinking not as God but as human beings do.
—Matt. 16:23

While our Master Jesus was living physically in our world, he had been frequently giving surprises to his disciples—many times in his speeches, sometimes in his performing miraculous deeds, but most of the times in his very life, shattering and shocking the people by his controversial behavior in public. One of them is the event of Palm Sunday.

At any time in life, Jesus never wished to be honored or glorified as a celebrity; he never permitted anyone to call him good (Mark 10:18) or to make him king (John 6:15). Though this kind of behavior of Jesus was not welcomed by the disciples, his attitude of humility was commendable to them when he said, "The Son of Man did not come to be served but to serve and to give his life as a ransom for many" (Mark 10:45). Jesus too commanded his disciples they should differ from other leaders: "Let the greatest among you be as the youngest, and the leader as the servant" (Luke 22:25–27). John the Evangelist discovered this attitude of Jesus not only from his lips but also in action when he washed the disciples' feet at the Last Supper (John 13:1–20).

Nonetheless, the disciples were bewildered to see Jesus—who was a humble and unostentatious person—accepting a pompous welcome from the public. Besides, they couldn't find any meaning in his funny and deriding desire to ride on an ass with its colt. This was because his disciples did not understand this. Also, they viewed by the natural light of humanness anything they came across in life, be it becoming disciples of Jesus or the dreams about their future by staying in the team of the Messiah.

However, our compassionate Master never left them in that same state of grim darkness. He promised before he left them that they would understand all his words and deeds through the Spirit. "The Advocate, the holy Spirit that the Father will send in my name—he will teach you everything and remind you of all that told you" (John 14:26). There was a different connotation about what the Lord promised and did to his disciples. In his narration about the Palm Sunday event, John wrote that, at first, the disciples didn't understand what was going on that day, but later they did. "When Jesus had been glorified they remembered that these things were written about him and that they had done this for him."

Here is the most striking factor the Spirit invites us to reflect in what John contributes to our spiritual life. According to the biblical scholars, John's Gospel is highly literary and symbolic, interpreting all the deeds and words of Jesus as "heavenly signs" for revealing the glory of God's only Son, who has come to reveal the Father and then returned in glory to the Father.

As closing remark, John writes, "Now Jesus did many other signs . . . But these are written that you may come to believe that Jesus is the Messiah, the Son of God, and that through this belief you may have life in his name" (John 20:30–31).

On this background, John interpreted the passion and death of Jesus as the sign of his glorification, as the Son glorifying his Father. Jesus's being lifted on the cross was an ascension in glory. In it, everything was fulfilled; by it, he would be the owner of the entire humanity. "When I am lifted up from the earth, I will draw everyone to myself" (John 12:32). As he was a paradoxical entity of a rare blend of humanity and divinity, he demonstrated how we, his disciples, should cope with and succeed in maintaining our own duality of body and soul, a rare blend of social and personal dimensions as we go through our earthly life, which is again another shocking blend of ups and downs, glory and fame, joys and sorrows, darkness and light, and certainly death and life.

His disciples, being subdued by natural order, couldn't grasp this blend factor. Only after being enlightened by the Spirit did they understand everything in detail. They then were ready to descend even to the hellish life for the sake of God's kingdom because they were convinced that they were, after all, ascending to heavenliness; they were rejoicing to be persecuted because it was a part of the rare blend of Christian life. We learn such an astounding fact from Jesus every day as we sit down before the Lord on the hilltop.

67. The Christian Personality Is
A Rare Blend of Glory and Suffering

When I am lifted up . . . I will draw everyone to myself.
—John 12:32

The whole dynamics of our Christian life is centered on our discipleship to Christ, our leader and guru who demands from us a clear understanding of his identity as the primary requirement to join his company. This we come to know by the friendly and very personal question he has asked his disciples: "Who do you say that I am?" Mark writes this in his narration about one of the best emotional events that have occurred in the life of Jesus and his disciples.

Jesus wanted, from his prime group of disciples, to clarify and verify the authentic version of the gossips that went around him. When they spelled out the reality of people's assertions, he immediately jumped up to the above-mentioned question. In other words, Jesus knew about what the public was saying about him. Hence, knowledge of the public gossips was not the main reason he put that question; rather, he slowly led his disciples to assimilate personally what his primary requisite from them was for their discipleship.

His disciples, through Peter, answered very well: "You are the Messiah." And Jesus was indeed very happy about it. However, he wanted to go further to what they lack in their knowledge about him. It was a good answer but an incomplete one. This was why Jesus corrected them, giving an additional note about his identity: "The Son of Man must suffer greatly and be rejected by the elders, the chief priests, and the scribes, and be killed, and rise after three days." He was trying to assert that he was not only a glorious Messiah but also a suffering one. He was truthful to what Isaiah predicted of him in OT (Isa. 50:5–9).

As a matter of fact, his additional note about his life consisting in a rare blend of glory and suffering was a big surprise and blow to his disciples. It surely led them in despair and a little bit of anger and disappointment. Their hurt feeling was exposed by Peter's rebuking of Jesus. "Get behind me, Satan," Jesus said to Peter with a vehement rebuke. "You are thinking not as God does, but as human beings do."

By the same token, Jesus too pronounced his own terms and conditions for anyone planning to follow him as his disciple: "Whoever wishes to come after me must deny himself, take up his cross, and follow me." That was a horrible, cyclonic blast for the disciples, but they just accepted their Master's stroke as a beloved gesture. They were in dismay till they received Jesus's resurrected Spirit, who not only enlightened them but also strengthened them to live the rare-blend discipleship life.

I am sure most of us may still be living in the same reaction of the first disciples. We may ask ourselves, "How exactly do we pull this off? Do we actually arrange to have ourselves scourged, nails pounded in our wrists and feet, and raised on a cross?" Undoubtedly, some of us—as martyrs and saints—are called to suffer in the same physical way in which Jesus has died. But not all of us are called to be so. Jesus expects his disciples to suffer and die "small deaths" in their daily life.

One series of deaths we encounter daily is the troublesome situations in human relationship as Jesus, the prophets, and his messengers like the psalmist have undergone. But they have stood on the ground of piety, honesty, truth, and justice. They have even questioned their opponents, "If anyone wishes to oppose me, let us appear together. Who disputes my right? Let that man confront me. See, the Lord God is my help; who will prove me wrong?" It is nothing but a reference to how each one of us psychologically and emotionally is affected daily by the oppositions, misunderstandings, and disagreements occurring in our human relationships.

There is another kind of small death we should undergo. While the first kind is in our relationship with equals, the second kind is in our relationship with those who are considered below us—the needy, downtrodden, and neglected ones. Through James, Jesus teaches that simply upholding our creed and faith is not enough to be called Jesus's disciples. We have to get out of our couches or comfort zones, say something about God's values, and do something about it among people so that our Father in heaven will be glorified. "What good is it, my brothers and sisters, if someone says he has faith but does not have works? Can that faith save him?" (James 2:14–18).

By our charitable commitments, we may lose our money, talent, and time, which perhaps will have been used for our self-gratification and self-entertainment. It pinches truly our undisciplined self; it makes us many times feel we have lost a lot. This is our daily cross. Jesus tells us today that we have to follow him in taking up the crosses that come our way.

68. The Mind-Boggling Human Family Tree

I am the root and offspring of David, the bright morning star.
—Rev. 22:16b

I am reminded of a saying posted in one of the church's signboards that reads "Our family tree traces back to the cross of Christ." Very true, but we should also add to this beautiful statement by enlarging it through the scriptural prism of the cross: "Our family tree traces way back to the Triune family of God."

Jesus has revealed and instructed us that the origin and source of all humans born in this world is none other than his Father God. And therefore, those who move around his cross invoke God as "Abba, Father." According to God's eternal plan, humans must worship only him and him alone.

Before Israelites have been chosen as his exclusive children, humans have been ignorant and indifferent to the divine desire. However, in the light of Christ, we are convinced that every human born in this or any planet has the right to be called God's children. This is what Paul has claimed when he has preached at Athens.

Pointing out to an altar dedicated to an unknown god, among the shrines constructed for Greek gods and goddesses, the apostle attested that the God unknown to the Gentiles was the One he preached. He too said, "He is the God who made the world and everything in it. He himself gives life and breath to everything, and he satisfies every need. His purpose was for the nations [humans] to seek after God and perhaps feel their way toward him and find him—though he is not far from any one of us." Paul too reminded the hearers of one amazing saying by one of their poets: "We are his offspring" (Acts 17:22–30).

When God the Father made certain humans in the form of team or community to be his representatives, he proposed how his offspring in this globe should behave and reciprocate his fatherly love. Being by nature a jealous person, he too repeatedly detailed how humans should love him: "Hear, O Israel! The Lord is our God, the Lord alone! Therefore, you shall love the Lord, your God, with your whole heart, and with your whole being, and with your whole strength" (Deut. 6:4–5). Remembering his undivided parental love, he wanted them to love him in return with filial devotion. Regrettably, neither his leaders nor his chosen children— as most of the Gentiles—behaved as the Father proposed; instead, they were arrogant, self-centered, and very stubborn in fulfilling his love will. The eternal family tree was seemingly being annihilated and uprooted.

But God the Father, the Source of Life, never lost his heart. Scriptures declared that we got the very good news of God by sending to the human children his beloved Son, who was from the beginning part and parcel of the godly family tree, from where the entire creation came to exist. Through the cross of obedience, self-immolation, and love fulfillment, not only did Jesus save every human during his Palestinian life but he, through his resurrection, also became an energy, a movement, and a loving resource whom he told us to call as the Holy Spirit.

The Christian life starts, proceeds, and ends in the name of the Triune God—Father, Son, and Holy Spirit. Before Jesus has ascended to heaven, he has commanded his disciples to baptize us in that mysterious name (Matt. 28:16–20). "Baptizing" and "becoming Christians" mean sinking deeply into a marvelous religious faith in the Triune God. We honor a God who lives in the community of a covenant relationship with us; that means a God who makes us like his blood relatives, a God as close to us as a marriage partner, a God who prefers us to his own Son as he has let Jesus give his life for us, a God who keeps stirring us through the Spirit with the inspirations of love, tenderness, compassion, and courage.

As a marvelous result of being baptized in the faith of the Trinity, we are privileged not only to be inducted as a member of the community of God, the church, but also to be inserted once again in a more renewed way into the family tree of Father, Son, and Spirit. The Triune God, in himself, is a unified family of three persons. What makes our Christian community so exceptional and unique is the belief that we, though divided in various ways, are unified as one family, which is founded on the love of our Triune God, which "has been poured into our hearts by the Holy Spirit which has been given to us" (Rom. 5:5).

69. Our Life Not Trumpeted but Truly Triumphed

You will receive power when the Holy Spirit comes upon you.
—Acts 1:8a

The Christian faith enacted by Jesus in the paschal mystery doesn't end with his resurrection. Scripturally, its summit is his ascension, which portrays that he finally has become our triumphant Messiah-King and started reigning in glory over all creation. He has gained possession of all power and glory from his Father for his successful life accomplishment in this world for thirty-three years, after he has done everything required of him. We are so happy to hear such positive thoughts and claims about Jesus, the crucified Lord. Indeed, we feel proud of being one of the disciples and followers in this twenty-first century of such a dynamic leader with a high status.

We are also happy for another very important reason. It is for those promises he has left with us before he has departed from this world. He has offered his followers three important promises for their "quality life." He has promised that he will entrust his redemptive work to them. "You will be my witnesses in Jerusalem, throughout Judea and Samaria, and to the ends of the earth" (Acts 1:8b). "Go into the whole world and proclaim the gospel to every creature" (Mark 16:15). This means he trusts them, though he "would not trust himself to them because he knew them all, and did not need anyone to testify about human nature. He himself understood it well" (John. 2:24–25). The main reason he loves them very much as his own siblings is that he is fully sure that, with his intimate cooperation, they will be up to his dreams.

Another promise he has given his followers is that he will share with them his power and glory. "I am sending the promise of my Father upon you; but stay in the city until you are clothed with power from on high" (Luke 24:49). The power Jesus has promised consists in three fruitful and resourceful elements such as "power of faith," which induces us to be firmly convinced of the presence and actions of God and his spiritual messengers; "power of hope," which is a strong vision that there is always a bright tomorrow; and "power of love," through which we conduct our life and our roles with a balanced understanding of relationship, fellowship, and leadership.

History testifies that his disciples have realized Jesus's promise in their lives. When they have gotten his triple power, they have accomplished all that Jesus has predicted. "These signs will accompany those who believe: in my name they will drive out demons, they will speak new languages. They will pick up serpents [with their hands], and if they drink any deadly thing, it will not harm them. They will lay hands on the sick, and they will recover" (Mark 16:17–18). He too has promised that he will never leave them orphans: "And behold, I am with you always, until the end of the age" (Matt. 28:20b). Up to this day and certainly the days to come, the risen and ascended Lord stays in the church and in the hearts of his disciples and continues to work marvelous deeds that ordinary humans can never venture with and accomplish.

All these promises make us feel positive about our human life. Being a Christian is not worthless or useless. We are chosen by Christ at the time of baptism and confirmation to be his disciples. We too have accepted it. If we sincerely accept and follow Jesus as our Master and Leader, then all his promises will be realized in every one of us. Mainly, he will invest in us his power so that we can do marvelous works on his behalf. This power enables us to give a powerful witness to Christ in our earthly life. This power is also abundantly available to us to face various sufferings and hurdles and to live our faith and Gospel values. This power also helps us in our fight against the evil powers and dark forces of hell. It fills us with enlightenment and wisdom, with joy and serenity. This power assists us in repenting, forgiving our enemies, and loving everyone.

70. Powerfully Individualistic but Shamefully Disunited

These are the ones who cause divisions.
They live on the natural plane, devoid of the Spirit.
—Jude 1:19

We live by energy, we love energy, and we breathe energy. Our life ends when our internal system of energy ends. The most powerful forces are outside us. We feel them, but we don't see them. All these powers and energies are invisible. We see where they come from. We feel their results and know where and when they end. But we surely cannot understand their shape, their form, their color, and their dimension.

Above all these powers, we believe there is the most powerful and eternal power, namely, God. Though as any other we are incapable of seeing him, we are aware of his deeds to humans and the whole universe. While esteeming God as the Supreme Power, we believe in the light of the scriptures that he has shared his power with humanity on two occasions.

First, he shared his power with humans after creating the entire universe. He offered them the power of individuality. God gave us natural power to probe into the mysteries and unseen powers of nature.

We brought many of those natural powers under our control. This was why, with the psalmist, we loved to sing loudly, "What is man that you are mindful of him . . . You have given him rule over the works of your hands, put all things at his feet" (Ps. 8:5–7).

And the second occasion when the Lord of the universe shared his power was the day of Pentecost. He offered to the human beings the power of community—an energy to be together, a power to be united in diversities. The Bible told us the disciples were together as one family, praying for the power. When they got it, we noticed that their spirit of unity energized all the people of different races, languages, and cultures, hearing everything the disciples spoke in their own tongues.

It is indeed hard for a natural man to be together with other people. Individually, we are gifted to dominate, to control, and to possess. But God wants human not to be a loner. A person cannot be full and whole unless he/she becomes a community person. This is why God has poured down his power from on high to energize men and women to become a community. Traditionally, the church feels this is the day she is born. The church's main goal to be here on the earth is to be a sign of that second creation, the second shower of God's power of community.

St. Paul beautifully states (1 Cor. 12:3b–13) how the Holy Spirit becomes the center and core of making us live together. Without him, it's impossible for us to be together. However smart we may be, however diplomatic or politically correct we may behave, we humans will not arrive at a genuine unity or togetherness without the power of the Holy Spirit. Paul affirms that no one can confess Jesus as Lord except in the Holy Spirit. This means that any effort to build up a community on the basis of confessing Jesus as the Lord cannot be possible or genuine if it does not start, continue, and end in his Spirit. He also tells us that all the gifts, charismata, ministries, and talents come from the same Spirit, from one God, and for the one church. The individual manifestation, achievement, is given for the sake of common good, not for individual benefits. Plus, the same apostle reminds us it is by and in the Spirit that we are one body of Christ. Oneness comes by the presence of the Spirit.

These days, it is very hard to bring people together, not only the secular and the religious, not just different religious people but also and much worse those disciples who say they confess Jesus as their Lord, those who claim they have charismata from the Spirit, and those who are convinced that they are the members of the true body of Christ. We should be careful with those enemies inside the campus of the disciples of Jesus who work against the spirit of community.

Pope Francis, addressing a group of new leaders of the church in mission countries (September 2016), asked them to "watch out carefully the works of the devil in their missionary activities." Especially, he pointed out that "divisions are the weapon that the devil has most at hand to destroy the Church from within." Hence, he exhorted them, "Please fight against divisions, because it is one of the weapons that the devil has to destroy the local Church and the universal Church."

We see many Christians around the globe behaving very individualistically and being injurious to the unity of the church. We can easily identify those enemies of Christ. Any person who is always claiming his or her right and living an isolated life or not interested in or hateful to community life is certainly a mini-Antichrist; he/she is the agent of the devil who has sneaked into the Garden of Eden and snatched away the first parents from God. We need both the power of individuality and the power of unity or community. The only possible solution for eradicating scandalous disunity among us is nothing but the empowerment of the Spirit.

71. The Invisible Church within a Visible Church

All the nations will be assembled before him.
And he will separate them one from another.
—Matt. 25:32

One day as I was browsing blogs, I came across *The Cyber Hymnal*, a site in which a hymn written and composed by Kent E. Schneider is posted. It started with the verse "There's a church within us, O Lord; not a building, but a soul; not a portion but a whole; there's a church within us, O Lord." That offered me an inspiration to understand the intricacy of the identity of the church. There can be a church either within or even without the church.

Augustine, many centuries back, has already verbalized these amazing twofoldness of the church. He has termed them "the visible" and "the invisible." What he means is within this one church Jesus has established, there are two realities: there is a visible institutional church consisting of more than two billions nominally, but there is also an invisible church that is made up of genuine believers from all ages who are known only to God; these members of invisible church have actually been regenerated or quickened by the Holy Spirit, God's elect or true believers. Unbelievably, later, a good many theologians have added a fact to this ecclesiology, saying that this invisible church may include even those non–church members.

Augustine drew this debatable contention from the scriptures only, largely from NT. Jesus stated this through the parable of the wheat and weeds (Matt. 13:30). He had ruthlessly divided his own church members in these two categories. He separated them as one group lisping "Lord, Lord" but not doing God's will and the other not only saying "Lord, Lord" to him but also fulfilling what his Father expected them to do.

He too underlined that, at the Last Judgment, he would visibly divide his church members into two. One group, calling them as goats, would be cursed; and the other, as his beloved sheep, would be blessed. The only criterion for such a terrifying judgment is observing his new commandment of love. Both Paul and Peter have followed our Master's perception and written about it in their letters: "Set apart for the service of the gospel that God promised long ago through his prophets in the Holy Scriptures" (Rom. 1:2). "You are 'a chosen race, a royal priesthood, a holy nation, a people of his own, so that you may announce the praises' of him who called you out of darkness into his wonderful light" (1 Pet. 2:9).

These chosen ones are Christ's disciples who make the church within the church by their intimate and committed life in, with, and through Christ. And those are the Christians who see the true church of God daily in their vision and dream. John describes it in the book of Revelation (chapter 21) as the city where dwell those who try to wash themselves clean daily from their sinful stains in the blood of Jesus, who take the Eucharist—the body and blood of Jesus—as their daily spiritual nourishment along with God's Word, and who share their bread and savings with the community and the poor and thus try their best to be committed stewards of the Lord.

As a matter of fact, these are the people who—as a result of their intense commitment to their Master's new commandment of love— actually undergo daily martyrdom as the psalmist cries out, "We are thwarted by the evil surroundings." They become overanxious, unbalanced, and restless. It is for such friendly disciples Jesus promises, "Do not let your hearts be troubled or afraid. Peace I leave with you; my peace I give to you. Not as the world gives do I give it to you" (John 14:27).

So if we really belong to that elite group of Jesus and if we desire to enjoy a lasting peace in our lives as Jesus has promised, we have to uphold certain strategies in our daily life. We should never lose sight of our remarkable identity as the chosen race. We should make sure that our heart, mind, and body become a dwelling of the Triune God by obeying Jesus's word of love. As members of this spiritual church and close friends of Jesus, we should be engaged in reforming the entire church in its physical, social, and universal dimensions. We should try our best to get rid of its false ideological principles; only then will the world be a better place to live in. Finally, when a disagreement among us arises—which is very normal among humans—we should follow the footsteps of the early Christian disciples, namely, being wise enough submit our differences to the power of the Holy Spirit in prayer. Once we arrive at our Spirit-inspired decision, we can act with efficiency and sensitivity in problem-solving as the disciples have done in the early church (Acts 15:1–29).

72. The Easter Church Lives and Proclaims The Resurrection

The Lord has truly been raised.
—Luke 24:34

Humans are social animals. No man is an island. Each one of us needs to belong to a community for our survival, growth, and safety. As human beings, we belong to a global community of the human race. As Christians, we belong to a community we call the church, which has originated from the Easter encounter. Undeniably, it deserves to be called an Easter church as the risen Lord exposed to the world at its dawn.

The Easter church was a faith-filled and consequently Spirit-filled community. From the Gospel passage, we came to know that—together with Thomas—everyone in that community was bonded with the risen Lord as well as with one another by the basic and central point of the Christian faith that professed in season and out of season that Jesus is "my Lord and my God" (John 20:28). At the dawn of Christianity, the disciples of Jesus began preaching about the risen Jesus as their Savior. At the start, it was very difficult for them as they were surrounded by enemies of their way. Some people even doubted about the identity of Jesus as Thomas did. However, the Spirit of Jesus inspired them by his merciful touch and made them understand the truth about his unique identity: he alone is Lord and God and none other. Because of such Jesus-centered situation, all his believers were filled with his Spirit. He breathed on them and said to them, "Receive the Holy Spirit" (John 20:22).

The Easter Church was also a united and peaceful community. As we heard in Acts (2:42–47), the church members were together as one family in listening to the teachings of their elders; in sharing together in love and justice all their property and possessions; in celebrating the breaking of bread, the Eucharist; and in praying together continuously and regularly. The repeated greeting from the mouth of the risen Lord was "Peace be with you" (John 20:19, 21). That powerful wish brought permanent peace to the community. It was indeed a peace-loving community.

Decisively, the Easter church has been a joyful community. When the risen Lord has appeared to the disciples, they have been overjoyed. This joy, throughout the centuries, has been an important sign of the community of the risen Lord. The risen Lord gives complete joy to his disciples. The community that experiences such joy is ready to do any sacrifice. Peter, the apostle, testifies to it, writing in his letter, "In this you rejoice . . . even though you do not see him now yet believe in him, you rejoice with an indescribable and glorious joy" (1 Pet. 1:6–8).

As an outcome, the Easter church was a missionary community. The risen Jesus, after empowering the disciples with his Spirit, entrusted to them a grand commission. John wrote about this succinctly: "As the Father has sent me, so I send you. Whose sins you forgive are forgiven them, and whose sins you retain are retained." However, the three other Gospel writers elaborated it according to their vision (Matt. 28, Mark 16, Luke 24).

What is mentioned above is not a utopian dream. There are indeed numerous local Easter communities globally in the name of denominations and parishes made up of so many disciples whose faithfulness inspires the world. They are the ones who trust the Spirit's presence even in the midst of adversity. They are the ones who raise their children to do the same. They are the ones who accept their own illnesses as opportunities to reveal God's love to others. They are the ones who quietly feed the hungry and share their own resources with faithful abandon and shape the next generation so they will do the same. And they are the ones who gather their families in the face of approaching death and remind them that "the Lord is truly risen."

73. The Secret for the Survival of The Fittest Christians

Love never fails.
—1 Cor. 13:8a

It is said that a person needs just three things to be happy in this world: "someone to love, something to do with love, and something to hope for, as the victory of love." When we reflect on the situation of the early disciples, we can readily observe that they have found all three of those things in Jesus.

Scriptures inform us that, in Jesus, the disciples had someone to love and to be loved. Jesus's love for them, which was found its fullest expression on the cross, engendered in them a love for him and for God that they expressed in their love for others. In the Gospel, we heard Jesus talking with his disciples, expressing his love and concern for them: "I will not leave you orphans; I will come to you" (John 14:15–21). He guaranteed that their love for him would connect them to his Father; besides, he also confirmed that "as the Father loves me, so I also love you" (John 15:9).

In connection with their Master, the disciples had something to do out of their love. Having learned in Jesus's school of love, they were inspired to do something precious; they served the needs of others, and even when they were made to suffer for doing good, they persevered. They never forgot the first and the last lesson they underwent on the new commandment: "Love one another as I have loved you." It was this love command that urged them to perform so many acts of love, service, and sacrifice. They went from town to town, they proclaimed the Gospel of Jesus, and they baptized them in Jesus's name. They cast out unclean spirits from many possessed people; many paralyzed or crippled people were cured. And because of all these, they created an atmosphere of joy in wherever they stepped in (Acts 8:5–17).

In Jesus, the disciples too had something to hope for as the ultimate result of love. Their steady perseverance was fueled by their hope—a hope that probably made others wonder at their spiritual stamina. Explaining the sufferings early Christians underwent, the apostles exhorted all disciples to bear them patiently

like Jesus and for the sake of getting crowned by him
(1 Pet. 3:15–18). In this light, the disciples—who knew
that God would ultimately bless and protect them—had
been enduring any human suffering and, in many cases,
making it an occasion for proclaiming the Gospel. They
had an unsinkable hope, and it was evident to all who
met them.

Jesus expects us today to buy from him this
survival kit free of charge: Jesus is the one to
love, his love command is something to do, and his
Promised Land is something to hope for. On the
other hand, for most of us, that "someone to love"
is some human or humans, "something to do" is a
worldly enterprise, and "something to hope for"
seems an earthly accomplishment. However, we—the
committed disciples of Jesus, being enlightened by
the Spirit—know well the reality that not any human
or worldly enterprise can satisfy us all the time and
fully. Therefore, we need Christ alive as the ultimate
resource for our survival.

We are called to be in the world but not of the
world. We can neither withdraw in arrogant aloofness
from the world nor be fully victimized by worldly
pleasures and accomplishments. Surely, these are
the challenges of Jesus's disciples. But Jesus affirms
today that we are never alone or without resources
for whatever we are called on to be or to do. Always,
we should be mindful that Jesus is the reason for our
joy, our love, our faith, and our hope. This is the secret
contained in the "survival kit" the Master offers for the
survival of the fittest Christians.

74. Fear Can Kill Us, but Jesus's Disciple Conquers It

I will fear no evil, for you are with me.
—Ps. 23:4b

Fear is one of the rarest gifts from God that takes care of our survival. Fear helps us be cautious of what we use and handle in our daily life for better or for worse. But such wonderful feeling of fear should not become a dangerous factor such as "phobia," which in Greek means an irrational and intense fear of certain persons, situations, or things. In common usage, this term refers to the social phobia of negative attitudes or prejudices against certain persons or groups.

Biblical heroes like Jeremiah, the prophet, were not exempted from this fear complex, which was why they panicked: "I hear the whisperings of many: 'Terror on every side! Denounce! Let us denounce him!' All those who were my friends are on the watch for any misstep of mine" (Jer. 20:10). The Gospels portrayed at length how much Jesus's disciples were afraid of suffering, persecution, and other life challenges. Many times, he advised them not to be afraid of anything and anybody in the world. He wanted them to fear only one—his Father, the consolation of truth, love, and justice. His Spirit also, through his disciples, taught us that the total destruction of our life would happen only by violating and going against the fullness of truth, justice, and love.

Jesus always wants his disciples to be free of fear. On the contrary, we know from the Gospels how timid and puny his disciples have been, being intimidated by anything and everything until they have received the power from Jesus's Spirit.

Invariably, all humans have to go through three phases in our development. In the first phase, we are situated in a horrible surrounding where so much slavery, selfishness, maneuvering, injustice, insensitiveness, and coldness are pervading. At that period, many humans are like dumb Stone Age barbarians who are either not fully aware of what is going on or, for their survival, simply and coolly satisfied with them.

But when we reach the second phase of life development, most of us become aware of all the outside atrocities strangling us. We start reacting against the existing system or situation. Out of this reactionary move, the world has witnessed so many civil wars, community struggles, infighting, and so many isms and unions.

And in the third phase of human development, humans are supposed to act in a "proactionary" mode, mature enough and well balanced in their communications, in their dialogues, in their dealings and relationships, and above all in their leadership. Unfortunately, since "the original fear" holds its dominion over many of them, even though they have gone through the first two phases of development, they continue to live only a reactionary life. They are adults, yes indeed, but only in the physical but not in the emotional, intellectual, or spiritual level. While they react against us out of fear, they keep us in fear. Probably, you and I may be part of this group.

It is to these disciples Jesus says, "Do not be afraid of those who kill the body but cannot kill the soul; rather, be afraid of the one who can destroy both soul and body in Gehenna" (Matt. 10:26–33). In other words, Jesus advises, "Do not fear. Trust in God. He is your Father, who loves you so much." He expects all of us to join with the prophet in saying to God every day, "Yes Lord. We trust you; for to you I have entrusted my cause; you are with me, like a mighty champion; surely my persecutors will stumble, they will not triumph. In their failure they will be put to utter shame, to lasting, unforgettable confusion" (Jer. 20:11–13).

75. Abundance Belongs to the Divine; Its Sharing Belongs to Humans

Give them some food yourselves.
—Matt. 14:16b

In God, we observe abundance in love, justice, and generosity and abundance in blessings, resources, and gifts. We hear about this frequently from God's own mouth in scriptures. Plus, we read about his marvelous deeds of love and blessings.

Isaiah gives voice to God to proclaim about his abundance and sharing as well as his natural resources: "All you who are thirsty, come to the water! You, who have no money, come, receive grain and eat. Come, without paying and without cost, drink wine and milk!" (55:1–3). About the abundance of God's love, Paul describes his own experience and conviction: "For I am convinced that neither death, nor life, nor angels, nor principalities, nor present things, nor future things, for powers, nor height, nor depth, nor any other creature will be able to separate us from the love of God in Christ Jesus our Lord" (Rom. 38–39). In the miracle of the multiplication of loaves, we can notice the abundance of resources in the powerful hands of God: "They all ate and were satisfied, and they picked up the fragments left over—twelve wicker baskets full. Those who ate were about five thousand men, not counting women and children" (Matt. 14:20–21).

Whatever the abundance of God's gifts in this world be, we know very well they are not possessed or enjoyed by all humans equally. We find that there is no distributive justice in sharing the goods of God's creation. Why? Who is to be blamed? God? Not at all. God's Word is totally different. The abundance of everything is on his side. However, its distribution or sharing entirely depends on us humans. God, as we read in scriptures, has created and produced all his earthly goods and entrusted them into the hands of humans (Gen. 1:27–31) whereas the same God continuously has been exhorting us through his prophets, especially through his Son, that he has entrusted the stewardship responsibility to us, whom he has created for this purpose.

In the miraculous event of the multiplication of loaves and fishes, we see the disciples being conscious of the starvation of the crowd of Jesus's listeners, requesting Jesus to dismiss the crowd to go and find food in a nearby village. But Jesus has retorted, "There is no need for them to go away; give them some food yourselves." It is thus the Master instructs his disciples the duty of distributive justice. You have to share whatever you have earned and whatever you have safely stored with those who are crying for food, water, shelter, and other basic needs.

Regrettably, while 10 percent of humanity enjoys 90 percent of earthly resources, 90 percent of humans hold only 10 percent. The richest and the most affluent in humanity are tempted to be content, cold, indifferent, blind, and complacent about the physical and emotional starvation of those around us, both inside and outside our living territory. Many middle-class people also join this outrageous injustice and turn a deaf ear to the compassionate call of both the Creator and the Redeemer.

We are influenced by certain modern and traditional theories: some by Darwinism, which posits the superiority of northern races; others by Marxism, which analyzes structures of injustice; some others by neocapitalism, which seeks to remove market restraints; and many others by the old-fashioned Calvinism, which identifies hard work, early rising, thrift, marital fidelity, etc., as signs of divine election. The Gospel tells us the role of the disciples in Christ's plan of sharing. It is they who have given out the meal to the crowd. He has worked through the hands of the disciples, and he still operates the same way. Let us never forget that abundance is in his hands, while the sharing and distribution of it remains in ours.

76. In God's Vineyard, All Are Equal but with a Difference

My thoughts are not your thoughts,
nor are your ways my ways.
—Isa. 55:8

We know there are so many exhortations and admonitions written in the Bible that don't share our human opinions, nor do they correspond to the ideas and feelings of us who take pride in living in a very civilized and well-illumined postmodern age. One such scriptural passage is the flabbergasting oracle of God we read in Isaiah 55:6–9. This sort of God's proclamation should have been humiliating even for all the prophets, preachers, and teachers. But when we consider this scriptural message seriously, relating them to other biblical verses, we run into what seems to be an almost inescapable truth about the dimension of our human condition; plus, we get to discover some practical guidelines to swallow this bitter capsule of truth.

The eternal truth that God has been proclaiming from the day of creation is that our humanness is very fallible and limited, though he has created us in his image. We want to contain God in our wallet so that we can use his presence as a credit or debit card in buying or coveting anything we want at any time and at any place. But he will not behave loosely that way. We prefer him to be blind to all our faults and sins, and never should he chide us. But he never hesitates to reprimand us, saying, "You Scoundrels! Forsake first your wicked ways and turn to me for mercy." We wish him to be angry against all the evildoers around us, but surprisingly, he loves to be merciful to all.

We feel that human death is a big loss. God suggests that life is Christ and death is gain (Phil. 1:21). Some of us, especially the elderly, mourn and groan daily to get away soon from this world; we want to die before we die. But God points out through Paul that, though it is far better to leave this valley of tears and sufferings to be with Christ in heavenly mansions, he lets us remain in flesh for some more time for the benefit of our neighbors (Phil. 1:23–24). The Creator wants our sickbed or deathbed as the reverberating pulpit for proclaiming God's sovereignty and Christ's holiness.

The most excruciating truth of all is what we hear from Jesus in his parable of the workers in the vineyard (Matt. 20:1–16). We totally agree with Jesus that God is the Proprietor of this whole universe—which is, according to the Bible, his sole vineyard—and that he hires humans to cooperate with his works in his garden of life. Yet what we cannot digest is, at the end of his parable, Jesus echoes the gardener's declaration: "My friend, Take what is yours and go. What if I wish to give this last one the same as you? Or am I not free to do as I wish with my own money? Are you envious because I am generous?"

By this, Jesus seems to underline the plight of so many of us who have been toiling tirelessly in God's vineyard from birth, namely, we cannot expect from our Creator more than what he considers just and right to be handed down to us at the end of a day's work in his vineyard. Our human spirit expects that God will reward us more compared with other people during this life and in the otherworld. Serving him is our duty, but rewarding us is his prerogative.

Nonetheless, the Spirit encourages us to uphold this truth by enlightening us with an amazing truth: in the eyes of God, what we do is less important than what our attitude is toward him. What matters to him is our sincerity in living a life according to the promptings of his Spirit, nothing more or less; other things like our accomplishments or our performances are very secondary. He will remunerate us only according to our truth-filled relationship with him. It is this attitude that makes us different from each other.

77. The Nuance—Tips for Becoming Christian Adults

The Lord's will shall be accomplished through him.
—Isa. 53:10c

Adulthood in humans' life is not only the most precious period of life but also the most crucial and riskiest one. Not having the right and healthy idea about its greatness as well as its intricacies, some adults—behaving till their death as mama's babies—either never attain and enjoy its benefits or become a burden to the family and society. Being Christ's followers, we know how the Creator shuns such pathetic Christian adults.

What does God think of Christian adulthood? We are given a thought-provoking answer of God through Jeremiah (31:7–9). According to the Divine Mind, the worthy adults in his kingdom are those who are convinced of their origin and roots, namely, they were once enslaved by various earthly things and persons, but now they have been delivered by God as remnants of the human race; those who accept the reality of humanness, namely, they have come together from different kinds of backgrounds, races, nationalities, colors, mind-sets, IQs, disabilities, levels of downheartedness, roles, and needs, dreaming of a better life; and those who put indomitable faith, trust, and hope in the Creator, who has never left them alone. They believe that their God is not like a child who kicks the ball away and stands there enjoying how it is rolling; rather, he behaves like a father to them.

Yes, if we want to be worthy adults in God's kingdom, we should be fully conscious of our being delivered by the Father and also set apart from other humans as his representatives, proxies, and agents. However, to make us better adults in his eyes, we cannot falsely glorify ourselves for such exclusiveness. We read in a passage from the letter to the Hebrews that, like Jesus, we should have a peculiar heart of praising and glorifying only our God, who very early— even before we have been conceived in out mother's womb—has said to us, "You are my son, you are my daughter; this day I have begotten you" (Heb. 5:1–6). Hence, if we want to be true adults in God's kingdom, we need to freely and persistently live only for the accomplishment of God's design for us because that is the way Jesus has reached his adulthood as God has prophesied: "The Lord's will shall be accomplished through him" (Isa. 53:10c).

To attain and maintain this unique Christian adulthood, biblical scholars and spiritual sages have recommended to us to go through the NT and observe what Jesus has done in this regard; and also, they want us to see through Gospel events how Jesus's beneficiaries have become adults according to his heart. Unquestionably, as modern disciples of Jesus, we must try to get into the peculiar shoes of humans who have already been esteemed by Jesus as his worthiest adults.

For instance, let us take a miraculous event narrated by Mark (10:46–52). A blind man named Bartimaeus has been cured by Jesus. This healed person is brought by the Spirit before our eyes as a role model for reaching the outstanding Christian adulthood. First, the Spirit teaches us how to behave as a Christian adult in our prayer time before Jesus. He expects us to stop begging only for material goods but to cry out in prayer to become mature as the blind man, saying, "Jesus, Son of David, have pity on me." Even when the crowd has restricted and rebuked him, he has stood by his guns and is louder enough with his prayer.

Second, when the blind man has heard that Jesus is calling through his disciples, he has immediately left everything and rushed to Jesus. We should, besides praying, get the support of our fellow disciples in our families or parishes and rise and do what Jesus tells us. Third, like Bartimaeus, we should uninterruptedly demonstrate our faith in Jesus; and during that process of faith in action, we will become mature Christians.

In the kingdom of God, the only sign of reaching Christian adulthood is nothing but sharing testimonies about all that have gone along the way. Therefore, our becoming adults will be proved through our abiding in Jesus, walking with Jesus on his way, and glorifying God with joy, exclaiming the marvelous deeds he has done not only in the past, in the Bible, or among the saints but much more in our personal life, how we have attained the Christian adulthood. This is the secret of cherishing and managing our Christian adulthood fruitfully.

CHAPTER VIII

WALK THE WALK OF THE MASTER THROUGH THE DAY

78. Walking in the Land of the Living

I believe I shall see the Lord's goodness in the land of the living.
—Ps. 27:13

By all the poets and authors, especially Judeo-biblical writers and Christian authors and teachers, human life is considered a journey from womb to tomb. Every town has got two graveyards: one is literally a yard outside the town where the dead are buried; the other is unfortunately inside the town where many live and move as if dead humans walking with no life. The Spirit calls us with some inspiring scriptural passages to know more about this journey and the way to walk through it energetically and fruitfully.

The psalmist (Ps. 116) vows that he will walk in the land of the living. He means it is a land where his relatives and friends, including their cattle, live together joyfully and productively as a bonded community and as a nation where humans live and move consciously as the people of God. However, we are tempted to ask ourselves, "How can we go through this life, the valley of tears and darkness?' The Spirit beckons us to see through and learn from the lives of Abraham, Jesus, and his apostles.

The main lesson from these great persons' lives is that our God is a "living lover" to them and demands our covenantal response to his love. When God called Abraham (Gen. 22:1–18), the great patriarch immediately responded, "Here I am." Then God asked the unthinkable. Abraham's enthusiasm for doing God's will was put to the ultimate test. Nevertheless, when God called a second time, the answer was the same: "Here I am." Even though he knew what was being asked of him, Abraham was able to maintain his fervor, and he was willing to surrender to an action that appeared to quash his hopes for the future.

Jesus, on his part, behaved like Isaac and obeyed what his Father asked to do. He emptied himself, came down from heaven, took the form of a slave, and underwent an ignominious death. At the onset of his journey of redeeming mankind, Jesus willingly replied to his Father, "Here am I Lord, I am ready to do your will." He was very firm in his answer and lived up to it till his last breath. Throughout his journey in this world, Jesus went through terrible trials and tribulations. Yet he accepted them and consciously lived as an obedient Son of God. For such a remarkable fervor and faith, God "elevated him to sit at his right hand."

We are fortunate enough to be disciples of Jesus, who through his life and words has shown us the way of surviving and succeeding in the land of the living. As he got a remarkable recognition from his Father, he longed that his disciples too would receive such appreciation. He constantly advised them to take up their own crosses and follow him. They truly accepted it at first as they started their journey of life, but they occasionally, and some very frequently, drifted away from his values. He tried to convert them into his side and strengthen them in their discipleship by many miraculous deeds, personal discussions, and even showing a little glimpse of his true divine personality on the hilltop of Tabor (Mark 9:2–10).

Indeed, like any other humans, they were struggling to cope with the faith demand from heaven as shared by Jesus. We knew, after being empowered by the risen Lord's Spirit, they were renovated. They truly walked in the land of the living despite dungeon and fire. They smiled with inner joy to suffer for the sake of Jesus. The world would have maligned them, saying they were scum and foolish and making them a spectacle to the world. But because of their staunch faith, they never let themselves become down spirited. Their hearts were constantly uttering what Paul wrote: "If God is for us, who can be against us? God who did not spare his own Son but handed him over for us all— how will he not also give us everything else along with him?" (Rom. 8:31–32).

We have started our journey with Christ in baptism. If we browse our life journal, we will realize that most of us have started it well; but on the way, we have failed when faced with life challenges and when things we handle become too difficult. The Spirit asks us, "Are you today walking in front of God and in the land of the living? Or still lying in the graveside of the dead humans?" A legitimate question indeed.

79. Walking Empty Tombs But Carrying the Risen Lord

For you have died, your life is hidden with Christ in God.
—Col. 3:3

The postmodern society is horribly bombarded by thousands of opinions on millions of issues—legal, political, and religious—tearing the entire world. In the church, surely, we are well aware of how we are divided by opinions. In all matters of faith, every Christian has got personal opinions and dies with them. From the Gospels, we gather the same kinds of rifts and dissensions occurring among the primary team of Jesus, especially after his resurrection.

It's true that the first appearance of the risen Lord, as narrated by Gospel writers, was to Mary Magdalene, who later went and announced this good news to other apostles and disciples. It's true also that the apostles could not digest the opinion of a woman. They thought she was hallucinating. But this woman's opinion became popular and accepted finally by the entire global church.

In the realm of God, human opinion matters very little. Whatever be the talent of a person who has generated that opinion, unless it is connected with the risen Lord and his Spirit, it will never become popular and eternal. It is not the talented proclamation of Mary Magdalene that gives continuity to her opinion about the risen Lord. Rather, it is the Spirit of the risen Lord that has influenced and possessed her that has made it all possible. This is the truth that Gamaliel, a teacher of the law, has contended before the Sanhedrin about the unrivaled aftereffect of Jesus's resurrection factor: "For if this endeavor or this activity is of human origin, it will destroy itself. But if it comes from God, you will not be able to destroy them; you may even find yourselves fighting against God" (Acts 5:34–39).

And so is with the two-thousand-year-old proclamation of the church about Jesus's resurrection. The risen Lord has truly risen, and with his Spirit, he is at this moment pervading the hearts and minds of millions of people of this world. They have experienced him and his intervention in their lives. They encountered him in prayer, scriptures, and tradition. Because of the effective influence of the risen Lord, sinners like Mary Magdalene and many other disciples have once died truly in their sinful past but then risen to a virtuous new life. They are convinced now that "the old life is comfortable; the new life is demanding. Yet the new life is rich and the old life is barren."

These disciples, enlightened and enlivened by the risen Lord, emptied their entire body, mind, and heart; became liberated from all kinds of evil thoughts, words, and deeds; and began walking seemingly as "empty tombs" but truly carrying the risen Lord. Whoever saw their lives and not just heard their opinions became energized by the same risen Lord.

Being the disciples of Jesus today, our opinion about the risen Lord should also become our life. Consequently, our present life becomes a celebration of the reality that Jesus lives. Proclaiming about this amazing mystical death and resurrection, Paul exhorts us, "If then you were raised with Christ, seek what is above, where Christ is seated at the right hand of God. Think of what is above, not of what is on earth" (Col. 3:1–4).

We too should try our best in ripping off our sinful old lifestyle and upholding a new order of life: emptying sins from our body but filling our spirit with the risen Lord. Paul is right when he writes, "Do you not know that a little yeast leavens all the dough? Clear out the old yeast, so that you may become a fresh batch of dough, inasmuch as you are unleavened . . . Therefore let us celebrate the feast, not with the old yeast, the yeast of malice and wickedness, but with the unleavened bread of sincerity and truth" (1 Cor. 5:6b–8).

80. Keep the Law, and the Law Will Tend You

Obey, teach all that I have commanded you.
—Matt. 28:20

Judeo-Christian traditions uphold the source and dignity of the commandments of God by quoting him repeatedly, saying, "See, I have today set before you, life and good, death and evil" (Deut. 30:15–18). In other words, the commandments of God are to be honored simply as a resourceful guide for our survival and success in this world. These are supposed to be strategies for our life management. Very sadly, humans—especially we who have been born and bred in this postmodern age, being swayed by this sophisticated individualism—hate laws and regulations; considering these laws as limiting their freedom, they dream of how much happier life will be without so many dos and don'ts.

Such wrong attitude against God's commandments has originated not by mere outward "modern isms" but much more so from within, namely, out of ignorance of the richest benevolence of those commandments. Actually, God's laws are optional instructional manual for our life. There is an ancient adage: "Keep the rule and the rule will keep you." As this ever-guiding principle for a victorious life, God wants humans to take to heart all his commandments. Persons who are sincere to strive for a joy-filled and peaceful life in this world have been fully aware of this option God has entrusted to them.

Jesus is well aware of the facts that those laws are God's special gift to his people. They express his love for the people since, observing them, they will walk in his ways and come to share his life and happiness; they, in turn, show their gratitude for his love by obeying the laws and by sharing his love with one another. Hence, he has been totally conformed to those laws and zealous in institutionalizing and enhancing them in the hearts of his followers. "Do not think that I have come to abolish the law or the prophets. I have come not to abolish but to fulfill" (Matt. 5:17–27).

He was very sad to observe God's chosen people abusing his laws as they paid more attention to the letter and not to the spirit of the law. He was disturbed by the abusive efforts of religious leaders and teachers of his time, being engaged in hairsplitting interpretations of the law. This created a bad perception among the people about the relationship with God, which was no more based on love but on the legalistic observance of so many man-made laws. Therefore, he revisited those commandments and renewed them in their core spirit. He too capsuled them in a simple package so that his disciples, educated and uneducated, may keep these laws in their memory and be reminded always. "Love God with all your heart . . . and love your neighbors as yourself." He too asserted, "The whole law and the prophets depend on these two commandments" (Matt. 22:40).

After the age of enlightenment, the baby boomers and the millennials try to revisit and reinterpret those laws according to our situations and needs. I think there is no problem in it. Our current attitudes and actions express that God's plan of action is not dead; it is alive and growing. Like Jesus, we too can reread and revisit those laws. Nonetheless, our only problem lies in our engagement with the laws. On this matter, we should follow exactly what our Lord has entrusted to us as criterion for making choices. It is nothing but the package he has given to us. He has named it as his new commandment: the gospel of charity. The word "charity" that Jesus has used mysteriously includes all virtues, especially justice, freedom, and purity.

81. Our Enemies Indeed Are Neighbors in Need

Love your enemies and pray for them.
—Matt. 5:38–48

To many of us, most of Jesus's words may seem confusing, challenging, or very hard sayings to digest. One of them is that we have to love our enemies. Certainly, love for enemies seems madness to common reason and politically incorrect in the public square of modern society. Upon seeing so much evil in the world, especially when that evil affects us deeply, our reaction is always anger and perhaps revenge. But Jesus tells us not to let evil force us to fight it with its own weapons of evil. He commands us to fight it with the weapons of God himself: mercy, forgiveness, love of the evildoer, and prayer for the ones who have hurt us. Nonetheless, we see in history that good-willed followers of Christ firmly believe and continue to observe Jesus's command of loving enemies.

God's archenemy, the devil, who has started his rivalry against God from the Creation, is sowing evil continuously in the hearts of humans. The result is millions of tombs and monuments full of skeletons buried by wars of hatred, retaliation, and revenge. Even today, we hear and see such cruel, horrible, violent, and bloody conflicts globally being enacted in the name of religious affiliations or political isms. In this unending spiritual battle, we—the followers of Christ—discover that victory can be attained only by the strategy Jesus has used in his own life: forgiving, loving, and praying for those victimized by the cruel devil. He has demonstrated it to us while hanging on the cross. *However, we should never consider such a meek and forgiving style of life as surrender to the evil situations with a sour-grape attitude or that of pacifism. Rather, there is something more to it.*

According to Jesus's gospel of charity, our neighborly love should be based on need and not on one's own liking. Unfortunately, because of our self-centered perception, we make our own calculation in practicing the command of charity. According to it, we judge and divide our neighbors as those who like and love us, those whom we like and love, those whom we don't like yet love, and those who hate us and do all kinds of evil against us.

We are prone to showing love to the first three groups of neighbors, whereas we dislike and sometimes hate others. These are the ones whom we judge as sinful, alien, and unworthy to live with us. In other words, we—with our selfish shortsightedness—name certain neighbors as enemies. But in themselves, they are not. As any other humans, the so-called enemies also have their needs. Actually, they are the neediest people. Especially, they are in need of a merciful and compassionate touch from God through us. Jesus suggests to us to come out of our self-centered shortsightedness and to love the wrongly named "enemies" as our neighbors.

Jesus had an incredible dream about us, namely, we should be perfect as the heavenly Father is perfect. All that he lived, experienced, and preached centered on this motif. He defined this goal of perfection as "going beyond ourselves" and not living as average humans.

Our religious life must surpass that of the scribes and Pharisees and of the hardheaded and hard-hearted humans by loving our neighbors, especially our enemies. Loving our enemies is indeed a miraculous act, very hard to perform. Yet it is possible if each one of us closely stands by the cross remembering the words of Paul: "All belong to you, and you to Christ, and Christ to God" (1 Cor. 3:22–23).

82. Temptation Is Inevitable But Always Conquerable

Jesus was led by the Spirit into the desert to be tempted.
—Matt. 4:1

Temptation is simply a lure, enticement, inducement, or coaxing from within or without ourselves. The temptations, according to our Christian perspective, are the compulsions happening in the spiritual dimension of our life. They are the events occurring in the battlefield between good and evil, truth and lie, darkness and light, God and the devil. This battle is not happening somewhere beyond the space or in other planets; rather, it happens within each one of us.

Every spiritual temptation comes to us only when we are facing a situation or occasion to make choices for God. Satan enters in those situations and lures us either to reject or to deviate ourselves from our connections, our commitments, and our observances toward a loving God. The main cause of these failures is none other than the devil. He is a roaring lion, roaming about to devour all of God's children (1 Pet. 5:8–9). He is very smarty and performs his actions in a very subtle way; he never appears directly and shows his face of arrogance and cruelty to his clients. He comes in various disguises, like a serpent or a lovemate (Gen. 3:1–7).

This shrewd but fallen angel waits for the weak moments of humans to devour them. We are a rare blend of both physical and spiritual dimensions. However, in our hunger and thirst for fulfilling our basic needs physically and emotionally, we become weak. During those moments, Satan enters into our life to gobble us. Many of us at those moments, forgetting the other side of us—the children of God—like Adam and Eve succumb to Satan's temptation.

In the Gospels, we read that Jesus too, as a human, has been approached by Satan in his weak moments. But we know he hasn't yielded but driven him out of sight. Thus, Jesus is given to us as a role model in handling these temptations successfully. Very faithfully, he has used the Word of God as ammunition in his battle against his enemy. Besides, the most striking factor we have to understand is that Satan picks up only those who are good-willed people as his priority victims.

Before he was tempted by the devil, Jesus was at the Jordan, baptized by John, anointed by the Holy Spirit, and given recognition from his heavenly Father as his beloved Son; soon after, the Spirit led him to the desert to perform a forty-day retreat as an immediate preparation for his ministry. During this holy period, Satan entered to tempt Jesus, taking hold of his regular strategy of feeding through human weaknesses. He tempted Jesus to misuse his self-awareness, in other words, his own goodness.

The Christian life, indeed, is a risky business. It is a wild road jam-packed with temptations. Pope Francis is quoted, saying, "Temptation is our daily bread, so much so that if one of us says that 'I have never been tempted,' the right response would be, 'Either you're a cherub with wings or you're a little stupid.'" Satan continues to go after people who are like Jesus, who are spiritually well groomed, well educated, well trained, well positioned, and well aware of their identity. A disciple can never be more than the Master but can follow his footprints. One preacher very well writes, "When I am tempted I know how to win; I just hide myself behind the Cross." The crucified but risen Jesus surely will help us handle with care our Christian identity, our well-established discipleship, especially in our life's weak moments. Temptations are inevitable but always conquerable.

83. True Prayer Takes Us down To the Valley of the Needy

Lord, it is good that we are here.
—Matt. 17:4

Though God has pronounced "good" about his creations, our feeling about the earthly life is not that good. We lead a life filled with assiduous snags that hinder us to be Jesus's faithful and trustworthy disciples, sometimes even drifting away from him. Plus, it is like a journey of Abraham to a "land of destiny" unknown to us but known only to God (Gen. 12:1–4); it seems like we are living an exilic and deserted life, hoping for a better future. As committed disciples of Jesus, many of us feel often that we are surrounded by the lawless and unruly, the godless and sinful, the unholy and profane, the unchaste, murderers, sodomites, kidnappers, liars, perjurers, and so on (2 Tim. 1:9–10).

However, the Lord argues that our feelings are not at all genuine regarding our life on the earth. Yes, he has underlined that human life is burdensome. But he has promised he will make the burden light and the yoke easy. Observing Jesus's life, we discover some effective and productive tips to snatch the win. We know from all the Gospel writers that Jesus has never missed a single moment to commune with God. His heartbeats have been not only ceaselessly infusing within his blood but also inebriating his elevated spirit. However, he has chosen special hours and special environments to be immersed in prayer.

He usually preferred a hilltop environment to be secluded from the mob; as he had preached, "going to his inner sanctuary of spirit, closing all the doors of outside world, he prayed to his Father in secret." Such kind of commune with God was his primary tool to be nourished, strengthened, and renewed during his personal exilic journey. He too endorsed the one-heart-and-one-mind group prayer by taking disciples to pray with him.

In one such hilltop group prayer time, he shared with us another tip for winning against Satan. We should never be self-centered during prayer time as Peter did. And this was why he often rebuked the Master for desiring to go to Jerusalem to suffer and die.

We would notice the difference between Jesus and Peter during the hilltop prayer (Matt. 17:1–9). While Peter was preoccupied with not losing the split-second spiritual ecstasy he was experiencing, Jesus—despite his full awareness of his glorious transfiguration— seemed more attentive to conversing with his spiritual mentors and getting their advice and directions. More importantly, Jesus—being strengthened in his will to accomplish his Father's will—rushed back down to the valley, where his vision and mission would be realized. He never gave even a single minute to discuss with his disciples what happened to him at the hilltop; rather, he warned them not to mention it to other people.

Those tips of Jesus for managing our life in this world, in the light of the Word, are based on the covenantal relationship with the Supreme Being. From the beginning of human life, as the Bible underlines, God proposes to humans his covenantal love and demands from them the same. Jesus has obediently reciprocated his faith and love to his Father by emptying himself, becoming a very fragile human, and undergoing an ignominious death on the cross.

That is the way we, his disciples, must cope with this treacherous earthly life. The hardships we undergo during this deserted life must be borne with the convictions that, in this life, we have been called by God to be holy and that everything that happens in this life journey is designed already by the grace of God.

Our only concern should be to listen keenly Jesus's voice that says, "Undoubtedly, prayer time is good. But get up. Don't stay only on the hilltop, but get out, and go down with me."

84. Be the River of Living Waters From the Divine Spring

Whoever drinks the water I shall give will never thirst.
—John 4:14

Very surprisingly, in every moment of our life's frustration and confusion, the Spirit provides us guidance on how to quench our unending thirst during this deserted earthly life. In the Gospel story of Jesus visiting with the Samaritan woman (John 4:5–42), we see him and his disciples feeling thirsty as they are walking through the desert from Galilee to Judea under the scorching Palestinian sun. Jesus requests the Samaritan woman to give water to him and his crew. As the Spirit of God moves Jesus, using the natural and physical need of thirst for water, he discusses about the impending thirsts in life of not only the Samaritan woman but also every human being, and he offers the strategy for quenching human thirst.

God the Creator had never been tired of claiming himself as the Rock of our salvation. We read in the book of Deuteronomy (chapter 32) that he spoke through Moses how he had been their Rock who could bring out their life resources, breaking through any kinds of rocks found in this earth. In fact, he demonstrated his claim, as we hear in OT, with a miraculous deed. While people were stranded in the desert on their way to the Promised Land, in their thirst for water, they grumbled and groaned. God indeed listened to their cry, and he arranged cool water to flow from the hot rock (Exod. 17:3–7). And therefore, all his messengers, like David, exhorted their people to "acclaim the Rock of our salvation" (Ps. 95). Undoubtedly, God—to us who are marching on in this deserted life—is the Rock on whom we can rely and the source of the life-giving water.

Even the physical rocks that seem to be giving troubles to us in walking the walk of our Master can turn out to be the source of energy and nourishment as the living waters. Abiding in his Father, Jesus spelled out his own identity of being that divine Rock from whom we can receive spiritual waters that can quench our thirsts. Regarding this salvific water, he offered us two promises: (1) "Whoever drinks the water I shall give will never thirst"; (2) "The water I shall give will become in him a spring of water welling up to eternal life" (John 4:14), which was his reference to the Spirit when he said, "Rivers of living water will flow from within him" (John 7:38).

Humans of this postmodern age are affected by too many thirsts—thirst for power, dignity, freedom, pleasure, fulfillment, prosperity, and so on. According to Jesus, whatever we do by our natural, artificial, earthly ways to quench our thirsts will not confine or control all those thirsts. The one and only permanent solution for this plight is drinking the living waters that come from the heart, words, and sacraments of Jesus. To drink this living water means welcoming Jesus into our life; accepting his lifestyle of love; boasting in hope of the glory of God; boasting even of our afflictions, knowing that affliction produces endurance, which yields proven character, which brings forth hope (Rom. 5:1–8).

We observed in the Gospel story of the Samaritan woman how she tasted this living water. She was so intoxicated by this water that she went around proclaiming its greatness. Other Samaritans believed the witness of the woman but remained steadfast in their belief because they themselves had already tasted the living water. Similarly, let us not limit ourselves to the hearing of the greatness of Jesus, but let us experience his greatness in our personal lives so as to remain steadfast in his love. Plus, being the river of living waters from the divine spring, we flow through society to make it ever spiritually fertile.

85. The Anointed Soul's Sudden Awakening

While you have the light, believe in the light.
—John 12:36a

Helen Keller, who became visually impaired in her early childhood and remained in that status till her death, wrote about an experience, saying, "I came up out of Egypt and stood before Sinai and a power divine touched my spirit and gave it life." Later in her life, she went on to experience the beauties and mysteries of life with such clarity that she was able to share what she called her "soul's sudden awakening" with others.

The Gospel story narrated by John (9:1–41) is about one such person with a visual impairment who has been cured of his inborn disability by Jesus's anointing. It is a metaphoric explanation of the Spirit about every human's spiritual journey from blindness to sight, from unbelief to faith, from darkness to light. It is all about the daily encounter of us who have been enlightened by Christ in the sacramental anointing. All who get this spiritual anointing begin to see their own self and all that are outside them very differently.

First, we fully see that Jesus is our Savior, who helps us in this liberation process of coming out from blindness and darkness to a light-filled life. Jesus's anointing of the blind man in the Gospel has brought light and renewed hope into the man's darkened life. Liberated from his blindness, the man has begun to see and to believe in Jesus. His seeing and his believing challenge us to leave behind our personal darkness and to live in the light of Christ. In the same way, we begin to see that the one who offers us such healing anointing—namely, Jesus the Messiah—is our light. We begin to be fully aware that our life gets its fullness in him, through him, and with him.

Second, we see everything and every person around us as God sees it. We hear the Spirit telling us at every point of judging others, as it has been in the life of the prophet Samuel, "Do not judge from his appearance or from his lofty stature, because I have rejected him. Not as man sees does God see, because, man sees the appearance, but the Lord looks into the heart" (1 Sam. 16:1–13).

Moreover, after the Lord's anointing, our inner eyes are opened to see the fact that we are not alone in our journey of life, which is like a desert, like climbing up a high mountain, like floating over or swimming against the current of natural waters. This is because our mind and spirit are in full agreement with the truth that there is God in and around our life like a Good Shepherd. Therefore, we start feeling safe and secure, not living in timidity and fear (Ps. 23).

We too begin to know our true identity. We are weak, clay, dust; but at the same time, we possess a dignity and freedom that has previously eluded us. As Paul writes, we have once been darkness, but now we are light in the Lord (Eph. 5:8). We have been delivered from darkness and transferred to the daylight (Col. 1:13). In that bright light, we uphold the daring attitude as Jesus's disciples to call God our Abba, Father; we love to wear the faith glasses and see through our glorious identity of being anointed by Jesus as God's adopted children, plus Jesus's own possession.

With this enlightenment, we are endowed with the power of the Spirit; we start, with no inhibition or fear, proclaiming that Jesus is the Lord and Messiah, like how the cured visually impaired man has gratefully accepted and cooperated with the anointing Jesus has offered him. He has not only gone and washed, as directed, but also become a witness to God's anointed, Jesus. Since Christ has already won the ultimate victory, we are assured a share in his strength with which we initiate wherever we live, causing darkness to recoil; all our words and works contribute to the liberation and advancement of the whole human race.

86. Earthly Encounter with the Risen Lord

Were not our hearts burning while he spoke to us?
—Luke 24:32

The risen Jesus is alive today in our midst as he has promised before he has left this world, and the NT books and the church tradition uphold that he can be encountered by any disciple of Jesus. It is this unfathomable truth that Peter has preached as "witnessing" (Acts 2:14–32). As history proves, there have been innumerable incidents of encountering the resurrected Lord beginning from the day he has risen from the dead. According to my calculation, the risen Jesus's appearances reported in NT are twelve at different times to various disciples, ranging from one—like Mary Magdalene, Peter, Paul, and Jesus's brother—to five hundred as Paul points out (1 Cor. 15:6).

As Christians, we firmly believe that the risen Lord is still alive in our midst, knocking at the doors of our hearts, our families, our communities, and surely our personal and private lives. However, after hearing and reading all these testimonies found in the New Testament and church tradition, one question always arises in the modern minds: "Is this possible even today?" Can we experience such apparitions of the risen Lord as the disciples have had in the early days of the church? Many may contend that we don't. Because of this failure and disappointment, some of us are dejected and discouraged and even stop our pursuit of these marvelous encounters, maybe with a sour-grape attitude. But let us rethink our approach toward this faith fact.

If we, with the Spirit, dug into all those appearances of the risen Jesus, we can find some particular life situations in which the disciples met him. The encounters occurred when they were in search of the Master (John 20:11–18), planning to perform the usual rituals for Jesus (Mark 16:1), conversing about the Master's life and death (Luke 24:14), or living behind closed doors out of frustration and fear (John 20:19).

Particularly, in the Gospel of Luke, we read a narration (24:13–35) about two disciples encountering the risen Savior, which seems to be very closely related to our daily life situations. Like them, we are travelers in life; we too continuously converse, analyze, and meditate on the Master's personality and deeds. At the end of our spiritual and religious attempts, we fail and become intensely frustrated. In such a grim situation, we notice one of the wonderful, heartwarming encounters of the risen Lord happening in the lives of the disciples. They testify it clearly.

Unquestionably, every disciple of Jesus possesses the ability to encounter the risen Lord in prayer, in visions and dreams, in moments of suffering. However, that is not a regular occurrence for every ordinary human disciple of Jesus. There is one more very tangible, very visible, very plausible, and very regular encounter of the risen Lord in each one's life. He is found, touched, heard, and read in scriptures and surely in the intimate connection we have with the church. At the end of his earthly life, Jesus has left to us his unique path of human life as a self-actualization. This self-actualization of Jesus is found in the written scriptures and lived tradition, namely, the church. "Very surprisingly the heavenly Word became flesh and later more miraculously his flesh and Spirit became the Words of scriptures and Traditions of the Church."

Therefore, willingly and longingly, when I reach out to scriptures and when I involve myself in the traditions of the church more faithfully, I do encounter Christ, the risen Lord. He is walking with us. He is talking to us. Are not our hearts burning within us while we read and hear scriptural words, while we are in the church as Eucharistic Christians, and while we are caring the sick and the elderly as Good Samaritans?

87. Jesus's Spirit Is the Breath of Fresh Air

To each one the manifestation of the Spirit is given for the common good.
—1 Cor. 12:7

The struggle of understanding and communicating about the Holy Spirit, who is invisible but proactive inside Jesus's church, is perennial. However, NT writers have tried their best to do this job, especially in writing about the Pentecostal event. In spite of the differences, basically all of them agree on the fundamental truths hidden in the event and the modes of the Holy Spirit's manifestation, such as that there is a strict unity between Jesus and the Spirit and that with the descent of the Spirit, a new era in the history of God's dealing with humanity has begun.

John says in his Gospel that Jesus has breathed on the disciples and said, "Receive the Holy Spirit" (John 20:19–23). The Spirit is esteemed as breath or air, which is one of the constitutive elements of the universe. The breath is the extraordinary force that brings forth energy. Therefore, the Spirit is the creative force in God, in man, and in the universe. Everything that is good and true comes from the Spirit.

In the event of Pentecost, Jesus acted as his Father Creator did at the Creation of humans (Gen. 2:7), breathing his recreating breath into the selected humans who were open to such redemptive renewal. That breath seemed to the disciples, at times, like a tempest shaking houses and uprooting trees but not destructive and other times like a refreshing gentle breeze. The Spirit was always refreshing them in their understanding of Gospel values.

Such a historical event has become a nonstop occurrence for two millennia. In performing this remarkable act of breathing his fresh air, Jesus wants us to uphold one important point about today's church life. Any change that happens in the church or in our life because of the Holy Spirit is not a total topsy-turvy change.

On Pentecost, the Spirit brought forth a new system of religion. But it was not altogether brand new. The Spirit made disciples to maintain the symbols of the old era; they revered the sacred symbols of the past, all the while ruthlessly revising them. That was what we meant by the Spirit's actions in us as the breath of fresh air.

We know how millions of humans walk around in this world and, surprisingly, in the churches with their bad-smelling mouth. The air they inhale as well as exhale is very much contaminated. Therefore, other people notice how badly they speak and behave. One spiritual leader has identified three specific groups of Christians who live among us with a bad spiritual smell: uniformists, who prefer that everybody and everything in the church must be rigidly uniformed;

alternativists, who always have their own ideas about things and who do not want to conform their minds to the mind of the universal church; and exploitationists, whose only concern is to seek personal benefits and who consequently end up doing business in the church.

These bad-smelling Christians do possess many wonderful natural and spiritual gifts from the Creator God, but they use them for their self-gratification and self-glorification. Through Paul, the Lord tells all of us (1 Cor. 12:3–13) that we should use all our talents in the church for others out of love. Our human mind, on its own, is inadequate to understand Jesus and God. Jesus's disciples have only understood fully when he has breathed this Spirit into them after his resurrection and in the assembled church when it has received the Spirit at Pentecost. Certainly, it is not easy to do so because worldly temptations are many. This is why we should go to the Holy Spirit every day to be renewed in his breath of fresh spiritual air.

88. Privilege Entails Responsibility

Without cost you have received; without cost you are to give.
—Matt. 10:8b

Every breath we take is a gift. Every dawn and every sunset we are able to witness is a gift. Every family member, every friend, each and all is a gift. Every holiday and holy day we are able to welcome and celebrate is a gift. Every good book, movie, or play we enjoy is a gift. Every good teacher we have ever had is a gift. Every job that has enabled us to feed, clothe, and shelter ourselves and our loved ones has been a gift. God, the Creator and Provider, expects us to be mindful of all those gifts and blessings. God has done so much for us. We have received so much from him; therefore, he wants us to give them back generously and gratefully. All the gifts are privileges that require responsible responses.

God, who has liberated old Israelites from Egypt and made them his chosen elite race, has demanded from them their relentless love and gratitude toward him. We, the new Israelites of the twenty-first century, have received an unthinkable gift from him through his beloved Son, Jesus. Paul proclaims this truth: "Christ, while we were still helpless, yet died at the appointed time for the ungodly. God proves his love for us in that while we were still sinners Christ died for us. Indeed, while we were enemies, we were reconciled to God through the death of his Son" (Rom. 5:6–11). We have been endowed with a beautiful and unthinkable community experience of being redeemed by the love and mercy of God that has come through the life, death, and resurrection of Jesus, God's only Son. With the bountiful shower of all these gifts and privileges from God and his Son, what is expected of us?

As we read God expressing his desire in the Bible, we should pay attention to God's voice and keep his covenant faithfully. Also, we should express that covenant and love for God in the love and compassion we show to our neighbors, especially the needy and the weak. Having been given worth and dignity by that love—having been justified and sanctified by that love—we are to become the channels for passing on that love to others without evaluating how much they deserve it or their capacity to return our love.

Jesus too, on his part, expects us to become his faithful partners in building up his kingdom on the earth. As he has felt pity and compassion on humanity, he wants us to hold the same love and closeness to the sufferers, the hungry, and the poor. "At the sight of the crowds, his heart was moved with pity for them because they were troubled and abandoned, like sheep without a shepherd" (Matt. 9:36–38). We individually should lead a life of gratitude. Just as we have received without cost, so we should give, giving back our love to God by obeying him, telling him courageously as the Israelites did, "Everything the Lord has said, we will do" (Exod. 19:8a, 24:3). We will give back ourselves to the call of Jesus in helping him save the world. Harvest is plentiful; laborers are very few.

89. Spoiled Freedom Can Damage Our Spiritual Growth

Sometimes a way seems right, but the end of it leads to death.
—Prov. 14:12

Our Creator God perennially has been showing himself as a dutiful and generous sower and gardener who takes care of not only the entire creation but also, very attentively and exclusively, our inner land, the soul. In Psalm 65, David proclaims that "God is a hard-working gardener who stays continuously connected to his land, cultivates it, drenching its furrows and breaking its clods and once he sows, he regularly waters it and consequently prepares its grain."

God acts as a generous sower in nature. When we look at living beings, plants, and animals of all kinds, we see how much seed is generously sown. There is plenty of it, yet few spring up and reproduce fruit. There is same gardener, the same sower, the same natural ground or field; yet at harvest time, the world reaps different results and fruits. Yet the Lord of generosity himself keeps on sowing the seeds abundantly.

As a sower of human body and soul, the same God works with us more intensively for our spiritual growth. Our soul is nothing but God's product. The seed he sows in humans' creation is part of his image and likeness. This is why he is so attentive to our spiritual development. The human soul is a treasure land where he wants to dwell as his sanctuary and help us grow in his holiness more and more and bear in the world his godly fruits for his glory.

For this remarkable soul management, according to scriptures, God uses his powerful Word as ammunition and source of nourishment as well. Isaiah writes about the power of his Word: "Just as from the heavens the rain and snow come down and do not return there till they have watered the earth, my word that goes forth from my mouth shall not return to me void, but shall do my will, achieving the end for which I sent it" (55:10–11). From the days of Creation, we notice the results of God's mighty Word, with which he has created the universe and everything in it. When the time of fulfillment has arrived, God has uttered his final and complete Word, who has become flesh among us.

The very sad but interesting part of the good news about the heavenly Gardener is how his soul management in humans' lives seemingly meets failure. As we encounter in nature the fact that lavishing seeds are sown every season on the land but very few sprout and bear fruits at the harvest, God sows his powerful words in every human heart with no hesitation but only out of sheer love for us. Unfortunately, not all of us are receptive and fertile soil; some are like the walkway, some others are as rocky ground, and others are filled with thorny bushes. And only a few of them are like rich soil; even in these fertile grounds, some are good, some better, and some others best (Matt. 13:1–23).

The main reason for this is, as Jesus identifies, the human weakness of pride, arrogance, self-righteousness, superficiality, faintheartedness, worldly possessions, and anxiety. Most of us either misuse or abuse the greatest gift God has shared with us, freedom. The Gardener who has sowed the seed within us pours out his Word over that seed, which is nothing but an invitation, a call, and a challenge. Wherever God's Word is received properly, it yields a miraculously bountiful return. It is within our capability to obstruct the divine Sower's purpose and prevent or curtail its growth. Those who close their minds against him receive less. Let us be cautious of how we handle the greatest gift of freedom we enjoy in our land of freedom.

90. Our Burden Must Become Our Song

My soul, be at rest in God alone.
—Ps. 62:6

All preachers usually strengthen their audiences by quoting the hearty invitation of our beloved Jesus:

"Come to me, all you who labor and are burdened, and I will give you rest" (Matt. 11:28). Many of us may do some wrong calculation about such lighthearted words. But if we go deeper into the spirit of Jesus, we discover a huge spiritual treasure for our daily enrichment.

We should understand that Jesus doesn't invite us to take a nap when he says, "Come, I will give you rest." Undoubtedly, taking a short rest by napping, medically speaking, can result in less stress, more patience, better reflexes, increased learning, more efficiency, and better health. Jesus's intention is not to offer such petite rest; rather, he points out a spiritual pause and a place to rest and be refreshed so that we will be fortified in faith and energized in our service.

Jesus's invitation to pause and rest is deeply rooted in the spirituality of Israel. In Psalms, we hear God summoning us repeatedly: "Be still and know that I am God" (Ps. 46:11). "Be still before the Lord; wait for him" (Ps. 37:7). The Hebrew imperative "Be still," found in scriptures, has also been variously translated as "Desist," "Give in," and "Let be" as in an authoritative order to a contentious person to "shut up" or "stop it"; rather than be overwhelmed by life's troubles, we are to let go and let God act. Therefore, God's bidding is not simply to rest as in "Take a load off" or "Put your feet up." Being still and taking a rest refers to more than all these: it is to go deeper always with Jesus into ourselves, which I personally label "in traveling" into our inner sanctuary where the kingdom of God has been already established.

At that sacred space, we get to know who God is, get to listen more clearly to God's true voice and teachings, get to discover and be amazed of the marvelous pearls of God in Jesus. We will be very

242 I REV. BENJAMIN A. VIMA

close to Jesus, and we will listen more clearly to what he teaches us. Also, during those holy resting moments, as Jesus mentions, we will be the "little ones" who will be able to know and understand most of his heavenly secrets (Matt. 11:25). These heavenly mysteries are not merely some revelations about God's mysteries; they are very secondary. We will fully understand the most remarkable strategy for a successful life in this world and deeply come to terms with it. That hidden heavenly secret is leading a life of meekness and humility. In a Godward glance, to be meek means perfect trust, willing obedience, and lived faith; in its posture toward others, meekness means force of character and inner strength that invite admiration and a desire to emulate such virtue. These are the lessons we learn from the Lord when we come to rest in him.

As the results of our rest in and with Jesus, first, our attitude will be changed into Jesus's likeness, which is meek and humble of heart. Second, getting into the true restfulness of Jesus, we begin to feel—as Jesus has promised (Matt. 11:29)—that all of life's burdens are easy and light. Jesus's promise of an easy or well-fitting yoke does not mean that his followers will be freed of all challenges of unfairness or burdens of human roles and duties; he has not brought a Gospel of prosperity or that of comfort. When the burden of love and service is laid upon us and shared by Jesus, our loving yokemate, our hearts find peaceful settlement in him. Until then, we will be crying, as St. Augustine has done, "God! Our hearts are restless until they rest in thee."

91. Salvific Patience Is the Need of the Day

*If you suffer for doing good and you endure it,
this is commendable before God.*
—1 Pet. 2:20b

The entire Bible is abounding with the details of the eternal truth of God's Triune personality as the just and merciful Owner and Proprietor of our lives. In the book of Wisdom (11:12–19), for example, we hear a song of praise to that God of mercy and justice, the God of power and leniency, and we are asked to practice the same dual characteristics of God. God's power is made most manifest by being merciful. Mercy seems to be an almighty power at its best and most revealing. Those familiar with God are called to trust the loving power of mercy so that they need not be fearful. The psalmist too constantly sings and proclaims that the Lord is good, forgiving, merciful, and gracious (Ps. 86:5).

Jesus has preached the same truth as his eternal Gospel of mercy, which he portrays splendidly by the tiny parable of the weeds (Matt. 13:24–30). The good seed of God's kingdom, according Jesus, sown in us both by first (natural) and second births (baptismal), is very well sprouting and growing by the bountiful providence of the Creator. However, through some evil sources, both from inside and outside of us, bad weedy seed is being sown in and around us, and it also sprouts and grows very well. Through this metaphor, Jesus emphasizes that God is not the source of evil; rather, he is good in himself in everything. God, as our gardener, has sown only good seeds; but some enemy, an opposite force of God, has done the weeds. Satan's kingdom of darkness (as he comes at night) loves confusion and doubt. This evil enemy has taken part ownership of the field or at least has taken out a lease.

Imprudently and foolishly, most of the times, we love to move and have our being not in the light but in darkness. There is a part of our earthliness that wants to be left alone. It desires not to be tilled, cultivated, and of course weeded. Yielding to Satan's vicious analysis about God's command of avoiding the forbidden fruits (Gen. 3:4–5), most of us feel the tension of holding ownership of ourselves and our life; and consequently, we not only make our sacred inner field bad soil but also permit Satan to sow bad weeds in our hearts somewhere at some time.

Since such evil seeds and deeds are sown and spread lavishly in and around us when we are enlightened by the Spirit and led by him, we begin to see the ugliness and sinfulness of human life, and we start trembling before a God who is just in all his ways because we are told by our Master that there is going to be a harvest time during which the crop of wheat and the disordering weeds will be collected, one for burning and the other for union and life. Therefore, we feel desperate; and by all means, we try to destroy the weeds as early as possible. However, Jesus exhorts us to imitate God the Father in his patience.

We, the patient disciples of Jesus, are expected to see the best in others and not judge their motives or their actions; moreover, we are instructed by the scriptures that God is uniquely a merciful Father who acts as the prodigal son's father, being very lenient to any contrite sinner. Observing face-to-face clearly that the bad weeds—like the unbelieving, the heretics, the false teachers, and the backsliders—continue to grow in our midst, we are told to aim at being tolerant and merciful as God is. We belong to a hope-filled and enduring community of believers. Until the Judgment Day, let us put our heart and soul together patiently in cooperating with God in his gardening of his kingdom.

92. Merciful and Just Faith Guarantees Our Salvation

By grace you have been saved through faith.
—Eph. 2:8a

Many times, I ask myself, "Am I saved?" In other words, "Do I belong to the elite group of God in Jesus? Will I go to heaven?" I have valid reasons to doubt my salvation. Nobody, even God, has directly told me that I have been saved, nor has anybody from the heavenly government supplied me with an ID card. Only the church, where I belong to or registered in, embraces me and offers me all licenses to participate in any activity in the earthly kingdom of God. Nonetheless, I do not think any church can monopolize or guarantee my salvation. The right to enter into God's heavenly kingdom totally depends on the gratuitous mercy of God.

This is what Paul underlines in all his letters. Especially, when he puts forth the nuts and bolts of human salvation, be they chosen ones or Gentiles, he argues splendidly, "Just as you once disobeyed God but have now received mercy because of their disobedience, so they have now disobeyed in order that, by virtue of the mercy shown to you, they too may now receive mercy. For God delivered all to disobedience, that he might have mercy upon all" (Rom. 11:13–32). From the beginning of time, God esteems every human as his child. Because of his eternal love, those who seem foreign to us are not foreign to God, those who are marginalized are never marginalized by the King of kings, and those who seem to be a minority are not a minority to the Creator.

Through the prophet Isaiah, God clearly spelled out such truthful relationship with the humans. "The foreigner joined to the Lord should not say, 'The Lord will surely exclude me from his people.' And foreigners who join themselves to the Lord, to minister to him, to love the name of the Lord, to become his servants. Them I will bring to my holy mountain and make them joyful in my house of prayer . . . For my house shall be called a house of prayer for all peoples" (56:1–7). When we look up to Jesus to get more on this matter, we observe that his attitude is the same as that of his Father in esteeming our "faith enrollment."

One day Jesus was approached by a stranger to get his help or miracle. The person who asked his help was literally a stranger as she was a Canaanite woman, a non-Jew, who was esteemed by the Jewish community as pagan, a Gentile, and an alien who was to be scorned as a dog. Jesus took that occasion to teach us something his Father had proposed already, to look at those who seemed strangers or foreigners to us through the "specs of faith." He admired at her faith and said, "O Woman, great is your faith! Let it be done for you as you wish" (Matt. 15:21–28).

Those who are not like us, those on the margins, those who are outcasts or foreigners must be approached with the mercy and justice of God, whose compassion and love transcends geography, nationality, creed, and our own feeble human limitations. We, as his beloved children, should not create any check box and live in that cubicle as inclusive and exclusive persons. Surprisingly, God continually thinks of humans who are outside those boxes. His grace and mercy will not be contained in the puny boxes we manufacture out of pride, fear, and ignorance. He is even waiting even for our renewal of a mercy-filled and justice-oriented faith life.

The genuineness of our faith consists not in what we profess but in whom we profess. For salvation and for the miraculous intervention of God, it does not matter where we belong but to whom we belong. We should honor and respect all faiths found in different colors, in different dimensions, in different phases, and in different terminologies. Unarguably, our real salvation is guaranteed only by such compassionate, just, and tolerant faith.

93. Evil Never Prevails against Sturdy Faith

Stand up and go; your faith has saved you.
—Luke 17:19

Our religious or spiritual relationship with the divine and all that we perform and practice because of it seem to be full of challenges, surprises, rewards, and frustrations. Long-standing human experience proves that God, the prime CEO who always behaves as the sole Master and Proprietor of human life management, plays low key and invisible in all his undertakings, especially in the eternal war between him and the devil. Concomitantly, we too discover that the same God ultimately prevails in every fight. Paul—admiring the depth of the riches, wisdom, and knowledge of God—writes, "How inscrutable are his judgments and how unsearchable his ways!" (Rom. 11:33–36).

In the Gospel (Matt. 16:13–23), we find God, the heavenly CEO, secretly inspiring Peter to go first to answer Jesus's question: "Who do you say that I am?" This we know by the words of Jesus: "Blessed are you, Simon son of Jonah. For flesh and blood has not revealed this to you, but my heavenly Father." Then comes the investiture of power on Peter as the rock on which God's church is to be built, and the entire responsibility of godly binding and loosing has been entrusted to Peter. From the Gospel writers, we know how the delinquent and feeble Peter has been. Soon after this remarkable investiture event, we read how Peter has been rebuked by Jesus, saying, "Get behind me, Satan! You are an obstacle to me." He, the Supreme, is in control of all our promotions and demotions. He creates as he likes; he destines his creatures as he plans.

Such unsearchable deeds of God are numerous as we read in the scriptures. One that I admire most is his dealing with the man Shebna (Isa. 22:19–23). Shebna, a household treasurer in the court of King Hezekiah, was a wicked, deceitful, and proud man who had conspired with Assyria to attack Jerusalem. Seeing Shebna's malpractices, God proclaimed judgment on him through Isaiah. Consequently, Shebna was brought down from his prestigious position, while the same Lord raised Eliakim, a faithful and trustworthy servant of the Lord, from a lower position to become a great officer in the court. This is the way how God deals with his humans, demonstrating that he is in total control of everything.

While all these invisible, secretive managerial or providential activities are going on in the realm of God among human beings, though we cannot fathom his wisdom in this regard, we can notice a single behavioral trend in all his deeds. Invariably, he is so enticed and attracted by humans' strong faith, or chutzpah, that he offers wonderful power to those who possess it; if absent, he throws them out. Even if they are pagans, not belonging to the elite groups of society, or weak, sinful, and timid, he—looking through their chutzpah— receives them, elects them, and makes them solid rocks by his grace.

This was what Jesus did to Peter, who was so weak, fragile, and sinful to deny him, yet he found Peter's chutzpah from his public testimony about him: "You are the Messiah, the Son of the living God." He elected him as the first leader of his church and strengthened him by grace as an unshaken rock that then would never be prevailed by evil.

Definitely, by proclaiming that Jesus is the Messiah and witnessing to it by our personal and humble obedience to God's will, we will become genuine and true rocks on which God will build up his towers of glory and blessings and minister to his people who shelter faithfully in his house.

94. We May Die by Others' Wrongdoing But Always Rise by Our Forgiving

Forgive, not seven times but seventy-seven times.
—Matt. 18:22

One of the remarkable sayings of Jesus is "If you forgive others their transgressions, your heavenly Father will forgive you. But if you do not forgive others, neither will your Father forgive your transgressions" (Matt. 6:14–15). Though it may sound hard, most of us accept it warmly because we desire, as the Master states, to "be perfect, just as our heavenly Father is perfect" (Matt. 5:48). However, the same saying becomes the hardest one to be practiced when we hear the Lord saying at the end of his parable of the unforgiving servant (Matt. 18:21–35), "So will my heavenly Father do to you, unless each of you forgives your brother from your heart." We have to pay serious attention to the words "from your heart." The human will, as we know, doesn't perform its task of loving without the cooperation of human rationality for its final success. God's Word, therefore, offers us some valid reasons why we should forgive others from our heart.

First, as Jesus underlines in the parable, the amazing eternal factor is that God—who loves us and forgives us as soon as we beg for his mercy and pardon—expects us to be so in our dealings with others. Second, the duty of forgiving others emerges from the obedience to God's love commandment. "Remember the commandments and do not be angry with your neighbor" (Sir. 28:7). Third, from Jesus, we know that there is only one condition

God demands from us to be forgiven by him, and that is to forgive other people's sins and mistakes. "Forgive us our trespasses as we forgive those who trespass against us." He has surely based this crucial demand on the teachings of OT sages: "Could anyone refuse mercy to another like himself, can he seek pardon for his own sins?" (Sir. 28:2, 4). Fourth, the teacher Sirach tells us, "Could anyone nourish anger against another and expect healing from the Lord?" (Sir. 28:3). Hence, to get healing from the Lord, we need to forgive others.

Another valid reason for forgiving others is that we are still going to die. Surely, a day will come when we will die. Before we die, let us set right everything before God and others. We hear in OT, "Remember your last days and set enmity aside; remember death and decay, and cease from sin!" (Sir. 28:6). It means, with the heavy burden of hatred and vengeance, it is very hard for our soul to fly toward heaven.

There is also one more compelling reason for Jesus's disciples to forgive others. As God's children, we have initiated ourselves by our faith to intimately connect to our Father. Especially in Jesus, we too have made a covenant with God and his human family. Therefore, we have to live up to that promise. As OT points out, we need to "remember the Most High's covenant, and overlook faults" (Sir. 28:7). In addition, through baptism, we started living, moving, and having our being through him, with him, and in him. "If we live, we live for the Lord, and if we die, we die for the Lord; so then, whether we live or die, we are the Lord's" (Rom. 14:7–8).

Most of the time, we are hurt terribly by others only because they hurt our prestige, good name, or good life. Certainly, every hurt others inflict on us is a tiny, little death before we face the grand death. But as

Christians, our entire life—containing those deaths—belongs to Christ. Surprisingly, when we totally forgive wrongdoers, Jesus resurrects us to a new life, which may be also that of the opposite party. Our glory, our prestige, and our good name come only by our union with Christ. So others' sins or evil deeds against us do not in any way affect us; even it does, by the Christian forgiveness, we will be raised to a new life in Christ.

95. When Rejected, Don't React but "Proact"

The stone, builders rejected, has become the cornerstone.
—Ps. 118:22

As I was meditating on Jesus's parable of the tenants (Matt. 21:33–43), what struck me most was the biblical quotation with which Jesus was concluding his story. He quoted from Psalm 118, "The stone that the builders rejected has become the cornerstone; by the Lord has this been done, and it is wonderful in our eyes?" In particular, the scriptural term "the rejected stone" sparkled an enlightening sensation in me.

Undoubtedly, any stone—being a material thing, whether kissed or rejected—doesn't feel anything. But its reference to humans clearly suggests the feelings we experience, either feeling joy when good things occur or encountering a painful trauma if we are rejected or scorned. Jesus purposefully used this scriptural quotation to offer us some practical guidelines for tackling those painful feelings.

We are fully aware of the perennial truth that every privilege we enjoy comes with a price tag. "No pain, no gain." Some people who are granted the favor of being positioned as cooperators in God's deeds misuse it, trying to take advantage of others, of society, and even of God. We see this in Jesus's parable.

While enjoying the benefits, the rebellious farm managers withheld to themselves from the landowner. Because of their unjust dealings, when their landowner took some stern efforts to correct them, they felt uneasy and irritated; and very sadly, they began reacting against the landowner and tried all crooked and malicious ways to reestablish their "stony" status. Instead, had they "proacted"—namely, repented for their misdeeds and get pardoned from their Master and amended their ways—they would have been well treated by the compassionate Master, and he would restate them even to the dignified position of "cornerstone."

That is what Jesus wants us to do. Everything we handle in this world belongs to God as its one and only Owner. He has elevated all humans as his favorite "stones" and entrusted his vineyard as a lease. Though we are responsible in all our creative works, we are accountable to him. Unfortunately, most of us ignore this fact and take everything of it in our hands and do according to our whims and fancies. Besides, when his Spirit stands inside us and warns us, we begin to react against him.

As the inevitable result of this violent and imprudent reaction, whatever we perform and manage brings forth only bitter fruits at the harvest: "God looked for the crop of grapes, but what it yielded was wild grapes" (Isa. 5:2–4). Those fruits can be the twisted and bad behaviors of our own sons and daughters, the family feuds, the immoral situation of our nation, and all the social evils pervading the entire universe. When God finds that the results of our creations are not according to his expectation, he gets outraged. He dashes us out of his vineyard. "Yes, I will make it a ruin" (Isa. 5:6). Jesus echoes God's words and adds some nuance to them: "Therefore, I say to you, the kingdom of God will be taken away from you and given to a people that will produce its fruit" (Matt. 21:43).

However, even if we have been rejected by God, as many of our forebears, we can get the cornerstone position. The only thing we should do is, during those troubled days, as Paul advises, we must perform continuously some spiritual exercises such as "making our requests known to God in everything by prayer and petition, with thanksgiving; plus, keep on doing whatever is true, whatever is honorable, whatever is just, whatever is pure, whatever is lovely, whatever is gracious" (Phil. 4:6–9). This is the way, as Jesus expects, to proact against rejections.

96. Let Us Participate In God's Banquets of Quality Life

The feast is ready but those who were invited were not worthy to come.
—Matt. 22:8

We love to attend parties as well as to host them. Happy are the days of a good celebration, when we can forget our worries for a while, enjoy one another's company, and laugh, sing, dance, and be happy. We are lucky to have such a day now and then, a day of feasting and real joy. Scriptures tell us that God's entire life consists in simply hosting such parties where he offers sumptuous meals for his creations: "On this mountain the Lord of hosts will provide for all peoples a feast of rich food and choice wines, juicy, rich food and pure choice wines" (Isa. 25:6).

Jesus ascertained this heavenly party factor. He esteemed God as a King who hosts a continuous heavenly wedding banquet: "The kingdom of heaven may be likened to a king who gave a wedding feast for his son" (Matt. 22:2). Describing the joyful feast God hosted, in his parable of the prodigal son, he quoted the amazing words of God to his servants: "Let us celebrate with a feast, because this son of mine was dead, and has come to life again; he was lost, and has been found" (Luke 15:23–24).

Jesus, our Redeemer, also was a party person. He loved to participate in such parties. "John came neither eating nor drinking and they said, 'He is possessed by a demon.' The Son of Man came eating and drinking and they said, 'Look, he is glutton and a drunkard'" (Matt. 11:18–19). Gospels testify that most of his beautiful sayings came out of his mouth while he was dining. Above all, he chose the paschal feast dinnertime to institute the greatest miraculous banquet of the Eucharist.

Scripturally, the banquet hosted by God and his Son has a deeper meaning to it. The Lord God offers us the lively banquet of his salvation, liberation, and redemption. His banquet provides us all that we need physically, emotionally, mentally, and spiritually. God's party is a banquet of joy and forgiveness because he will destroy death forever and will wipe away the tears from every face. It is a banquet of rest and peace.

All of us know well enough that in a well-hosted, genuine party, we feel that all our inhibitions are gone. We feel one with each other. We too are ready to help and assist other persons in a way possible. In other words, we are out of ourselves. It is the same kind of feeling that God, in his Son, wishes for all of us, not just in one or two banquets but also throughout our lives. Like a caring parent, he provides us a beautiful life with all its resources. We can name it "quality life." This quality life—menu of God's banquet—contains also the capsules of contentment, fullness, and sportive spirit. Paul, being so nourished in God's daily parties, writes how he has felt about the aftereffect of them (Phil. 4:12–14).

God in Jesus invites us daily to this sort of banquet (Matt. 22:1–14). Very surprisingly, not all of us are ready to take it. Though God as the host will cook, prepare the table, serve, and even do the dishes, he never compels us to come and join the party. He simply invites us and leaves to our discretion. But according to God's survey for the past millions of years, "Many are called but a few choose to be chosen" to participate in the dinner. We humans, with our free will, can reject this invitation.

However, God's dinner party is eternal with no interruption. Blessed are those who go and attend that sumptuous dinner of life. They indeed get the nourishment and fulfillment thereof by filling to the brim their heart, soul, and body.

97. A Puffed-Up Self Will Pull Us down to the Pit

I have made you contemptible and base before all the people;
for, you do not keep my ways.
—Mal. 2:9

Thanks to our scriptures, every Christian upholds that all things that are occurring now, as well as at the end of our lives, are coming from God's hands as either his blessings or curses. Throughout our lives, we have been watching and witnessing many of our neighbors and friends shining in public as very good politicians and diplomats, church ministers, preachers, teachers, and elders who are honored, esteemed, popular, and glamorous at the pulpits and podiums in front of an audience. But we too have noticed some of them being cursed and humiliated in public. Surely, all of these spotlight the eternal truth that people who have once started well in their career and counted as blessings from the Lord can turn out to be curses and contemptible in the eyes of God.

Such atrocious phenomena occur first because those blessed ones, in the course of their lives, have sidelined God, and their puffed-up self has taken priority. They have created their petty kingdom and formed their own laws, for which they become strongly opinionated. Their unaccounted supremacy replaces God's own, and they begin to use even God's authority, his podium, and his words for their vainglory. They forget God is their one and only Father, Master, and Superior (Matt. 23:1–10). Many times, they abuse their titles and recognitions to delete God's power and glory. We read in OT that

258 | REV. BENJAMIN A. VIMA

the Lord has become very angry and cursed those whom he has chosen and appointed as his liaisons to his people because they have turned aside from his way (Mal. 2:2–9).

Second, as time goes on, many humans begin to learn the tricks of survival; and so most of the time, their words do not correspond to their actions. They say one thing in public and do another in private. Most of their statements seem to be mere fake news and unproven views. Jesus calls these persons hypocrites. Jesus has observed that there is no integrity between the preaching and the life of elders, so he has exhorted, "Do and observe all things whatsoever they tell you, but do not follow their example. For they preach but they do not practice."

Third, these community leaders always go against the will of God, who advises them to be humble. "The greatest among you must be your servant. Whoever exalts himself will be humbled; but whoever humbles himself will be exalted" (Matt. 23:11–12). It is pride that breaks the bond they have with God, that keeps them stonyhearted, that leads them to exploit and cheat others, especially the ignorant and the weak; sometimes pride takes an ugly shape of patronizing others and bringing them under their control.

Fortunately, church history testifies to an array of Jesus's disciples, like Paul, who have been fully aware of the admonitions of God and learned from Jesus's life and teachings to behave gently among their people as a nursing mother caring her children. But they have shared with people not only the Gospel of God but also their very self, and they have never imposed bigger burdens, though they could have done it. They have earned their livelihood by working night and day.

Because of such attitude and conduct, people have received from them not human words but those of God (1 Thess. 2:7b–9, 13).

To always get such uninterrupted blessings from the Lord and walk as source of blessings in the midst of our friends and relatives, let us strive to be obedient to God, truthful to our words, and a humble servant to others only for the sake of God.

98. Building up Our Strength in Discipleship

The one who began a good work in you
will continue to complete it.
—Phil. 1:6

In one of my Religious Communications classes at Loyola Chicago, during our question time, some of us asked our Jesuit professor a childlike question (most of us were still babies in our spirituality at that time): "When God and humans communicate to each other, what actions and reactions are going on between the two persons?" It was a relevant issue we thought because, during that class hour, we were studying on humans' interpersonal communications. The professor smilingly said that it was a wonderful question. And he added, "At every moment of our life, God communicates with us in whatever environment or condition we may live in. But at times, when he needs humans for his creative and redemptive agenda, he speaks to them with an intense and intimate communication technique." Then he went on describing some such events narrated in the Bible.

In all such remarkable incidents, first, we noticed God manifesting a glimpse of his glory, holiness, and power. When God appeared to his chosen messengers like the prophet Isaiah (6:1–7), for example, God communicated to him as the Lord seated on a high and lofty throne, surrounded by his angels, who were singing, "Holy, holy, holy." Together with this, Isaiah saw that the frame of the door shook and that the house was filled with smoke.

Second, we observed the communicator God encouraging his receivers to rise when they were found trembling and fearing. For instance, while Isaiah stumbled and considered himself very low and humble in the august presence of the divine, God through an angel touched the mouth of the prophet with purifying fire and said, "See, now that this has touched your lips, your wickedness is removed, your sin purged." Jesus, God's Son, behaved the same way when he communicated with his disciples. In the miraculous event of the unexpected catch of countless fish by Jesus's powerful order (Luke 5:4–10a), when Peter and other disciples were seized by astonishment and trembled at the sight of their Master, Jesus got closer to them and encouraged them with a positive prophecy: "Do not be afraid; from now on you will be catching men."

The third action of the communicator God in his interpersonal encounter with his chosen ones has been calling them straight away to follow him in his footsteps, if they has been chosen by the divine ordinance already. Plus, he too begins to share with them his strength and power. His plain order seems to be "Follow me" or "Go where I send you."

However, the reactions of the human receivers, standing on the side of these unthinkable interpersonal communication with the divine, always echoed their limitations and inabilities. Whenever God's chosen ones experienced the immense power of God, they felt unworthy and tried to resist his order. Listen at Isaiah crying out, "Woe is me, I am doomed! For I am a man of unclean lips, living among a people of unclean lips; yet my eyes have seen the King, the Lord of hosts!" And in the Gospel event of the numerous fish catch, we noticed Peter falling at the knees of Jesus and shouting out, "Depart from me, Lord, for I am a sinful man."

Once God's effective and intimate communication encounters humans, besides recognizing their human frailty, they simply offer total surrender to the Almighty. Isaiah and other prophets, despite their awe-crushed situation, did obey his order and began their journey of carrying God's messages to humanity on his behalf. Surprisingly, we found that Isaiah—as soon as he heard the calling of God—took personal interest in it and volunteered to go as God directed him. "Then I heard the voice of the Lord saying, 'Whom shall I send? Who will go for us?' 'Here I am,' I said; 'send me'" (Isa. 6:8). The same is true for Peter and the disciples of Jesus. When the Lord commanded them, "Follow me," "Immediately they left everything and followed Jesus" (Luke 5:10b–11).

Every one of us is called by God at every moment of our lives as he is standing at our gate and knocking at our door; especially at times when we truly and honestly give him a specific time of solitude exclusively for him, he deals with us as he has dealt with Peter and Isaiah and other holy men and women. God calls us sometimes to what may seem like impossible work. But when we listen with the intention of saying yes and doing what we can, he provides what we need.

99. Quality Prayer for Quality Discipleship

When the Son of Man comes, will he find faith on earth?
—Luke 18:8

In our plan of walking with Jesus as his disciples, we are fully aware of our inability to cope with all his demands. Jesus knows it well, and therefore, he has offered us a support system in our journey of discipleship. That is called prayer, through which he hears the outcry of the poor and of the fragile disciples who are longing to stay in his company.

Indeed, we are "praying people." There is no doubt about it; otherwise, we will not be his disciples. Most of us pray not only here but also at various times, occasions, and ways. In our prayer time, we usually adore the Lord as our only God; we sometimes spell out to him what kind of God we worship. Whatever name we give him, we want to make sure we are present in front of him. We include in prayer many praises and thanks for his greatness, fidelity, and goodness. We express to him our weaknesses and mistakes and ask his forgiveness. In addition, we list out many petitions and intercessions to him.

Some of us take this prayer effort seriously as their duty or daily need. Most of us take this as an extracurricular activity or as an appendix to the humdrum main affairs of earthly life. So many pray before they go to accomplish certain serious and important jobs. Others pray only when bad and evil things occur such as death, accident, separation, and deception. Because of such anomaly, fakery, frustration, and silliness found in countless uses of prayer, many among us have drifted away from any kinds of prayer efforts. Also, some of us are feeling desperate that many of our prayer efforts become barren.

In this regard, our Master's advice is this: whatever be our aim, style, mode, and kind of prayer, it must possess an important ingredient that is called perseverance if it is to be a genuine and resourceful prayer. He wants to show to all his disciples that they should pray continually and not lose heart. In this connection, he presents to us a widow as our role model who has finally gained her victory by her impudent attitude and persevering attempts (Luke 18:1–8).

Our beloved apostle Paul defines the term "perseverance" very succinctly: "Pray unceasingly." If praying unceasingly means endlessly reciting prayers on our knees, we are in big trouble. However, if praying unceasingly means living, breathing, walking, interacting, laughing, and loving in a constant spirit of prayer, then this is achievable. Perseverance is the basics for the victory of Jesus's disciples in their process of becoming the most worthy disciples.

Let us take any saint in church history or any holy person mentioned in the Bible. Their lives would tell us that they could not and did not achieve their aspirations to become worthy disciples till their death, but one thing was certain: they were beloved sons and daughters in whom God was well pleased. He was pleased not much on what they had accomplished for Jesus or on their Guinness World Record of reciting 1,001 prayers with no interruption. The only reason for God being pleased with them was that they persevered in prayer and action.

In the Bible (Exod. 17:8–13), we read about a historical record breaker in the prayer of perseverance. He was Moses, whom God loved very close to his heart. Even though Moses had his miraculous staff in his hands, even though he climbed up the mountain and prayed, the Lord did not offer his request, namely, a victory to the Israelites against their enemies. Moses never lost his heart. He persevered in prayer, lifting his hands. His style of praying may seem and sound funny and bizarre. Yet God finally granted a historical victory to his people because of Moses's perseverance in prayer.

Victory, defeat, failure, success—all these are part of human lives. Prayer is not something that interfere the plan of God and changes God and his will. Rather, our prayer of perseverance suggests that our hearts are melted, open for God's grace, and ready to cope with whatever his will has designed for us. Such a persistent prayer practice requires a relentless faith in God, in Jesus, and in their promises and predictions about our prayer efforts.

The mind-blowing efficacy of persistent prayer is compared to that of God's Word in the book of Isaiah: "My word . . . shall not return to me empty, but shall do what pleases me, achieving the end for which I sent it" (55:11). So does he declare in the book of Sirach: "The prayer of the lowly pierces the clouds; it does not rest till it reaches its goal; nor will it withdraw till the Most High responds" (35:21). And Jesus has sworn to his disciples before he has left from this world, "Ask for whatever you want and it will be done for you" (John 15:7b). All of God's promises will be fulfilled if only we persistently cling to him and abide in his love with unwavering faith. That is the quality prayer Jesus recommends.

100. True Witnessing to Christ Is By Nothing but the Truth

Consecrate them in the truth. Your word is truth.
—John 17:17

Every time we present ourselves to the Lord wholeheartedly, he reminds us of our duty of witnessing to him and his Gospel while we are still kicking around in this world. His voice is very intense today more than ever before as we encounter so many hurdles and oppositions in this modern age of total secularism and worldliness. He reminds us to follow the footsteps of his messengers found in the Bible. One among them, who is very close to his heart, is none other than John the Baptist, who has deliberately witnessed throughout his life for Jesus—the Way of truth for life, by the truth and nothing but the truth.

John's first witnessing to the natural truth started at his conception and birth by strange happenings that directed the public's attention to the mysterious and transcendent presence and interaction of the Almighty. They were miracles that included an angel announcing the good news of his birth, old parents conceiving him, his father having been punished to be dumb but then stunningly recovering his power of speech, and his leaping for joy at the presence of Messiah's mother while John was still an infant in his mother's womb. Above all, he witnessed to the Almighty by the name "John," given by the angel and literally meaning "God is gracious," when it was finally accepted in an awesome way by his parents and relatives.

As an adult, John witnessed to the spiritual truth through his choice of milieu for his entire life, which bore witness to a different, otherworldly reality. He became a man of the most austere desert and totally separated himself from the world to give testimony to another world, and within his solitude, he was able to hear the voice of God. His simple and unglamorous clothing bore witness as well. His preference in location, food, and attire demonstrated a counterculture going against the prevailing wisdom of his day. He testified by his unobtrusive lifestyle to how important it is to be simple and detached from the things of this world.

Being aware of John's unrelenting life of witnessing to God's kingdom values, Jesus praised him in public: "What did you go out to the desert to see—a reed swayed by the wind? Then what did you go out to see? Someone dressed in fine garments? Those who dress luxuriously and live sumptuously are found in royal palaces. Then what did you go out to see? A prophet? Yes, I tell you, and more than a prophet. This is the one about whom scripture says: 'Behold, I am sending my messenger ahead of you, he will prepare your way before you.' I tell you, among those born of women, no one is greater than John; yet the least in the kingdom of God is greater than he" (Luke 7:24–28).

Beyond all the above-listed elements of his witnessing, John's message was the most intriguing factor that placed him as the third person with Jesus and Mary in God's salvific history. His message was all about Jesus, the truth and nothing but the truth, whom he pointed out to people as the Messiah, the Lamb of God who would take away their sins. He too verified to them Jesus's glorious and powerful identity. And he underlined that every action of Jesus was the one and only source of salvation.

In this regard, he witnessed his unworthiness and limitation before Jesus. "One mightier than I is coming after me. I am not worthy to stoop and loosen the thongs of his sandals. I have baptized you with water; He will baptize you with the Holy Spirit" (Mark 1:7–8). John not only preached a message but he was also the message of truth. He was an authentic witness because he himself was authentic. That was why people couldn't resist a witness like him. As Paul would proclaim about his contribution to God's salvific plan, "John heralded his coming by proclaiming a baptism of repentance to all the people of Israel" (Acts 13:24–25).

John's ultimate witness to the truth came in his death, and that too was caused by his unrelenting testimony to Jesus's Gospel value of truth and fidelity in human relationships. King Herod personified those human beings who, from the beginning of time until the end, chose to live a lie rather than in truth. There were thousands of leaders in human history, both in the political and religious arenas, who had been elected, selected, and promoted by nothing but lies. In their midst, from the depths of the dungeon, John's martyrdom had been a testimony that every discipled leader of Jesus must never be afraid to proclaim the truth and nothing but the truth.

101. We Make a Life by What We Give

When the Son of Man will come with
his angels in his Father's glory
He will repay everyone according to his conduct.
—Matt. 16:27

As Christians, we are asked to profess that our Jesus is the glorious and victorious Christ the King. This acceptance and affirmation of his unique leadership does not relate to the historical factors of Jesus of Nazareth as being a Galilean Jewish rebel who has lived some two thousand years back or a sage who has founded his own "better way" to reach the Supreme Being or a feudal king who has emerged in the beginning of third century to counteract and topple down all then existing rulers of the world.

Rather, our primary reason for this proclamation is that we encounter today the same Jesus, Mary's son, personally and communally as the resurrected Lord in his Spirit, moving and leading at his will around the globe; that this leader cannot be contained or restricted only to a few, even to the so-called Christians, but to every living creatures with no discrimination, labeling, or profiling; that "in Jesus, who was raised from the dead as firstfruits" (1 Cor. 15:20), "we all have redemption by his blood, the forgiveness of transgressions" (Eph. 1:7) "God set forth in Christ, as a plan for the fullness of times, to sum up all things in him, in heaven and on earth" (Eph. 1:9–10); and that we are so proud of being inducted into Jesus's Church and share the same power and dignity of being assigned as the proxies of his leadership, plus the assurance of entering into his heavenly mansions of eternity.

While we feel so happy and proud about our sharing with Christ his supreme leadership, leading others to our true and complete destiny, God reminds us to reflect over the handling of such dignified leadership. In the kingdom of God, the one and only definition of leadership is "imitating Jesus, loving others with justice, loving with truth, and serving them with love."

Through the prophets, God declared the unique style of his leadership: "I myself will look after and tend my sheep. As a shepherd tends his flock, when he finds himself among his scattered sheep, so will I tend my sheep! The lost I will seek out, the strayed I will bring back, the injured I will bind up and the sick I will heal" (Ezek. 34:11–17). That was the style of leadership Jesus performed and preached, and undoubtedly, that would be the measurement with which he would be judging all his discipled leaders on Judgment Day.

The one and only benchmark with which he is going to measure our lives is nothing but a love-saving love, life-giving love, truthful love, justice-based love, and surely action-packed love. This act of charity toward the needy and the neglected will be properly handled by us only when we unite ourselves with the Spirit of the resurrected Christ and see his presence in others as if they are the proxies of Christ (Matt. 25:31–46).

As one of the foremost authorities on this leadership style, Saint Teresa of Calcutta, who has lived and practiced it, is quoted saying, "Undoubtedly we will be judged at the end by the words of Jesus: 'I was hungry and you gave me to eat. I was naked and you clothed me. I was homeless and you took me in.'" Yes, let us never forget, we make a life by what we give as we make a living by what we get.

102. Who Is Worthy of God's Personal Gifts?

Blessed are the meek, for they will inherit the land.
—Matt. 5:5

Jesus was sent to us only to answer that question validly. From his birth up to his death, his only preoccupation was to fulfill that goal. We observed God finally proving his prophecies about Jesus's role of gift giver to humans. "See, your savior comes! See, his reward is with him" (Isa. 62:11–12). Plus, "the people who walked in darkness have seen a great light . . . You have brought them abundant joy and great rejoicing" (Isa. 9:1–2). At the birth of his Son, God demonstrated that a particular group of people would be blessed with his gifts through his Son and that they should be like shepherds (Luke 2:8–20).

Throughout the history of God's involvement with his people, God declared himself to be their Shepherd. Actually, he preferred to be called Shepherd more than any other names because he knew the intrinsic and intense tender loving relationship existing between a shepherd and his sheep. He claimed himself so. He loved, therefore, to delegate his kingly power to humans to a shepherd boy like David. He wanted shepherding to be the model for leaders of his kingdom on the earth.

Very sadly, those leaders whom he chose failed him in this regard. He took the whip in his hands and tried to straighten them out. However, he didn't see any change in humans' behavior. Hence, when he decided to become Immanuel in the form of Jesus to demonstrate his principle and policy of human behavior in his kingdom and to proclaim who would be eligible to share the gifts he brought, he was very choosy in bringing shepherds as his first visitors, admirers, and companions.

Those shepherds' routine tasks for centuries most clearly reflect God's own. Their daily life has been consisting in watching over their flocks, defending them from the prowling predator, leading them into good pasture, rescuing the lost and foolish stray, tending the wounds, and bringing them safe home to the fold. That is what God has willed that his Son, Jesus, should testify to, behaving as the Good Shepherd. He too has demanded all his followers, especially those who are chosen to lead his flock, to perform their ministries in his church as genuine shepherds as he is.

There were some more splendid messages God wanted to convey to us through these shepherds' activities at the birthday of Jesus. During the hours of Jesus's birth, the baby, Mary, and Joseph were alone except a few animals. At that moment, we found God seeking out simple people as their companions, who were none other than those poor and humble shepherds. As one preacher commented, the reason for such choice by God was that they, living in poverty, would not be dismayed at finding the Messiah in a cave, wrapped in swaddling clothes. By the coming of Christ, his Son, any socially neglected humans such as the shepherds would never again be despised as having a menial task or as being vagabonds. A whole new dignity would descend upon them.

The next turning point in the story was, after seeing the historical scenario with their own eyes exactly as they were told by the angels, the Gospel said, "The shepherds returned, glorifying and praising God for all they had heard and seen, just as it had been told to them." In other words, they started looking at the world they lived in with new eyes; they understood the real meaning of events that looked ordinary, though outwardly. And finally, let us also remember what the shepherds did next: "They made known the message that had been told them about this child. All who heard it were amazed by what had been told them by the shepherds."

Just as the shepherds have been invited by God, we are chosen by Christ and his church to be sent out today into the world to share the awesome truth God has brought through his Son. Jesus reveals himself to us in the midst of the ordinary incidents of each day. We have to be alert so as to discover Jesus in the simplicity of ordinary life, and he wants us to proclaim him to the world only through our simple and humble shepherding of those whom God sent to us for our caregiving. Pope Francis splendidly and metaphorically is quoted saying, "The shepherds should smell of the sheep."

103. Become His Epiphany Today By Assimilating His Epiphany

Through you I will manifest my holiness
in the sight of the nations.
—Ezek. 20:41b

The term "epiphany" is probably an alteration of the Greek *epiphaneia*, meaning "appearing, manifesting, or showing forth." Historically, it has been used to point out exclusively the manifestations of a supernatural or divine reality. In modern usage, it also denotes any moment of great or sudden revelation in which humans strikingly perceive something in a new and clear perspective.

It is a historical fact that, from the day of Creation, humans have been craving for God's chilling and thrilling manifestation in his power and glory. Not only the Gospel writers but also all the apostles and disciples who belong to Jesus's team in the first century have been inspired by Jesus's godly Spirit to go through his life's events, his sayings, and his accomplishments and discover what and how he has manifested his identity and nature. In other words, every step, every moment, every lip movement is his epiphany. "When you read this you can understand my insight into the mystery of Christ, which was not made known to human beings in other generations as it has now been revealed to his holy apostles and prophets by the Spirit, that the Gentiles are coheirs, members of the same body, and copartners in the promise in Christ Jesus through the gospel" (Eph. 3:2–6).

We were told by Matthew, in his narration about the magi's visit to baby Jesus (Matt. 2:1–12), that a unique manifestation of divine glory through baby Jesus was offered to the magi as the representatives of the Gentiles. We also read that the magi, who came from the East, offered to baby Jesus three gifts of gold, frankincense, and myrrh. According to traditional interpretation, those gifts were the symbols that contained the content of his Epiphany: the gift of gold symbolized the kingship of Jesus, the incense expressed his divinity, and the myrrh foretold of Jesus as a typical human who would undergo passion and death.

We observe in NT books and in church tradition that Jesus has manifested the presence of the invisible God in him by all the events of his life, especially as a helpless child lying in a manger and as a young man dying on the cross, the ultimate revelation that God's glory is love. This means that Jesus is the revelation of God as one who offers himself to us in love. At his birth, we encounter the revelation of the purpose of his incarnation: that God and we, God's creatures, might enjoy each other in the embrace of love. We too uphold in our religion that, in Jesus's birth, the OT prophecies about the redeeming Messiah have been fulfilled. Referring to the arrival of the magi who represent humanity from all corners of the globe, Isaiah writes, "Nations shall walk by your light, kings by the radiance of your dawning. Raise your eyes and look about; they all gather and come to you" (60:1–6).

This story takes us back to our day-to-day life, in which God continues to manifest himself in glory, power, wisdom, and love through Jesus's presence. Our belief in this matter is based on the promises of Jesus that he will be with us till the end of ages. He has promised to come in the forms of neighbors, the needy, the enemies, the sinners, and our community bonded in faith and prayer. We also know he manifests himself in natural resources, creative achievements of humans, natural disasters, and other social events. He too is present in each and every one of us in our inner sanctuary and manifests himself through inspirations, inner conscience, creative thoughts, visions, dreams, and certain mystic experiences.

Unfortunately, there are many among us who still do not want to accept our spiritual worth and our marvelous capacity to see the manifestations of God in our midst. This is for two reasons: (1) we are not humble and poor in spirit, but we behave hardheadedly like King Herod; and (2) we don't come to terms with the inspiration of God for perfection and don't dare to change our usual path of life like the magi have obeyed the angel's advice. Only when we are drawn by the daily manifestations of Christ and, as their effect, when we begin to modify and purify our life path do we also become the manifestations of his presence for others.

104. Give Respect and Get Respect

Over all these, put on love that is the bond of perfection.
—Col. 3:14

We, in Christianity, are fortunate enough to be brought up from early childhood with many golden rules and resourceful sayings and proverbs that stay permanently in our hearts and direct us to walk in the right path. Unlike old religions that proclaim some hateful sayings such as "Tit for tat, an eye for an eye, and a tooth for a tooth," our Teacher Jesus has given us many precious love-based sayings. One among them is "Do to others whatever you would have them do to you" (Matt. 7:12). In simple words, we can say this as "Give respect and get respect."

Paul gives a detailed description of the term "respect": "Put on then, as God's chosen ones, holy and beloved, heartfelt compassion, kindness, humility, gentleness, and patience, bearing with one another and forgiving one another, if one has a grievance against another; as the Lord has forgiven you, so must you also do. And over all these put on love, that is, the bond of perfection" (Col. 3:12–14).

God expects us to give this kind of respect to every human, especially our family members. Knowing the importance of such relationship, he has inserted it into his commandments: "Honor your father and mother," which is the fourth commandment of God. Very surprisingly, he placed it just after the three commandments that are to be followed in our relationship with God, this being the first commandment among all the others that are about our relationships with our neighbors. Expounding it, the teacher Sirach writes, "God sets a father in honor over his children; and a mother's authority he confirms over her sons" (Sir. 3:2). He too has talked about its results: "Those who honor their father atone for sins; they store up riches who respect their mother. Those who honor their father will have joy in their own children, and when they pray they are heard. Those who respect their father will live a long life" (Sir. 3:3–6).

We witnessed this sort of magnanimous and respectful behavior among the members of the Holy Family at Nazareth. Joseph, who had a dream at midnight and had been admonished by the angel of

God to flee to Egypt, got up immediately; woke Mary and the child Jesus, who were in deep sleep; rose and took the child and his mother; and departed for Egypt. Surely, Joseph—being a person of justice—would have explained about his dream to Mary; so respecting each other, they managed to adjust to the critical situations they were in. Though their son, Jesus, was longing to stay in his Father's house, as Luke confirmed, "he went down with them and came to Nazareth, and was obedient to them" (Luke 2:51).

Certainly, this sort of behavior is not possible for any human person. Human nature always is prone to judge others, to put down others, to seek self-gratification, to compare and contrast with others. These are all human techniques for the survival of the fittest. But this kind of self-oriented relationship never brings forth any peace or joy, only fight, war, separation, and hatred. Therefore, scriptures recommend to us first to give respect to the Lord; and then automatically, the element of true respect will be present permanently in our human relationships.

As the Gospels underline, the entire family in Nazareth lived and moved based on God's Word and will. They were respecting God as their Supreme Sovereign and Master. Mary, Joseph, and Jesus had more than their share of problems and woes, especially when the very reason and heart of this family was Jesus, their bewildering son. They did everything for him. What was typical of the Holy Family was that, in everything, they sought God's will. This too would be characteristic of Jesus; God's will was to be his food and drink.

Most of the time, we lose our respect for each other at times of crises like job problems, sicknesses, weaknesses of people, and so on. If we follow the footsteps of the Holy Family, honoring God as our priority and respecting and honoring our family members, we will preserve and sustain our peace and joy. Let us never forget that, for a Christian, the Golden Rule is a three-way process: "First give respect to God and automatically the mutual respect among the members of the family starts existing."

105. The Restored and Enhanced Human Authority

He taught them as one having authority.
—Mark 1:22

Our scriptures, being inspired by God's Spirit, make us understand the supremacy, sublime sovereignty, and immense power of God among his creations. At the same time, they too offer very reasonable arguments for the human authorities we hold in the family and in society.

All great leaders in history try to articulate their plans as promises about how they will be using their power and authority for the future continuation of their mission or work for the welfare of society. Very sadly, most of these leaders, political and religious, fail in their promises. God knows the limitation of humans in this regard. Hence, through his Son, he has offered some guidelines for using our God-given authoritarian power and executing his plan in this world.

We read in the Gospel about Jesus's splendid handling of his authority (Mark 1:21–28). The people were astonished at his teaching. That was because they heard him uttering words that were not empty; they even had power to drive out evil spirits. His words got powerful and forceful because he made the wavelength of his relationship with his Father very intimate.

Unquestionably, Jesus was the realization of God's promise through Moses: "I will raise up for them a prophet like you from among their kindred, and will put my words into the mouth of the prophet; the prophet shall tell them all that I command" (Deut. 18:18). Nonetheless, we found in Jesus's life a sincere and faithful commitment to God's expectations of his prophets. He knew God demanded his messengers to speak, in his name, only his words and not theirs. But if the prophets didn't obey as he willed, he cursed them. "If a prophet presumes to speak a word in my name that I have not commanded, or speaks in the name of other gods, that prophet shall die" (Deut. 18:20).

Not only did Jesus deliver his authoritarian speech but they also were accompanied with deeds of an exemplary life, acts of healing others, and surely concentration on targeting to cast out evil spirits from others. People, therefore, testified on this, saying to one another, "What is this? A new teaching with authority. He commands even the unclean spirits and they obey him."

All of us—in our families, in our communities, and around the globe—are possessed at one time or another by various types of evil spirits like jealousy, pride, anger, grudge, partiality, revenge, laziness, and many others. To expel these from our hearts, we still need the powerful and authentic words of Jesus, which are surely transmitted from his committed disciples.

When we are healed by his authoritative words, we become stronger and more powerful. We can speak and act as wounded healers. We will be chosen as God's prophets in our limited milieu, and either he will be glad to bless us if we, in our executing power of ordering or disciplining, speak the balanced truth as God proposes to us and never rely on human authorities or power centers' influences or he will punish us as he has cautioned through Moses.

When we are attuned to the good Spirit of God, we can surely discern the difference between good and unclean spirits. As Jesus, we may be bestowed with the spiritual power to cast out those demons around us. Nonetheless, we know we cannot all the time turn out to be miracle workers of healing the sick. Jesus tells us we have the power to make our people whole and wholesome; that means he wants us to make everyone around us become like him, that is, completely human, good, and whole persons not only physically but also in all our life's dimensions. If we want to enrich our prophetic power, as Paul advises, we must try our best to be free of worldly anxieties, and we must be spiritually anxious about the things of the Lord and how we may please the Lord with no distraction whatsoever (1 Cor. 7:32–35).

106. How to Make Our Burden Light And Our Yoke Easy

*Keeping our eyes fixed on Jesus, the
leader and perfecter of faith.*
—Heb. 12:2a

Many times, I have been approached by my church members as their spiritual mentor, exposing their life's burdens and drudgeries. Whenever I hear their problems, my inner spirit reminds me of the scriptural passages about the groans of a just man, Job: "Is not life on earth a drudgery, its days like those of a hireling? I have been assigned months of futility, and troubled nights have been counted off for me. When I lie down I say, 'When shall I arise?' then the night drags on; I am filled with restlessness until the dawn" (Job 7:1–7).

All humans born in this world—holy or unholy, weak or strong, prudent or imprudent—are undergoing such miseries and desolations. Suffering will always remain a scandal or at least a mystery. We can try to act as if it doesn't affect us, denying that it exists or running away from it, but there is no real escape from it for a Christian. It is written into our existence since Christ has died on the cross. Though we will never understand it fully, we know in the light of God's revelations that all human sufferings are meaningful and saving, if we bear them as God expects us to.

In this regard, the important advice God offers us is to listen to his Son's counseling words on this matter and try to spend each and every day of our life as Jesus has done. The best of Jesus's exhortations on pulling through our life's drudgeries is "Come to me, all you who labor and are burdened, and I will give you rest. Take my yoke upon you and learn from me, for I am meek and humble of heart; and you will find rest for yourselves. For my yoke is easy, and my burden light" (Matt. 11:28–30).

How did he manage all his burdensome experiences in life? We knew well the nature of his yoke. He was literally a vagabond walking under the hot Palestinian sun, on hilly and deserted locations, on thickly populated villages and towns, through the dusty roads, and in the midst of many of his enemies. Foxes had holes, but he had no room to lie down and take rest;

plus, with no big bag of savings accounts, he and his disciples were always waiting for somebody to invite them for dinner. In sum, Jesus was literally like one of us in undergoing life's burdens, worse than that of Job.

However, Jesus never lost his peace, serenity, dignity, hope, and joy. He left with us a paradigm of how we should live our day-to-day life of pain and suffering. In the light of the scriptures, we came to know that the daily chores of Jesus were marked by his three primary preoccupations. First, he immersed himself daily in prayer with his heavenly Father. Mark wrote, "Rising very early before dawn, he left and went off to a deserted place, where he prayed" (1:35). There were references in the Gospels about Jesus praying throughout the night. In between those prayer hours, Jesus never missed any event or scheduled programs of healing and doing good to people. Thus, Jesus started every activity in prayer and ended it in prayer.

Second, Jesus preferred to stay among the needy people throughout the day. In the Gospels, we heard that when it was evening, after sunset, needy people brought to him all who were ill or possessed by demons. The whole town was gathered at the door (Mark 1:32–34). All kinds of people, especially those who were downtrodden and poor, reached out to him, and he extended his healing and loving hands to them with no discrimination whatsoever.

Following the Master's footsteps, his disciples, like Paul, would untiringly take the burdens of others and alleviate their maladies. The great apostle asserted, "I have made myself a slave to all so as to win over as many as possible. To the weak I became weak, to win over the weak. I have become all things to all, to save at least some" (1 Cor. 9:19–22). The committed followers of

Christ for centuries understood well how to make life's burden light by holding one conviction of sharing the blessings of the Gospel they proclaimed (1 Cor. 9:23).

We are at one time or another miserable, depressed, negative, discouraged, desolate, and gloomy. But when we are closely related to Jesus, we hear him continuously saying that in the midst of the burdens of life, we should go to him not only to get his healing and wise counseling but also to learn from his life the right and efficacious way of maintaining our peace and joy in darkness. Plus, we learn from Jesus that the brokenhearted people should not only stop upholding this positive attitude in their sufferings but also encourage others in their suffering times as well. There are many among us who are wounded in spirit and waiting for us to heal them from their pains and sorrows and liberate them from the demons that plague them. These wounded people may be in our homes, neighborhoods, and even enemy camps. We must be ready to go beyond our likes and dislikes. That is the only way for a Christian to be a merrymaker and a jolly good fellow even in pains, sufferings, and perils.

107. Lower Ourselves toward the Needy As Jesus to Us

Be imitators of me, as I am of Christ.
—1 Cor. 11:1

In the Gospels, we read many miraculous contact happening between Jesus and humans afflicted by physical, mental, and spiritual illnesses. Holding strong faith in the healing power of Jesus, we too long for such kind of healing contact, especially during our dark days of illness. However, we should know there are some necessary requirements from our side to realize our dream of being healed by Jesus.

The primary requirement is we should understand the compassionate heart of Jesus. Let us take, for example, one miraculous healing event narrated by Mark (1:40–45). It is about the miraculous healing of a sick person (leper) who has been suffocated by an incurable and abominable disease. In Jewish culture in Jesus's time, leprosy has been considered very abhorrent and abominable, one given by God as a curse or punishment for sins (Deut. 13:44–46).

We observed Jesus in this Gospel event reacting, acting, and reciprocating to the leper as if a lover. First, he was moved with pity. The word "pity," in its genuine meaning, pointed out one's feeling for others, particularly sentiments of sadness or sorrow. Jesus's only concern was reciprocating to the needy person with sincere love. He stretched out his hand and touched his needy partner. In human communications, gestures (body languages) are better than mere words. Being fully aware of human limitations, Jesus showed his love to the needy as his Father did in his love affairs with humanity, only in actions. As a climactic love act, Jesus offered a beautiful and amazing gift to his love partner, the leper. Using his power of the Word becoming flesh, he cured the sick person by uttering the miraculous words "I do will it. Be made clean." The leper was then and there made clean.

As a second requirement for the unbelievable, miraculous healing contact with Jesus, we are told to utilize the maximum possible human involvement. The leper himself is given to us as a model to imitate. All the actions of the sick person in his encounter with Jesus are remarkable and to be seriously noted.

He knelt down with respect and humility in front of the Great Healer. With the sense of trust, he begged Jesus to cure him. He too communicated to Jesus what was bothering his mind, namely, he was unclean. We too can notice in his communication with the Master certain faith and recognition of Jesus's independence and dignity. He added a faith-filled proclamation to his appeal for healing, saying, "If you wish, you can make me clean."

Amazingly, when we observed what happened in the life of the healed leper, we found him unmistakably obeying Jesus's first demand. He would have gone and showed himself to the clergy of the temple and offered the due offerings prescribed by Moses. He would have gotten his license to go out of his ghetto and walk freely in open places with the crowd. However, he was so taken up and overwhelmed with joy, gratitude, and love for Jesus, the Healer, that he overlooked Jesus's second demand of not publicizing the happenings between him and Jesus. The Gospel said that he publicized what had happened to him in his unfathomable contact with Jesus and showed everybody his license of being cleansed by the Great Healer.

Jesus—by his loving interactions with us—recreates us, renews us, molds us, shapes us, grooms us, heals us, and fills us; and surely, in a mysterious and stunning way, he begins to use us for his glory and for humans' eternal life. Being healed by the merciful encounter of Jesus, the apostle Paul has imitated his Master in all possible ways. Whether eating or drinking or whatever his deeds, he has done everything for the glory of God. We too must do the same. Being grateful for all of Jesus's breathtaking encounters, let us go around the world proclaiming those loving deeds in the form of our own humble charitable deeds to the needy. Are we daring enough like Paul to propose to our beneficiaries, "I did it. Can you?"

108. Workable Solution
For Today's Economic Crisis

Whoever is begotten by God conquers the world.
—1 John 5:4a

For better survival in this modern world, God's Spirit summons Christians daily to go deeper into the startling interactions of the risen Lord in our midst. Very specifically, we are asked to enter into the life of the first community of Jesus's disciples and meditate on their quality life in the risen Lord.

We read in the book of Acts (4:32–35) that the early Christians were "of one heart and mind." This was testified in their behaviors such as no one claimed that any of his possessions were his own, they had everything in common, and they would sell all their properties and distributed the proceeds to each apostle according to need. The obvious result was that there was no needy person among them.

Such bewildering behavior may be either not well understood by today's Christians or simply rejected and nullified by modern skeptics. But we should never forget that the economic values that these early Christians have cherished are those of Jesus Christ and loudly preached by his apostles. They have followed exactly what the Lord has commanded them: "If you want to be my disciples sell all your possessions, give to the poor and then follow me" (Mark 10:21). It is indeed the hardest saying of Christ, yet the first Christians have lovingly followed it because of their inner encounter with the risen Lord.

As John wrote in his letter, they esteemed their faith in the resurrected Lord as their victory and based every bit of their earthly steps and enterprises on that belief that they were the children of God, who is love (1 John 5:1–6). They obeyed very meticulously, word for word, God's loving command that we should love our neighbors as our brothers and sisters. This command, seemingly a utopian dream, was not burdensome to them because they had been regenerated by the Lord.

Today more than ever before, we are indeed very much frightened at the looming financial crisis around the globe. Our society soon has to deal with the difficult situation of being populated by more than three billion humans, among whom there are too many elderly citizens; and the immoral and godless solution promulgated by many is to lessen the number of older people. The "right" to die is quickly becoming the "duty" to die, especially when millennials feel how costly it is to keep older people alive; and regrettably, some of them viciously state, "You've lived a full life, but now you cost too much. Time to step aside."

This kind of cold and ungrateful attitude is the result of the wrong handling of our social and economic values. It is here we see the good old values followed by our early Christians. Esteeming every citizen born in this world as the child of God as we are and in the spirit of the risen Lord, we should rise to solve the impending problems in our own way. It need not be called as any isms, like communism, socialism, totalitarianism, or capitalism; but simply, let us call it Christianism. We must start our life again from our initial faith on the risen Lord.

Like the apostle Thomas, who initially did not want to believe in the resurrection of Jesus (John 20:24–28), we may be wavering in our faith belief. But he finally bent down to the risen Lord and responded in faith loudly, "My Lord and my God!" We should soon reconcile with it and get stronger in that faith.

In this way, all the quality life the scriptures promise will be ours. The early Christians have borne powerful witness to their contemporaries by this kind of quality life consisting in unity, oneness, forgiveness, peace, truth, justice, and love. Undoubtedly, with the impact of our formidable faith in the risen Lord, we will be energized to follow what the early Christians have done in our efforts to solve our current financial problems.

We will begin earning our livelihood in a straightforward way and not by crooked means, spending it meticulously and not lavishly, saving it or accumulating in just ways and not dishonestly, sharing what we own with our needy family members, sharing willingly with senior citizens a portion of what we earn and save in life, and last but not the least sharing what we possess with the needy citizens of today, the downtrodden sections of the global society. This is the only way to solve our global economic problems.

109. Daily Testimony to Peace Results in Forgiveness

You are witnesses of these things.
—Luke 24:48

Though we Christians are divided by various traditions, we feel one and united strongly with one single appealing cry to Christ: "Save us, Savior of the world, for by your cross and resurrection, you have set us free." Unquestionably, this sort of faith teaching may sound new and weird to many modern minds who are being swayed by new philosophies and views.

Christianity never hesitates to recognize this historical and salvific fact and its valuable contribution to humans. The central message of the apostolic preaching has been that Jesus of Nazareth, who has died and risen, continues to resurrect all humans and offers them salvation and liberation. Their message has come out of their vivid memory about what the Lord has proclaimed to them: "Thus it is written that the Messiah would suffer and rise from the dead on the third day and that repentance, for the forgiveness of sins. And as John testifies, Jesus is expiation for our sins, and not for our sins only but for those of the whole world" (1 John 2:2).

Jesus's death liberates us from all our sins. This assertion was made by the risen Lord himself to his apostles when he appeared to them before he left for heaven. And he wanted them to be faithful witnesses to this truthful fact: "That repentance, for the forgiveness of sins, would be preached in his name to all the nations, beginning from Jerusalem" (Luke 24:35–48). Jesus's disciples, being faithful to their Master's grand commission, had been making their continuous appeal to people, exhorting, "Repent, therefore, and be converted, that your sins may be wiped away" (Acts 3:19).

Scripturally, sin is a denial of the Triune God and excluding him from our life as our forebears have done in human history. As Peter has pointed out in his preaching about the cruel deeds of Jesus's own people (Acts 3:14–15), today we too deny Jesus, the holy and righteous One; sometimes we even plan to put him to death in and around our life, acting out of ignorance as our forebears have done. The church upholds that Jesus has redeemed us from such sins by shedding his blood as a scapegoat.

In tandem, Jesus has initiated also another dimension of our salvation, namely, through his resurrection from the dead, he has liberated us from the dark and gloomy situation of our life, being buried in the murky tomb. Our earthly life imposes on us too many troubles and frustrations. Everywhere there is pain and death; no one is exempted from worries. There is no peace and therefore no sleep.

To gain true peace, God told us that his Son is the source of liberation and peace. The Gospels narrated that the risen Jesus stood in the midst of the apostles, even if the doors were locked, and greeted them, "Peace be with you." He understood their fear and trouble. He encouraged them not to feel so, and as a plan of action, he exhorted them to look at his life, which had been totally damaged by his enemies; he showed them his scars of crucifixion and wanted them to believe his risen presence and interaction. That was the Gospel message God offered us: Jesus is the source and guide in our life's challenges.

The fact of getting forgiveness for sins and liberation from peacelessness happened first to his first team of disciples. Our Master commanded them to be witnesses of the amazing things that happened to them and in their midst. He also wanted them to witness to the transformation they experienced. After getting plentiful repentance for their sins, they experienced relief from distress; true joy settled in them. And as the psalmist sang, as soon as they lied down in bed, they fell peacefully asleep (Ps. 4).

Today we are called to be his living witnesses. When our manner of witnessing becomes a way of life and when our manner of living becomes itself a credible witness, then we will be able to offer the worthy testimony that will enable others to recognize and accept the truth of the good news by which we are saved.

110. A Unique Way to Enjoy A Fuller Life in This World

*I came so that they might have life and
have it more abundantly.*
—John 10:10b

Whenever we point out that our Master Jesus is the only Savior of humanity, the world is outraged. That sort of zero-tolerance attitude regarding salvation has been contemptuously scorned by most of humans both outside and inside the church. However, let me share here what the Spirit asks us in renewing our faith by understanding this critical issue in the light of scriptural verses.

This kind of assiduous claim was preached undoubtedly by apostles like Peter, proclaiming that "there is no salvation through anyone else, nor is there any other name under heaven given to the human race by which we are to be saved" (Acts 4:12). He meant plainly that the only way to be saved and enter into heaven is through Jesus Christ. Apostles held such a seemingly intolerant claim because our Master Jesus had claimed so. He was quoted in John's Gospel (chapter 10) stating that he is the Good Shepherd and the human race is his sheep and that all the others who claimed to be so are simply thieves, hired men, and many times wolves in sheep clothing. He ascertained also that, one day, all humans would be one flock under his leadership.

Such an unwavering claim, posted in the NT books as well as in church tradition up to this day, didn't begin overnight, nor did it belong to a genre of historical conspiracy theory as some friends proposed. It blossomed out of the personal experiences of early church members with the risen Lord's Spirit. Peter, for example, who had sinfully denied his Master, was radically changed by his encounter of the risen Lord. No longer was he focusing on himself.

In Acts (3:1–19), we read about a healing Peter performed to a crippled man. We heard Peter saying to the physically impaired, needy man, "I have neither silver nor gold, but what I do have I give you: in the name of Jesus Christ the Nazorean, rise and walk." Then we saw Peter performing the miraculous deed through which the crippled immediately got sufficient strength to his feet and ankles. However, we noticed that Peter was resolute in making the crowds know that this was not his work but entirely that of the risen Jesus. He made his public profession of faith: "By faith in Jesus' name, this man, whom you see and know, His name has made strong, and the faith that comes through it has given him this perfect health, in the presence of all of you."

There are numerous miraculous encounters, such as Peter's, that have happened between the apostles and their risen Master. It is surely from those factual and personal encounters that has come their astounding statement that their Master is the sole Savior and Lord of the universe. As Jesus has claimed himself, all of us—his followers—till this moment unhesitatingly believe that he is the only way of truth for us to live a fuller life. It is undebatable to state that he is the foundation of our salvation. "He is the stone rejected by you, the builders, which has become the cornerstone" (Acts 4:11). If he is not the foundation of our lives, we have no foundation at all to survive. We should always remember his bewildering claim (John 10:10).

This is what our faith statement is all about—Jesus. If we add anything to or subtract from this creed, we betray Jesus and his Gospel. All the practices that we perform in the name of the church, all the doctrines and dogmas we formulate or interpret and promulgate, must be totally focused on only Jesus and his values of love because we firmly hold that it is in Jesus that we see "what love the Father has bestowed on us that we may be called the children of God" (1 John 3:1).

There is indeed some valid reasons why the postmodern age people reject such claim. They point out, because of this exaggerated exclusive claim, that too many wars and deaths have happened in the past. Thanks to the risen Lord's Spirit of renewal, most of us try not to repeat those blunders. However, still, some among us—instead of eradicating the abused forms of this claim—make another blunder of completely erasing the centrality of Christ in human life and proclaiming a gospel of humanistic love with no reference to Christ's love. Such a distorted attitude has had its repercussions, such as violence, atrocious killing of babies, families broken to pieces by divorce, glorification of undisciplined homosexuality, euthanasia, and so on.

One thing must be underscored: our style of proclaiming that Jesus is the one sent by God to liberate humans from maladies might have been wrongly botched over the decades, but its content and goal still persevere, vivid and truthful: Jesus's way of sacrificial and compassionate love is the only truthful way for humans to enjoy a fuller life both here and in heaven.

111. How to Live Sparklingly And Bear Fruits Abundantly

Whoever remains in me and I in him will bear much fruit.
—John 15:5b

There are so many references in the Bible to explain to us, through metaphors and images, what kind of relationship God longs to keep with us. They are concerned not only with our external encounters with him but also with the interactions taking place interiorly between ourselves and God in Jesus.

Before Jesus has departed from this world, during the Last Supper, he has revealed to his disciples many mind-blowing truths about our interior connections with him. One among them is (John 15:1–8) "I am the vine, you are the branches." It is all about an ontological connection, a very intrinsic relationship between him and us. The branch cannot survive if it is separated from the parent vine. Jesus is right when he says, "Just as a branch cannot bear fruit on its own unless it remains on the vine, so neither can you unless you remain in me. Apart from me you can do nothing."

Jesus too has promised that by abiding in his love and word, we will bear much fruit. The words "much fruit" refer to a quality life of fulfillment and a lifesaving life. When we believe in Jesus Christ, partake of his mysteries, and keep his commandments, his person becomes—through the Spirit—the living and interior rule of all our activities. John, referring to this fact, exhorts us in his letter, "Children, let us love not in word or speech but in deeds and truth" (1 John 3:18).

Undoubtedly, loving through words is a part of human love. But deeds are the better symbols of true love than mere words. We have an excellent example in the life of Paul, who has offered us one of the magnificent poems on love.

In the beginning of his ministry, as all of us experience, he had some "starting trouble." He indeed used his wonderful, mesmerizing words to witness that he was a disciple of Jesus and no longer a persecutor of Christians. Unfortunately, people just did not believe him; his life was threatened by them, and his friends had to send him away to a safer place. Only later, when he really proved his love of Jesus by his total service of the community, was the world ready to accept him, plus accepted his faith proclamation (Acts 9:26–31).

Only when we love in deeds can we know that Jesus lives in us. God's love is, in some way, similar to electric power, which cannot go through us if it doesn't go into us. It is an eternal fact that God does not love us because we are good; rather, we are good because God's love is working in and through us to others. This is why Jesus has said, "By this, is my Father glorified, that you bear much fruit and become my disciples." Many times, Jesus has emphasized that he is the only person who is sent by the heavenly Father to offer us the quality life of fulfillment and lifesaving life. Today he emphatically reiterates that he is the sole true God-grown Vine. Even though there may exist some competing vines around us, Jesus has been proved as the true Vine, which is the most life giving, the most nourishing, and the most dependable.

As his intimately connected branches, we are challenged, nourished, encouraged, and advised by his life and words. God, being the faithful Gardener, will prune us to help us channel all that is life giving into our lives and actions: selfless love, sacrifice, voluntary cross carrying, feeding others, clothing others, visiting others, comforting others, serving others, forgiving others, healing others, reaching out to the marginalized, protecting defenseless lives, and even giving up our lives for others. It is for this much fruit-bearing life we are summoned by the Spirit of the risen Lord.

112. To Win Victory in Our Combat against Evils

Take courage, I have conquered the world.
—John 16:33b

We are naturally born weak, cowardly, barbaric, self-centered, self-interested, and possessing some survival kits and many diplomatic and cunning first aid tools. At the same time, we are gifted by God in Creation with many natural talents such as wisdom, understanding, counsel, fortitude, knowledge, piety, and fear of God. Unfortunately, as we decide many times to abuse these marvelous gifts, not only do they bear fruits that are very temporary but they also bring havoc to ourselves and others. This is our perennial problem.

Our forebears have believed and taught us in their limitations that our spiritual enemies are three: world, devil, and body, of which the first two reside out of us and the third part of us. The elders' teaching is both right and wrong. It is right in the sense that all three enemies create lots of spiritual and moral problems in our life, but the wrong side of their teaching is that they forgot to tell us these three evildoers cannot win in their attacks against us unless and until the fourth enemy, which is existing within us, yields to them.

We know very well from our scriptures that the human spirit, which was breathed by God into our body in Creation, had been damaged by the first sin and thus broken into two spirits, "fleshly and spiritual. For those who live according to the flesh are concerned with the things of the flesh, but those who live according to the spirit with the things of the spirit.

The concern of the flesh is death, but the concern of the spirit is life and peace . . . and those who are in the flesh cannot please God" (Rom. 8:5–8).

It is about this fleshly spirit that Paul warns us to be careful (Gal. 5:16–26). Our spiritual spirit is open to God; desires him and is drawn to him; is attracted by goodness, beauty, and truth; and yearns for completion in God and to see his face. In contrast, our fleshly spirit—which is the inner part of us—alienates itself from God, being rebellious and obstinate, and can become the gateway to sin, the arena in which sin embeds itself; and to an extent, it can turn out to be sinful itself.

Paul, therefore, uses the term "flesh" in his letters to mean physical flesh, human body, humanity as a whole, human descent, and human relationships to make us understand that our human physical life is transient, frail, and provisional in contrast to the eternal, unchanging, and powerful realm of the spirit, which is the only sphere of salvation. However, a part of our inner spirit has become so damaged, twisted, and weak that it has failed against our spiritual enemies from outside. Thankfully, our weak spirit—assisted by the Holy Spirit—draws us to desire what is best, upright, good, and helpful.

As we heard in the Gospel (John 20:19–23), before Jesus was taken up to heaven, he breathed on the disciples, reminding them that by receiving his breath of the Spirit, the already residing spirit of the Creator within them—though a damaged one—would be renewed and rejuvenated. He emphasized that the Spirit, through whom he would be going to stay with them, would act like an advocate, a counselor, a peacemaker like a dove, a purifier like fire, a mover like strong wind, a productive, strong glue that would bond all diversified people together under his wings like an eagle.

Therefore, let us be convinced of the astounding fact that it is possible to win the battle against our spiritual enemies by living in and by Jesus's Spirit. Paul gives emphasis to this truth, writing, "I say, then: live by the Spirit and you will certainly not gratify the desire of the flesh."

When we make use of our natural gifts, very mistakenly, most of the time, we join hands with the evil spirit. Our activities undertaken with talent, intelligence, IQ, diplomacy, cunningness, etc., frequently are planned and executed with evil intention and motivation such as self-gratification, vengeance, jealousy, pride, and fake prestige; and consequently, we know the results are too bad. But when we connect every move of ours with the Holy Spirit, all that we think, speak, and do—making use of our God-given talents—bear excellent and solid fruits.

113. How to Be the Bread of Life for Others

Let us love not in word or speech but in deed and truth.
—1 John 3:18

Remember, while Jesus claimed himself as the Light of the world, he too preached to us, "You are the light of the world" (Matt. 5:14). While he claimed himself as the source of living water, he also stated that we too would be the source of that water: "Whoever believes in me . . . Rivers of living water will flow from within him" (John 7:38). We read in the Gospel Jesus saying that he is the Bread of Life that came from heaven and everyone who received him would inherit his life (John 6:22–65). The same Lord commanded his followers to do the same sort of life giving in their lifetime. This we knew from the light he gave us through his life and sayings, that we his followers too must be the same toward our neighbors.

Unfortunately, the life-giving promise has Jesus proclaimed has become a sort of bone of contention; it has been used as a religious veneer that has split us into many religiopolitical groups. The funny part in this tension is, whereas all of us truly respect and love our human life, we differ from in the style we share the same life with one another. People of goodwill, in no way, debate on these statements of Jesus: "Take and eat; I am the Bread of Life" and "Take and drink my Blood which has been shed for you." Actually, in this hurry-burry, speedy world, we don't have enough time to dwell on this. Plus, scriptural scholars and church fathers have already discussed enough on this matter. Today more than anything else, we are concerned with the core message in those statements Jesus has proposed to us, namely, how to appropriate his salvific life and how to share it with our fellow human beings.

Unquestionably, every human is created with the rare blend of material and spiritual lives. The Creator has designed us in such a way that we should make the best use of this life to extend and expand it and to repair and renovate it. On this common holy and divine ground, we humans are living, moving, and having our being. Very sadly, because of our pride, arrogance, and even ignorance and weakness, we fell short of the Lord's expectation. We always love to use our freedom for choosing our own whimsical style of obeying the divine's call to give and share our life. We even forget the Creator's will that our life is not meant to be only for ourselves but mainly for others who are still struggling to enjoy that life.

God demanded us to be the bread of life to the needy rather than to our own gratification. Father God tried his best to straighten us out through his messengers, such as the prophets and judges. But again and again, we failed him. Hence, he was patient enough and finally sent his own beloved Son, Jesus, to instruct us and direct us in this awesome issue: what is the genuine style of sharing and giving ourselves as the bread of life to others?

Jesus has demonstrated this unique style of giving life in his very life. Paul explains it in a very succinct way: "For you know the grace of our Lord Jesus Christ, that though He was rich, yet for your sake He became poor, so that you through His poverty might become rich" (2 Cor. 8:9). In detail, he also expounds it in his letter to the Philippians (2:6–8). All NT books profusely discuss Jesus's remarkable pattern of life giving. Besides, they too declare that Jesus has demanded from us such style of giving our life.

Jesus himself is the embodiment of life giving. His style of giving life to humans is nothing but emptying himself, becoming poor, and enduring patiently the breaking points of sufferings because of his amazing obedience to God and ultimately giving up his very earthly life to share the same life with everyone who comes to him. He has lived as a broken bread, a bloodshedding body, a shared meal, and surely an annihilated Valentine who has foretold about the

climax of his own love affairs with humans. "No one
has greater love than this, to lay down one's life for
one's friends" (John 15:13).

As the prophet Isaiah preached about what kind
of fasting and giving God expected from us, Jesus
lived and proclaimed it till his last breath. "Is this not,
rather, the fast that I choose: releasing those bound
unjustly, untying the thongs of the yoke; setting free the
oppressed, breaking off every yoke? Is it not sharing
your bread with the hungry, bringing the afflicted and
the homeless into your house; clothing the naked when
you see them, and not turning your back on your own
flesh?" (Isa. 58:6–7).

According to the scriptures, if we go on saluting
our self-centered behavior of enjoying this earthly
life as a lone wolf, one day we will breathe our last
shamefully and with regrets. In contrast, by giving
up our very life—its beauty, energy, riches, talents,
intelligence, and certain of our bullheaded, perverse
teachings—we are guaranteed by our Master that
we will be blessed with eternal rewards: "Amen, I
say to you, there is no one who has given up house or
wife or brothers or parents or children for the sake
of the kingdom of God who will not receive back an
overabundant return in this present age and eternal life
in the age to come" (Luke 18:29–30). "Give and gifts
will be given to you; a good measure, packed together,
shaken down, and overflowing, will be poured into
your lap. For the measure with which you measure will
in return be measured out to you" (Luke 6:38).

114. Are We Inside or Outside God's Kingdom?

Whoever does not gather with me scatters.
—Matt. 12:30b

As there are two sides in a coin, our life—related to God in Jesus—is made of both its inside and outside. Disappointingly, many of us love to play the colonial game of divide and rule and choose either-or. Consequently, our Christian life gets its worst condition.

From the start of his public ministry, Jesus preached his Gospel truths in so many ways, especially by his life and miraculous, charitable deeds of healing and casting out demons from the needy people to offer them a quality life in this world. Through the same ways, he demonstrated the establishment of God's promised kingdom among humans. But many people around him didn't accept his sincere intentions and performances, even though they considered themselves residing inside God's realm. Some named him as a disciple of Beelzebub; many others considered him mad, quite out of his mind. Because of such callous arrogance and sheer ignorance, many rejected him till his death; some others joined first his team but then left him, while many others conspired against him to the extent they caused him to die on the cross.

In the eyes of Jesus, not only were such self-righteous people standing outside God's kingdom but their sins would also not be forgiven by God. He stated they were sinning against the Holy Spirit, namely, they turned their backs on God by rejecting God's teaching and guidance. In other words, they totally fit to be inside God's kingdom. These people were like our first parents, living and enjoying God's garden of life yet refusing to listen to his word and disobeying him by eating the forbidden fruit (Gen. 3:9–15). This resulted in their being expelled from the garden. They were then on the outside and subject to all kinds of distress and suffering, left—by their own choice—on their own.

Jesus was aware of our human weakness that can make us deaf to his continuous knocking at our inner spirit and indifferent and stubborn to recognize him and his words of truth, life, and way. Hence, he used an event in the Gospel (Mark 3:20–35) to teach us a positive lesson about living fruitfully always inside his kingdom both before and after our death. Pointing out those who were sitting around him and at his feet, like Mary of Bethany, listening to him—namely, those who are inside with him, sincerely being ready to commit themselves to his Gospel—he said, "Here are my mother and my brothers. For whoever does the will of God is my brother and sister and mother."

What Jesus meant was that the new way he established by his coming in their midst was the source of a valid and fruitful relationship his disciples should hold between one another; he was inaugurating a new family trend. In this family, disciples are brothers and sisters to one another not on the basis of blood, culture, race, nationality, or any other conventional group but solely based on their faithful commitment to God's will—acknowledging him as our Lord and Brother and God as our Father.

Paul reminds us frequently in his writings about how we neglect Jesus's dream of a macro human family because of our human fragility and weakness. As we grow older, we succumb to the gradual decline of our human abilities; plus, we are weighed down by many troubles. That may cause us to be afraid of our safety and security; whatever and whoever strange and new we face in this life seem to threaten us. Especially, we are tempted to feel as if our greatness and individuality are slowly dwindling. And therefore, we too slowly avoid any kind of relationship beyond our cozy and traditional safety network we have built on blood, law, race, and caste.

However, in the Spirit of Jesus, Paul advises us not to be groaning and mourning endlessly; rather, we should be filled with hope. "We are not discouraged; rather, although our outer self is wasting away, our inner self is being renewed day by day. For this momentary light affliction is producing for us an eternal weight of glory beyond all comparison, as we look not to what is seen but to what is unseen; for what is seen is transitory, but what is unseen is eternal" (2 Cor. 4:16–18).

As genuine disciples of Jesus, we must keep listening to and obeying Jesus's word of God's will that we should not only abide inside the heart of Jesus permanently but also, with no bias or fear whatsoever, extend and expand our relationship to his macrofamily. In other words, in the name of our Christian inclusiveness, we should in no way be exclusive regarding all our fellow humans.

115. God's Word, Already Sown, Sprouts by Our Efforts

Work out your salvation with fear and trembling.
—Phil. 2:12c

In the kingdom Jesus has established, God works and harvests his fruits with us and, sadly, without us also. This means God's work will be carried out whether we cooperate or not. The stunning factor is that if we choose not to cooperate with God, God's plans will not be frustrated, but we ourselves will be the losers.

God has already sown the seed of his power, his love, his wisdom, his holiness, his sanctity, his joy, and his peace inside humanity. We are not fully sure how many centuries back he has begun this marvelous work. It has been hidden, it has been buried, it has been watered, it has been enlightened, it has been nourished by the same Gardener for centuries. In general, the Bible names this seed as God's Word. He has sown his Word in all the environments of the universe— mountains, oceans, planets, stars, and particularly every human heart. When each creature grows from that Word as it is designed, he can transplant, break, or prune it, if need be, as he desires.

Just as any seed would take its proper duration for its maturation, so did the Seed God had sown took its own course of growth—sprouting, blossoming, flowering, and fructifying. While this God's Seed took so many centuries to grow to its full structure at one point of human history, as the Bible loved to proclaim through prophets and apostles, it was none other than

Jesus of Nazareth, Mary's son. A benevolent time came in his eternal creative works when God revealed that the Word he had sown in his creations was none other than his beloved Son, Christ.

NT books underscore it profusely. Especially, we find in the Gospel of Mark a clear portrayal of this remarkable and mysterious fact being expounded through the parable of the seed (4:26–34). Jesus, God's Seed, has been hidden, simple and humble in appearance like the mustard seed, but always has been in God and with God (John 1:1–5).

The historical process of the Word becoming incarnate has become a model for every human being for how to make the seed of God—sown in our birth—sprout, bloom, and grow to its full stature. The amazing factor in human creation is the unthinkable potential discovered in every human. If any person cherishes the Word sown by God within oneself with loving tender care, they will—as trees portrayed in the Bible—put forth branches, bear fruit, and become a majestic cedar. "Birds of every kind shall dwell beneath it, every winged thing in the shade of its boughs" (Ezek. 17:23). And as the psalmist sings, "[He/she] shall flourish like the palm tree, like a cedar of Lebanon shall grow and shall bear fruit even in old age being vigorous and sturdy" (92:13–15).

When Jesus has said "the kingdom of God," he means it is the power, glory, status, realm, or environment of God that is present within us, in our midst, and is near us. He has emphasized through his parabolic teaching that this realm and environment of God—sown as a tiny, little mustard seed at our conception and then watered, nourished, and safeguarded by our personal, spiritual, and religious efforts with purity of intention—will grow and bear solid and valid fruits if we remain with him always. That is the promise of our Master: "I am the vine, you are the branches. Whoever remains in me and I in him will bear much fruit, because without me you can do nothing" (John 15:5).

Paul, who exhorts us about our responsibility in managing our salvific gracious gift, is also never tired of telling us that those of us who earnestly work hard to manage our inner gardening of God's Seed should be always courageous, although we know that while we are at home in the body we are away from the Lord, for we walk by faith, not by sight. And we should be ready to face the judgment seat of Christ so that each may receive recompense, according to what we have done in the body, whether good or evil.

116. Great Is the Nation Where People Live by Disciplined Freedom

Repay . . . to God what belongs to God.
—Matt. 22:21b

By celebrating certain national feasts like Independence Day happily and colorfully, American citizens demonstrate our pride about our heritage of enlightenment and freedom, through which our modern civilization has been blessed with technology, science, and material possessions. It is true we are so creative that we have discovered so many ways and styles to find pleasures at their maximum. Nonetheless, we also should acknowledge the dark side of our independent lives. We, knowingly or unknowingly, have built up and maintained a culture of death, depression, and anxieties; we are experiencing a culture of reverse values, of disbelief and violence, of poverty of spiritual contentment. Because of our mismanagement of unbridled human pleasures, they have turned out to be pernicious to our prosperous and healthy life.

The evils are simply our own making from the atrocious contract we make with the evil spirit of unbridled freedom. Unquestionably, freedom by itself is the greatest gift the Creator has shared with us. This freedom brings forth independence, which automatically produces individuality. And because of individuality, we differ from each other; and consequently, there exist variety, diversity, and division.

While we enjoy this remarkable blessing of freedom, we are anxious about our survival among us. We compare and contrast ourselves with others; we are afraid to face their competition when we hunt to fulfill our basic needs of food, shelter, sex, love, safety, self-esteem, and self-actualization. Our weakness compels us to prefer a safety network, namely, a group of our own based on the only anthem "Salute me, help me, support me, and if need be play and fight with me." To build and manage such safety network, we intelligently make use of cunningness, lies, and some artificial groupism—glues of race, color, creed, caste, class, blood, and clan.

Indeed, God appreciates the beautiful differences existing among us·but wants us to make the best and fruitful use of our divisions in justice, truth, and mercy. On the contrary, because of our cranky, illogical, and biased presumptions, we make human life miserable and deplorable. Thus, evil takes its throne slowly but steadily in and around our lives and deforms our colorful and awesome independence.

Because of such darkened freedom, we are freaked out by certain kinds of superimposing but very artificial, fake, and paranoid assertions such as "We are greater 'cause I am the greatest, but they are not even great" and "I am okay, and you may be okay, but they are not okay." This pinheaded and overinflated resolve and attitude toward individualism has come out of the remains of world wars and even the Cold War.

There is nothing wrong about our efforts not to lose heart and to maintain one's equilibrium of heart and mind, thinking highly of oneself, upholding self-esteem and self-respect as much as possible. God's Spirit in the Bible stresses this fact and offers us certain positive teachings about our greatness. "You are the light of the world; you are the salt of the earth." "Don't think you are born to slavery but to freedom. You were once no people now you are holy people, holy nation, and separated from others."

However, our Triune God never expects from us a maniac roundup of the most astounding blessing of freedom. He has offered our independence personally, socially, and nationally at a high cost of inspiring some of our forebears even to shed their blood. We should be law-abiding citizens. Many consider that they are truly law-abiding persons because they are very careful in observing traffic rules and paying taxes faithfully. That is not a sufficient explanation of "law-abiding." America has been founded on God's great law, which is a package of moral, social, and spiritual commands. These commands are the rudder for keeping us on the right course, the protection that keeps our salvation secure. As they instruct the receptive minds of believers on the earth, they lead safely to the kingdom of heaven. If we fail in them, we know the results from the baby boomers' shaken and toxic history as well as from the horrible stories we hear today of our children, the millennials.

The historian David Goldfield, in his book *The Gifted Generation*, explored in detail how some leaders in the past—despite partisan differences—possessed a deeper, richer vision for America, the great nation. According to him, presidents like Harry Truman, Dwight Eisenhower, and Lyndon Johnson considered America as a beneficial force in the globe with its commonwealth ideal of mutual responsibility that strengthened individualism by promoting equal opportunities for all its citizens. "These leaders too believed," Goldfield wrote, "that America could not be whole until everyone had the opportunity to succeed. They knew from personal experience that government was not only good but also necessary to address society's inequalities."

This is exactly the echo of the Gospel values Jesus has been sowing for two millennia into our hearts. Every nation, which takes pride in God whom its people trust, must be very grateful not only for its founders and its constitution but also for so many leaders and prophets breathing and preaching, even bleeding, to maintain such nobility and greatness of our nation. Through his Word, he continues to emphasize to us that if we want our freedom to bear abundant and valid fruits, we need to know and live with a disciplined (not unbridled or licentious) freedom as the crucial guideline for making the right choices for the prosperity of our nation and thus making it "the great and the beautiful."

117. The Magnanimous Way of Helping the Least Ones

Whatever you did for one of these least
ones of mine, you did for me.
—Matt. 25:40

So many times, our preachers have exhorted us to share and care of the poor and the needy, who are crowding around us. And they too emphasize their message of charity by quoting Jesus Christ, who as the Judge at our final Judgment Day will either bless us or curse us according to the good we perform to the least ones. Now who exactly are the least? There are millions and millions groaning and mourning in two dire needs. One crowd of people cry for filling their stomach, for getting proper health care, for getting good job, for good friends, for being released from bad tragedies, for liberation from dense psychological darkness, and so on. And the others—though well fed, clothed, and sheltered—are in a depressive mood for not knowing how to grow better, how to come out of childishness, how to get into the shoes of Christ, and so on.

Those of us who dream of becoming charitable saints, like Mother Teresa, feel restless fretting over the impending problems of humanity of our time. The littleness of our frugal earnings and the shrinking of our savings drive us dejected over our inability and our helplessness in this hopeless situation. The Spirit of Jesus never lets us down and be as couch potatoes.

In the event of Jesus's miraculous multiplication of loaves (Mark 6:34–44), we heard the same natural human reaction of the disciples when their Master asked them to feed thousands of hungry stomachs with the tiny, little bread and fish available in their hands. They retorted, "There is a boy here who has five barley loaves and two fish; but what good are these for so many? Two hundred days' wages worth of food would not be enough for each of them to have a little." But Jesus continued pestering them, repeating, "Give them some food yourselves."

Jesus was fully aware of their limitations and his own immense power received from his Father. He was well read in what the miraculous, marvelous deeds his Father performed through his prophets like Elisha (2 Kings 4:42–44). This prophet, receiving a devotee's offering of twenty barley loaves, ordered to give them to people to eat, but one of his servants bothered about and questioned the prophet's unrealistic effort of feeding hundreds of people with few breads. But Elisha tranquilly replied, "Give it to the people to eat, for thus says the Lord: You will eat and have some left over."

This is the way Jesus expects his disciples to manage any life's problems, retaining peace and calmness, despite our limitations in doing what we can afford to do to the least of Jesus. He then will do the rest. His Spirit lists out some scriptural tips for us to attain this remarkable ability. He exhorts us to assure ourselves of the eternal truth: "The Lord is near to all who call upon him, to all who call upon him in truth. He gives them their food in due season. He opens wide his hand and satisfy the desire of every living thing" (Ps. 145). Consequently, the Spirit persuades us to totally surrender everything to the Lord and become his prisoner. That is what Paul and most of Jesus's followers have done. Paul loves to call himself as a prisoner for the Lord, and in that unthinkable calmness, he could

314 | Rev. Benjamin A. Vima

advise others from his dungeon that they should cherish Christian values such as humility, gentleness, patience, forgiveness, peace, and unity (Eph. 4:1–6).

When this remarkable kind of mind-set is established and maintained within us, the Spirit of Jesus—who has made our inner spirit as his abode— begins to urge us to share what we possess or procure as the "widow's mite" with the needy, helpless, and starving people as much as we can within our limit, as much as possible, and as much as it is needed. We become fully aware of the fact these unfortunate humans can find the compassionate God only through these sorts of kind gestures. Plus, after we hand out and share our possessions and bread, at the end of the day, we should never wait for the praise and appreciation from our beneficiaries; rather, like Jesus with humility, we should either fly away or shut ourselves in our private chamber and tell the Lord smilingly as any faithful servant, "We are unprofitable servants; we have done what we were obliged to do" (Luke 17:10).

118. The New and Astounding Way Of Earthly Living

This is the bread that the Lord has given you to eat.
—Exod. 16:15

Christianity, in its first century, was not labeled as a religion or any sort of institution. Rather, it was named as "the Way." Early Christians were called "followers of the Way."

Hence, with whatever catchy terms the modern communities or groups of Christians may be labeled, if they are gatherings of Christ's disciples, the relevant identity of them all is nothing but "the Way." What do we understand by this term? The primary meaning is the members of any of this auspicious Way communities are living and moving in Jesus, who is the only Way of truth and life amid many other earthbound pathways.

According to Jesus, his way is surely narrow and en route to "beyond this world." He advises, therefore, to go beyond the present situation of our life. Nonetheless, he too underlines that, in our dealings with God, we should not separate this present moment from the past.

We read in the Gospels that the people living in Jesus's time ignored the power and identity of Jesus behind the miracles they saw, asking him some more miracles so that they could believe him. They said to him, "What sign can you do that we may see and believe in you? What can you do? Our ancestors ate manna in the desert, as it is written: 'He gave them bread from heaven to eat.'"

This was the mistake of the old Israelites in the desert. They were so worried about today's bread that they did not trust that their God, who had done wonderful things in their past, especially during their liberation journey to the Promised Land, would do the same. They grumbled against God (Exod. 16:2–15). Jesus cautioned us not to behave that way. Our life journey in his way would be filled with so many steps or phases of repentance, change, and renewal. And perhaps we may be engaged in many innovative programs of enrichment during the present stage of life. This sort of preoccupation should in no way make us forget the great things that the Lord had done throughout our life.

Remembrance is a sign of gratitude. With the renewed mind of Christ, we should remind ourselves of the marvelous deeds of God in our past and connect this present situation to the past endeavors of God done in our lives out of his compassion and mercy.

Also, the Lord inspires us through his scriptures to see the Giver beyond the gifts. Everything that is happening is simply a sign for us to reach out to God, who is the Provider. We should never ask in ignorance, "What is this?" as the old Israelites in the desert, but any feeling we communicate in public must be one of awe that witnesses to the awesomeness of God and his unfathomable deals.

Moses stated that it was a food beyond the natural and artificial. He explained to them it was bestowed by God. And the Lord God also pointed out to them, "So that you may know that I, the Lord, am your God."

The Israelites were being called to accept the manna and the quail as gifts and to see beyond those gifts to the God, who had brought them from Egypt and was guiding them to freedom and a new way of life. We noticed the same ignorance and indifference of the people at Jesus's time, unable to see what was beyond his miracles (John 6:24–35). They ignored the power and identity of Jesus present behind the miracles and therefore asked him some more miracles to do. Jesus answered and said to them, "This is the work of God that you believe in the one he sent."

Everything in this universe is a sign and symbol of the goodness, beauty, and wisdom of the Creator. Any event that occurs; anything we handle, we see, we touch, we feel, we come in contact with; and everyone whom we relate to are simply the outer signs of God, the Creator, the Provider, the Redeemer, and the Judge. Therefore, we have to go beyond these things and see what and who is beyond all these.

This is the "new way" that we follow with our renewed mind and heart in Jesus. Referring to this new way, Paul writes, "You should put away the old self of your former way of life and put on the new self, created in God's way as you were taught in Christ" (Eph. 4:17–24). Indisputably, to follow such renewed way is very hard. It offers us an intense challenge in daily life; however, if we try to follow our Master's directions, surely, as he has promised, our yoke will be easy, and burden will be light.

119. Climbing up to the Hilltop Requires Heavenly Food

Get up and eat or the journey will be too much for you.
—1 Kings 19:7b

The eternal truth is while God is a supreme mystery, our human life too is a mystery, which is—be it very tiny—a bundle of problems and issues, though short lived but with continued struggle. It is a challenge many times imposing on us heavy burdens of unfair treatments. Indeed, such a critical life situation may make us, negatively speaking, discouraged and depressed. But the Spirit of God moves us to rethink of our mysterious life very positively and to rise and walk productively by using God's amazing resources.

We are exhorted in scriptures to esteem our life in this world as a journey traveling from one end to the other. It is a journey of our inner spirit hidden but active in our body and not just from womb to tomb. Rather, it is a journey from an eternal origin to an eternal destiny, namely, from God to God. It is like mountaineering to reach its peak as Hilary of Norway has done for the first time ever to reach the Everest of Himalayas. It's not just a struggle but also, positively, a sportive effort to reach our destiny.

In this journey of climbing, our goal is to reach the mountain of the Lord as the prophet Elijah has tried to go to the mountain of God, Horeb (1 Kings 19:1–4). This "hilltop of our life," as I label it, is a destiny of pure love and justice, filled with peace and joy. Paul portrays it as a life in reality, free of all bitterness, fury, anger, shouting, reviling, and malice; it is full of kindness, compassion, forgiveness, and love. In other words, the hilltop life—for which we are destined—is simply a life of the children of God imitating exactly God our Father in Jesus (Eph. 4:30–5:2).

We know it is indeed a hard journey to pull through as we read about Elijah fleeing to escape the cruelty of his king and queen: "[He] went a day's journey into the wilderness, until he came to a solitary broom tree and sat beneath it. He prayed for death: 'Enough, Lord! Take my life, for I am no better than my ancestors.'" The compassionate God never leaves us alone in all our hardships of climbing. This truth has been confirmed frequently in the Bible. Especially, we are told that our Creator has been fulfilling his promises of offering all that humans need.

Let us go back to the episode about the prophet climbing up God's mountain. Being very tired of not only physical but also psychological trauma from hunger and thirst, the prophet "lay down and fell asleep under the solitary broom tree, but suddenly a messenger touched him and said, 'Get up and eat!' He looked and there at his head was a hearth cake and a jug of water. After he ate and drank, he lay down again, but the angel of the Lord came back a second time, touched him, and asked him to get up and eat. He got up, ate, and drank; then strengthened by that food, he walked forty days and forty nights to the mountain of God, Horeb" (1 Kings 19:5–8).

The divine promise of supporting us in our troublesome climb up God's hilltop has continued through Jesus. Whereas in OT times God has directly bestowed this food through his angels as he has done to the prophet to lift him from all his worries, today he offers us this living bread from heaven through Jesus. To our surprise, John puts words in Jesus's mouth to explain Jesus's mysterious personality and identity. Jesus claims himself as that bread from heaven given by our Father to nourish us in our life journey (John 6:41–51).

Generally, the term "bread" brings to our mind a powerful resource that offers life nourishment, satisfying hunger and giving joy to community, family, memory, and life. This is what Jesus means when has he promised that he himself is the source of the nourishment we need on our daily journey toward our destiny of godly life. As Mother Teresa has remarked about us who live and move in the developed nations, we—the people blessed by God with material and physical bread—are the ones who need very badly this bread from heaven. According to the assessment of this saint, we have a long way to go on our journey to find our destiny and to reach God's hilltop peak.

120. Let Us Long for Main Dishes in God's Banquet

The Lord of hosts will provide for all peoples a feast of rich food.
—Isa. 25:6

Most of you, like me, enjoy any party that includes fun, drink, and tasty food. In every country, race, and tribe, we notice that people host sumptuous dinners on special occasions like weddings, anniversaries, birthdays, and so on. Through the scriptures, we are aware of the most sumptuous banquet being hosted eternally by God in the name of his Son; and with no discrimination whatsoever, the entire humanity is invited to participate in it. The Bible claims that all that we enjoy as physical food, talents, IQ, and natural resources are indeed the contents of God's banquet, which he has prepared as he has created humans. Sometimes it is labeled as a banquet of wisdom (Wis. 9:1–6), banquet of joy, banquet of love, and so on.

Jesus, summing up everything that has been said about God's banquet in OT books, has highlighted his own sacrifice of his body and blood as the "banquet of life" for the world." According to his promise, his banquet is nothing but the source of our salvation. Many church fathers and biblical scholars and preachers point out that, from the sensational news that scriptures offer us about God's banquet, we can understand what sort of menu he serves us in his banquet. Besides the side dishes of his physical, intellectual, and social gifts, the main courses he places in our plate are eternal life, godly wisdom, sacrificial love, uncompromising justice, and never-ending heavenly bliss.

God's banquet is unarguably the result of his unconditional love for us. Nonetheless, it is so remarkable and heavenly that God expects some prerequisites from those who decide to participate in and enjoy it. First, we are asked to be fully aware of the greatest difference between the banquets that humans host and that of God. Though both are lavish, human banquets are limited only to certain guests. But God, to his banquet, invites every human being with no discrimination whatsoever. Anyone who is hungry is enough to hear and accept her invitation. They may be a slave, a servant, poor, or dumb. He proclaims, "Let whoever is naive turn in here; to any who lack sense I say, 'Come, eat of my food, and drink of the wine I have mixed!'" (Wis. 9:4–5).

Second, those dishes served in God's banquet definitely will all nourish our spiritual hunger. However, they are all covered dishes. We cannot easily open the covers and eat them as we like to. It is all in the hands of the banquet Host, God himself, who has to open them for us in his time. But he will provide us more than what we look for if we fulfill his second condition, which is to go on longing for such food, developing a deep hunger for the main dishes. Not all scriptures of the world religions say that God offers himself as food. Only Jesus has highlighted this truth, which we call the incarnational aspect of Christian life. Being the Son of God, Jesus boldly claims he is God's banquet. Jesus desires, therefore, that we should long sincerely for such eternal food.

We firmly believe that, in his banquet, we receive all his attitudes and life's quests to be godly, to be wise, to be just, to be loving, to be blissful, and thus to be a genuine Christian. As Paul advises us, "We will watch carefully how we live, not as foolish persons but as wise, making the most of the opportunity. Adhering and assimilating Jesus' life, his attitudes, and his words will enjoy all the main courses in the Banquet he serves; consequently, we will be filled with the Spirit, singing and playing to the Lord in our hearts, giving thanks always and for everything in the name of our Lord Jesus Christ to God the Father" (Eph. 5:15–20).

121. Do or Die—The Choice Is Ours

As for me and my household, we will serve the Lord.
—Josh. 24:15b

Life is made of millions of multiple choices. Great is the person who chooses the right choice at the right times and right situations. This assertion holds good especially when we dare to make choices for God in Jesus Christ as our only way, truth, and life.

God always emphasizes that, at every decision-making occasion in our lives, especially about adhering to a church or religion, we should not distract ourselves at any time from him as our fundamental choice and to focus our attention on him and his Word. We observe this divine will in many incidents narrated in OT.

For example, we read that Joshua—assuring his and his family's faith, saying, "As for me and my household, we will serve the Lord"—bid a challenge to his people: "Choose today whom you will serve, the God who brought safely and bestowed you a land or the gods your ancestors." To him, all people answered, "Far be it from us to forsake the Lord to serve other gods" (Josh. 24:1–18). This was the way all biblical heroes got their final victory, by deciding for God and taking sides with God's principles.

The same was true for Jesus, who was the Joshua of NT. He wanted all his disciples take to heart all the challenges he proposed to them to inherit the eternal life. Those who heard him have been able to understand and accept most of his words and works. Unfortunately, when he proposed to them to participate in the banquet he would be hosting for their salvation, they were shocked, and many of them found Jesus's teaching too hard to understand. Some were scandalized, others confused and unconvinced. The best option before them was to quit. Jesus sadly watched them leaving. But he didn't dilute his teaching. Nor was he prepared to compromise to keep the flock with him. Rather, he went on repeating his extraordinary claim and unbelievable bid. He perfectly knew their weakness (John 6:66).

The only additional bid he made was to his disciples who were closely connected to him, mainly his apostles. He asked them in a stringent but smiling style, "Do you also want to go away?" More than anything else, this question was a bombshell to them, creating horrible shock waves in their spirit. But the twelve stayed put with him, responding with Peter, "Master, to whom shall we go? You have the words of eternal life" (John 6:67–69). They did not opt for a divorce from him.

Though they didn't fully comprehend the mystery to which Jesus directed them, they didn't leave; they stayed with the one who could feed them eternal life.

Jesus continues today in challenging us to have faith in him. This indomitable faith carries us to the point where we surrender all our rationality and will to his love and try to understand his challenges more, especially that of the heavenly Bread of Life. Very sadly, many of us may plan to leave him in ignorance and disbelief. Our relationship with Christ is very intrinsic and intimate like that of two lovers for eternal life.

Paul knew it well, and he lived as his Life Partner expected. The love between the two was so intense that Paul could utter, "Yet I live, no longer I, but Christ lives in me; insofar as I now live in the flesh, I live by faith in the Son of God who has loved me and given himself up for me" (Gal. 2:20).

In that same fervor, exhorting married couples to hold such relationship with one another, Paul offers us a clue on this mysterious relationship we should hold with our Master, Jesus: "He who loves his wife loves himself . . . even as Christ does the church; for this reason a man shall leave his father and his mother and be joined to his wife, and the two shall become one flesh. This is a great mystery, but I speak in reference to Christ and the church" (Eph. 5:21–32). Indeed, we cannot live with Christ without adhering to his church because each one of us is only a member of Jesus's body, the church. So Jesus asks us with a wounded heart, "Do you also go away from the Church as some of your own household members, community members do?"

122. True Religion Is
Simple, Integrated, and Authentic

You disregard God's commandment
but cling to human tradition.
—Mark 7:8

Among the people who claim they are affiliated
to Christian religion, even from their cradle, many
don't practice it as God demands from them and
consequently never benefit from it as they should.
Perhaps we may be included in that club by our
carelessness or indifference to be fully aware of the
right understanding of Christianity and its important
characteristics.

First, God offers us Christianity as a simple religion
that shuns complicated views, ideas, and practices; from
its true Judaic origin, it contains transparency and
unfussiness. When the Lord has bestowed his precepts,
he said, "In your observance of the commandments of
the Lord your God, which I am commanding you, you
shall not add to what I command you nor subtract from
it. Observe them carefully" (Deut. 4:2). God is simple,
and therefore, he wants his children to be simple and
expects them to observe simple religion, a simple way of
relating to him. John Wesley calls it "the simplicity of
intention, and purity of affection."

The laws given by God through Moses were
initially rather simple in their governance of the
relations between God and humankind as well as the
relationships between human beings. Unfortunately,
those laws evolved eventually into a complex maze of

legislation. By the time of Jesus, people were loaded with unbearable burden of thousands of laws and prescriptions, both oral and written. The worst thing Jesus observed was that those people who were very meticulous in observing all tiny, little prescriptions totally forgot the core of the demands of God (Mark 7:1–23). He made known his grievances against this behavior, pointing out that their dedication to so many minute details skewed their judgment and sensibilities. Also, he criticized how their observance devolved into external rituals that were very conscientiously performed but were becoming less and less informed by interior holiness. Jesus loved and proclaimed only a simple religion.

Second, God demands from the members of Christianity an observance of a religion of integration. "Integration" is defined as "a combining of parts or objects that work together well." This is the real consequence of our observance of religion in simplicity with no distortion or distraction.

Jesus's main instruction to his disciples was not to follow the disintegrated religion of the Pharisees, who were giving only lip service and not heartfelt obedience. We noticed him exploding from despair and a bit of anger whenever he saw and spoke about those Pharisees: "Well did Isaiah prophesy about you hypocrites, as it is written: 'This people honors me with their lips, but their hearts are far from me; in vain do they worship me, teaching as doctrines human precepts'" (Mark 7:6–7). He emphasized that every religious performance we do outside must correspond to what we profess, what we say outside must be connected to our heart, and our outward appearance should resemble our inner soul.

Third, God expects the followers of his Son to observe a religion of authenticity. Authenticity denotes the genuineness or truth of something, its legitimacy and validity. If we hold on to a religion that we esteem as so great and a source of love, peace, and justice, then we should prove it by our life. The Spirit instructs us in the letter of James (1:22–27) that we should follow a true religion that is simply doing and living by exactly what we hear from God. In that letter, we are given a simplified version of a true religion: "Be doers of the word and not hearers only, deluding yourselves. Religion that is pure and undefiled before God and the Father is this: to care for orphans and widows in their affliction and to keep oneself unstained by the world." Do first what we try to speak and speak what we feel within us.

True piety is not a practiced and soulless routine but a holiness that arises from within a heart that is consciously in love with God. This is the right way of practicing our religion to bring down peace and blessings on us.

123. God's Glory Shines Forth in Human Ailments

He should make the leader to their salvation
perfect through suffering.
—Heb. 2:10

The main intention of God in bestowing a special blessing to our mouth and ears is for our physical senses to be opened widely and broadly to see and proclaim his lavishing openness. In Creation, he acts like a spendthrift. In forgiving, he behaves like a crazy father. In liberating, he disguises himself as one-man liberation army. And above all, in relating himself to the sick, the poor, and the broken, disabled people, he stands like their one and only champion.

In OT, we read God demonstrating his championship for the welfare of the poor, the weak, the sick, the fearful, the blind, and the deaf and dumb. He encourages them through Isaiah: "Be strong, fear not! Here is your God; he comes with vindication; with divine recompense he comes to save you" (Isa. 35:45).

When his Son, Jesus, came to us, he made him execute such mind-set of his benevolent fatherhood and also proclaimed it by many miracles of curing disabled humans. He anointed Jesus as Christ and made sure that Jesus should start, proceed, and end his life in that spirit and goal: "The Spirit of the Lord is upon me, because he has anointed me to bring glad tidings to the poor. He has sent me to proclaim liberty to captives and recovery of sight to the blind, to let the oppressed go free" (Luke 4:18).

In accordance with his anointed fervor, we see Jesus traveling around Palestine doing good to all the needy. While all the Gospel writers fill their books with so many specific healing events Jesus has performed in his public life, Mark sums up all of them, writing, "When it was evening, after sunset, they brought to him all who were ill or possessed by demons. The whole town was gathered at the door. He cured many who were sick with various diseases, and he drove out many demons, not permitting them to speak because they knew him" (1:32–34). The same compassionate Lord underlines his special concern for those needy people in James's letter: "Did not God choose those who are poor in the world to be rich in faith and heirs of the kingdom that he promised to those who love him?" (2:5).

Also, God wishes all our senses to see through the suffering Messiah a weeping God in those fragile people. We know our susceptibility to all physical, psychological, and emotional ailments, sicknesses, and shameful and incurable diseases. Indisputably, our humanity has no complete escape from such maladies until we die. Though we cannot and should not attribute all these sufferings and evils to the sinfulness of humanity, they are closely and intrinsically connected to the disconnection of the body and the spirit.

Besides all the words and deeds of God, which we heard in the Bible, toward those who suffered such disorders, we observed Jesus's continuous and intense care and love shown to the disabled. His first thought at their sight was "It is so that the works of God might be made visible through him" (John 9:3). He meant that every malady, every suffering, every sickness of human beings has a glorious and challenging story of humanity with and toward God.

Let us be very certain that, if we are fully conscious of the merciful interactions God in our life and if we participate willingly in his compassionate caregiving ministry, we will discover the mightiest glory of God actively demonstrated by so many miracles happening in the sufferers. As the first miracle, these sick persons are consoled, nursed, and strengthened by our godly love in action. The second miracle is that we come to know more visibly that these desperate and socially rejected people are the true friends of God. It is through them we gain God's favor and his blessings. And as a third miracle, we will notice that these physically impaired persons become the right and effective source of our faith. Anyone who believes in God experiences this power and also shares this power with others. That is what occurs when we stand by these ailing humans.

The most amazing miracle—which we will encounter when we reach out with no discrimination to the poor, the disabled, the handicapped, the sick, and the physically, emotionally, mentally, and spiritually impaired—is that our inner spirit will feel overwhelmingly that we truly imitate God. James, in his letter, very succinctly addresses this amazing factor. He pinpoints the human weakness of making hasty and faulty judgments of others based on preconceived notions and outward appearances; he too exhorts us to make as our own the mind and heart of God, who does not show partiality (2:1–5). Therefore, God advises us today to appreciate and glorify not the sickness but those who are sick because we encounter in them his miracles of compassion.

124. The Only Way to Uphold Supremacy Is to Be Childlike

Whoever humbles himself like this child is the greatest in the kingdom of heaven.
—Matt. 18:4

Every human craves for power, primacy, supremacy, prestige, and number 1 status in life. There is nothing wrong for us to desire to become first in this competitive world. Moreover, the Bible acknowledges that our Creator—by creating us in his likeness and image—has shared with us his supremacy, honor, glory, and power to control the creation. Unfortunately, human history is filled with wars, infighting, murders, killings, and destruction of human lives mostly because of such unrestrained human ambitions.

The Gospels state how the first disciples of Jesus held the same power-seeking human attitude. When Jesus noticed it, he did not condemn the desire to be first. Competition and development are part of human life's survival game. God in Jesus never denied this. The human ambition for growing, climbing up, and progressing can very well come from God himself. Jesus did indeed have the desire to be the first, for God wanted it to be so.

We should be very clear about a factual truth about Jesus. From the onset of his life, Jesus aimed at to be number 1 in God's kingdom. He too longed to possess the glory and power as a chivalrous person. This was why we heard him praying aloud to his Father, "Father, the hour has come. Give glory to your son, so that your son may glorify you, just as you gave him authority over all people, so that he may give eternal life to all you gave him . . . Now glorify me, Father, with you, with the glory that I had with you before the world began" (John 17:1–5). And God confirmed Jesus's uniqueness when he said from heaven, "This is my beloved Son, with whom I am well pleased" (Matt. 3:17). God made us understand that it was his will for Jesus to become the firstborn of a multitude of brothers and the supreme head of the church.

As I have mentioned earlier, to become a favorite of God and taste his glory in our life is every human's birthright. Therefore, what Jesus has condemned is our wrong ways of speaking and acting to win and covet the primary and glorious positions in life. Jesus has given in detail some heavenly tips to realize validly and legitimately our ambitions of being the first. We read in Mark the summary of them in a succinct way. He narrates Jesus's foretelling to his disciples for a second time about his passion and death to make them know how he has been preoccupied with fulfilling his Father's will despite its perilous hardships.

This simply suggested how he built his life and its schedule on the intense consciousness of designing and fulfilling every one of his dreams in accordance to his Father's will. As Paul would verbalize (Phil. 2:8–9), Jesus—from his very conception—held firmly his unrelenting attitude of surrendering himself to the will of God, taking the form of a slave. "He humbled himself and became obedient unto death, even death on a cross." It was by this fixation that Jesus was fully convinced that he could realize his ambition of becoming number 1. Therefore, God has highly exalted him and bestowed on him the name that is above every name.

While Jesus was preoccupied with this remarkable program of life, we see the apostles being worried with one worldly issue, namely, if their Master died, who would then become the leader of their group? They were going on arguing about which of them was the greatest in the eyes of Jesus. When he asked them what they had been talking about, they were highly embarrassed. Knowing their inner turbulence but undisturbed by their pathetic attitude, he began giving them a tip to be elected or to be promoted in his team. He offered a beautiful strategy with which they can win their dreamy supremacy. "If anyone wishes to be first, he shall be the last of all and the servant of all" (Mark 9:35). He wants them to be humble, simple, and serviceable with no other self-gratifying strings attached. He invited them to assert themselves as leaders who serve instead of seeking to be served.

To help them cultivate this attitude, Jesus placed a child in their midst. He stated that they should be fully and totally depending on God as a child to the Father, and they too should receive his own childlikeness. "Learn from me, I am meek and humble of heart." This is the only way to establish our greatness, glory, and supremacy in this world, fully coveting peace, rest, hope, and happiness in this war-stricken and rifted society.

125. Be a Blessing
For the "Little Ones" and Not a Curse

I have other sheep that do not belong to
this fold; these also I must lead.
—John 10:16a

As disciples of Jesus, we have been called to take part in God's one and only work of universal salvation of the entire humanity. Among his people, God is so concerned with the "little ones." When some of us get strengthened by him, he expects us, in turn, to support the little ones.

First, Jesus expects us to possess a passionate concern for the salvation of all who claim they belong to his sheepfold. There are many sheep in Jesus's sheepfold who is spiritually very poor, and so many of them are physically and socially weak, unable to live a normal life. Jesus has called them "the little ones" and promised a very big reward to those who care for these vulnerable sheep. "Anyone who gives you a cup of water to drink because you belong to Christ, amen, I say to you, will surely not lose his reward" (Mark 9:41). Besides, he too warns those who are scandalizing these little ones, telling them that they should be severely punished. "Whoever causes one of these little ones who believe [in me] to sin, it would be better for him if a great millstone were put around his neck and he were thrown into the sea" (Mark 9:42).

The reason why Jesus expects us to hold such concern for the little ones is that we, as the people of God, form one body, one organism. In this body, there can be members who are weak in their faith and small in their understanding of what a spiritual life is. If the stronger members of the body mislead or put down the weaker ones, it affects the growth of the entire body. This is why he even wants the valiant members of the church to punish themselves by maiming their organs that are sources of scandal to the weak.

Second, our Master tells us that when we do not possess such passionate concern and love for God's little ones, we end up being the worst hindrance to God's salvific work. When we minister to the salvation of our little ones, God expects us to use all that we are endowed with. Unfortunately, as James writes, there are too many of us who become so selfish and very self-oriented that we enrich ourselves and forget the little ones. Thus, the elite and developed sheep not only scandalize the little ones and make them more vulnerable and subservient to the evil spirit but also do harm to their own salvation (James 5:1–6).

When we do not have a passionate concern for the little ones, we are prone to seeing our own good name, good position, and self-glory. Pride begins to rule us. Thus, even the good works we do in the name of Jesus, the church, or charity turn out to be a big source of scandal to the little ones. In our pride, we begin to exclude others and criticize their good works. We give room for infighting and jealousy. We notice this as a perennial problem in God's community.

In OT, we read God empowering seventy elders with the gift of the Spirit and making them prophets. He too granted his Spirit to many others outside the "holy campus." This was protested by those inside that elite group. But Moses advised them not to be jealous because it was the will of God (Num. 11:25–29). In the same way, we heard from the Gospel some apostles who were contaminated by their fake and illegitimate "supremacy" complaining to Jesus against someone from outside the campus driving out demons in his name. But Jesus replied, "Do not prevent him" (Mark 9:39).

This means Jesus wants us to recognize, appreciate, and include others in this ministry of salvation. In the body of Christ, everyone has the right and duty to be an instrument of God's healing and merciful love. There is no room for jealousy in Jesus's kingdom. God has empowered everyone with his Spirit for the benefit of the entire community.

Each member or soul is precious to God. It is true that each person is responsible for his own salvation. However, as mentioned earlier, there can be weak and delinquent members who are vulnerable to be misled by the actions or words of others. Jesus tells us today that our duty as his disciples is to lead God's children to salvation and not to be obstacles in their way. Any sacrifice is worth making when it is for the salvation of a soul, even if it means sacrificing our life as our Master has done.

126. Being Blessed Is The Fruit of Being Consecrated

Consecrate them in the truth. Your word is truth.
—John 17:17

"The Lord may bless us all the days of our life!" This is what we wish and pray whenever we stand in the sanctuary of the divine. And the entire Psalm 128 enlists all the promised blessings we want to be filled with—being favored by God; prospering with the prosperity of Jerusalem, meaning heavenly riches; enjoying everything we accomplish by our own hands; having a long life; and possessing a peaceful life. Now the question is how we humans can be blessed with such a remarkable life. Being bored with and unsuccessful in following private and social media views and opinions, many of us may be fed up and frustrated. The reason for such experience is that we are so excited with the scriptural promise that we overlook its requirement.

The psalmist in the same Psalm writes, "Blessed are you who fear the Lord! Blessed are you who walk in his ways!" Enlightening us in this matter of blessed life, we read in NT, "He who consecrates and those who are being consecrated all have one origin" (Heb. 2:11). This biblical verse underlines that all the disciples of Jesus are consecrated with our Master, Jesus, who has prayed earnestly for such gift for us at the Last Supper: "I do not ask that you take them out of the world but that you keep them from the evil one. They do not belong to the world any more than I belong to the world. As you sent me into the world, so I sent them into the world. And I consecrate myself for them, so that they also may be consecrated in truth" (John 17:15–19).

In a biblical and Christian traditional sense, a "consecrated life" to the Lord means to become God's possession totally. Look at the vessels and other clothes we use at the altar. All are consecrated and dedicated to God for the sole purpose of using for God and by God. This means they become God's properties. Everything should be used according to his will. It is simply like the consecrated life of Jesus, who has done everything from his conception to his death with sacrificial love to fulfill God's purposes, namely, to bring quality life to God's children. Our Christian life becomes qualified as consecrated or holy only if we lower down our fake self deep into the Sheol of sufferings, sacrifices, and finally death of any kind as our Lord has undergone.

God's call to a consecrated life is not exclusive to some religious sisters and brothers. It is a clarion call to every Christian. Because of background and need, each one of us may choose a different status in life. As our Lord has pointed out, some are born to be single, others choose to be single for the sake of community development and many others by natural causes, and most of humans choose married life and build up their own life-giving, life-producing, and life-sustaining families. All, in every status, are called to be consecrated.

Jesus verifies this fact of life as he recommends a sincere consecrated attitude and style of leading a pleasant and fruitful married life (Mark 10:2–16).

And Paul, discussing how we should lead a new life, portrays the consecrated style of married life: "As the church is subordinate to Christ, so wives should be subordinate to their husbands in everything. Husbands, love your wives, even as Christ loved the church and handed himself over for her" (Eph. 5:24–25). Indeed, the spirit of new life urges every Christian couple to enjoy the relationship as that of Christ and the church, living with sacrificial love, a selfless life, and a humble and stable relationship.

I know how hard it is for every one of us to fulfill God's demand of a consecrated life. Certainly, we are made of both light and darkness; however, we can strengthen ourselves in a consecrated life more and more by our religious and spiritual endeavors and by trying our best not to salute all the enticement of our own darkness. We may fail in conducting our lives in a consecrated way, but when we fail, let us believe and hope our Christ is there always to empower us with his forgiveness, love, and admonition and lead us to heaven. Once we are with God, we will finally live only a total life of light, which is nothing but the blessed life that we wish for.

127. The Eternal Anomaly of the Gift of Wisdom

Wisdom gives life to those who possess it.
—Eccl. 7:12b

"Fear of God is the beginning of wisdom." This has been the biblical verse often used by our elders in their exhortations on discipline. We perhaps know the meaning of "fear of God," but most of us may not know much about what "wisdom" means. All our sages and saints who have been probing into the term "wisdom" describe it as breaking through the silence of nature and the loneliness of humanity; they too confirm that wisdom demands an explosion of darkness of life, and it is a painful journey to the other world beyond what we see before our eyes. In the light our forebears have shed on our quest for wisdom, we may assume that wisdom is something beyond our ordinary life's perception; it is getting into the inner circle of our life to understand what it tells us to live right.

According to the book of Wisdom, when we possess this wisdom, "All good things together will come to us; and countless riches will follow it" (Wis. 7:7–11). This is why King Solomon, in his prayer, could tell the Lord that he prefers the gift of wisdom to material riches and power (1 Kings 3:1–15). Undoubtedly, wisdom is more valuable than any material good. However, we have to be cautious in demanding for this gift.

NT writers and church fathers pronounce that this remarkable gift of wisdom is nothing but the Word that comes from God, specifically Jesus Christ, who is the Word incarnate. Along the same line, the author of the letter to the Hebrews writes that the Word of God, namely, wisdom, is very "sharp, sharper than any two-edged sword. It penetrates and divides the soul and spirit, joints and marrow" (Heb. 4:12–13). This reminds us of the age-old saying 'Truth always hurts." Let us remember here the provoking statement of Jesus, who is the personification of wisdom: "Do not think that I have come to bring peace upon the earth. I have come to bring not peace but the sword" (Matt. 10:34).

However, it is worth paying the price of being the receiver of wisdom. Once we possess wisdom, we start working out our own plan in life; we know the knack of shopping around life's important seasons. Wisdom helps us in the choice of our career, job, and partner in life. Through wisdom, we learn how to live life profitably; we get the power to work hard to earn enough money in a just and right way according to God's norms. Money brings us properties and pleasurable entertainments; it leads us to earn popularity in and around our family and community. Thus, we get power over other people. At this pleasant juncture of trying to live happily thereafter, again, wisdom enters into our lives and really disturbs our peace of mind, telling us the wise words of Jesus: "You are lacking in one thing. Go, sell what you have, and give to the poor and you will have treasure in heaven; then come, follow me" (Mark 10:21).

If we feel very sad and down and not ready to accept his command, the same wisdom also feels sorry for us and hits us with a sharp-edged sword: "How hard it is for the rich to enter into the kingdom of heaven" (Mark 10:23). Doesn't it sound weird? The heavenly wisdom that encourages us to choose the right status in life, a suitable job, a taste for hard work, and a thrill to be sincere and duty conscious and in turn provides us enough riches and good positions now names us foolish. It curses us with no entrance to heaven and orders us to give away all that we have earned and secured to the poor and the needy. It is indeed an anomaly.

The exhortation of our Master may hurt our self-image and pride. Nevertheless, positively speaking, it will have its reward from our Judge in heaven;

negatively, it does not permit us to become as oversize as a bubble. We know the characteristic of the bubbles. The bigger they become, the more vulnerable they turn to be a victim of destruction.

128. Let Us Not Act "Dumb" In Handling "Dump" Boxes

The measure with which you measure
will in return be measured out to you.
—Luke 6:38b

I am sure, in many of our big cities, we can find locations of blue USPS collection box facilities for us to dump some of our mails or even packages. On specified hours, they are being collected by our post office workers for arranging their deliveries. In the same style, in many of our churches, especially in Catholic shrines, we see this kinds of boxes taller than an ordinary post—collection boxes in which the devotees are supposed to dump their gifts and donations with their written special intentions. Hence, in earlier days, these boxes have been labeled as the "dump boxes."

The practice of taking and dumping collections in religious circles has been a longtime ritual for pleasing their gods. Very disappointingly, humans who empty them or get the collections from those boxes or baskets do not spend the money for which it has been filled, or those who fill those boxes do not hold the right intentions over their gifts. In Christianity, it may be the same situation because of ignorance and carelessness of what our Master has instructed on it.

As his custom, Jesus went regularly to the temple and synagogues. He would have watched the disorderly and unjust ways of the collection ritual. As we read in the Gospel of Mark (12:38–44), he became furious and angry over it and vehemently criticized it. In his time, like the scribes, almost all religious leaders were corrupt and money and honor mongers. This was why he reprimanded them, saying, "Beware of the scribes, who like to go around in long robes and accept greetings in the marketplaces, seats of honor in synagogues, and places of honor at banquets. They devour the houses of widows and, as a pretext, recite lengthy prayers. They will receive a very severe condemnation."

Jesus may sound like he was totally against the custom of collecting tithes in the form of money and other goods. Yes, he was indignant toward the horrible abuses and misuses occurring in this kind of religious practice of offerings, but he never replaced these practices. He knew well that there were valid reasons for such practices of offering to God. He accepted these rituals, therefore, as symbols and signs of the outward expression of our love response to God.

God expects every one of his children to show in deed their love and gratitude toward him and his love. There is only one twofold commandment to please the Lord, and that is "Love your God with your whole heart, whole mind, and whole soul and with all your strength; and to express such love visibly and tangibly, love your neighbor as yourself."

Undebatably, Jesus observed these practices in accordance to his Judaic religion. However, as the

Son, he knew the deeper mind of his Father. He was quoted saying when he came down to this world, "Sacrifice and offering you did not desire, but a body you prepared for me; holocausts and sin offerings you took no delight in. Then I said, 'As is written of me in the scroll, Behold, I come to do your will, O God'" (Heb. 10:5–7). He was very clear in his approach to the religious ritual of tithing and offering but not only this ritual; any practice that we do in the name of religion must be so appropriate that it pleases God, the great and the holy. Hence, as he opposed the wrong handling of such ritual, he offered his disciples the right way of dealing with this wonderful religious custom of offering, tithing, and donating to religions.

The Bible gives us two widows as role models in the correct way of tithing or offering, one in OT (1 Kings 17:9–24) and the other in NT (Mark 12:38–44). Pointing out what the poor widows have done, the Spirit of God instructs us that offerings, in the sight of God, should be a sign of our total acceptance and recognition of God's providence. Never should we give only what is surplus in us; rather, as those exemplary widows, we should try to give what we really can with a sincere motivation and single-heartedness. Whatever we have belongs to him; he is the owner, and we are only the stewards and instruments in his hands. Therefore, we are ready to offer everything to him, even our own self, if need be. Selfishness has no room inside heaven. Every bit of our selfishness must be broken to pieces and burned in the fire of love. It is one of the reasons why Jesus appreciates our offerings to God.

Besides, even though God does not need our offerings or money, he needs our efforts continuously to empty ourselves and make him fill us; he offers to many of us ample and lucky chances and opportunities to gather his riches and become prosperous. Such divine benevolence is for nothing but to be the cooperators in his job of providence, especially to those at the low level of their life. God, through Jesus, commands us in all religious practices that we should include the love of neighbor. Every outward act we do as an expression of our love to him must be either through the love of others or together with the love of the same. We can have a private conversation with God in prayer and in religious ceremonies, but if it is without any relation to our neighbor, who is there outside, such a purely self-centered religious act cannot be a genuine expression of our love to God.

The giving of ourselves and of what we possess, even if they are like the widow's mite, is mightier than all prayers and other religious practices. God, on his part, will surely reward us as he has done in the case of the widow in the Old Testament. That poor widow of Zarephath has offered to a hungry and thirsty man of God what is available in her home—a small cupful of water and a little cake. For such hospitality, "the jar of flour did not go empty, nor the jug of oil run dry, according to the word of the Lord spoken through Elijah" (1 Kings 17:10–16).

Let us also remind ourselves of the golden promise of Jesus regarding his reciprocal gifts to us when we do these wonderful and generous religious practice of paying our tithes to the church with full understanding, without break, and without murmuring: "Give and gifts will be given to you; a good measure, packed together, shaken down, and overflowing, will be poured into your lap" (Luke 6:38a).

129. An Amazing Family Tradition With a Difference

Whoever does the will of God is my
brother and sister and mother.
—Matt. 12:50

"Family" is defined as a fundamental social group in society typically consisting of two parents and their children. These members of a household live under one roof. It is a group of persons who share common ancestry. This means it is a group of people derived from a common stock—the family of human beings in accordance to the Creator's design and goal. This is the right description of a "traditional family," which we have learned from our church teachings. We are also offered the Holy Family of Nazareth as the right pattern for such traditional families.

Surprisingly but actually, in this modern world, such a form of family system is becoming a smaller and smaller majority. We encounter different forms and shapes of family such as single-parent families, foster families, blended families, etc. Many Christians perceive that these kinds of postmodern families cannot be called holy because they drift from the original, traditional family system. But in the light of scriptures, our church proves it is possible.

In the Gospel of Luke, we read about the family where Jesus was born and bred. Joseph, according to tradition, was a widower who married Mary; therefore, all children from his previous marriage were esteemed as stepsons and stepdaughters of Mary and stepbrothers and stepsisters of Jesus. And Jesus was the foster son of Joseph and not his real son. Hence, the Holy Family of Nazareth cannot be included as among the traditional families. This sort of departure from the traditional style of family living can be traced in the lives of many biblical characters.

For example, the prophet Samuel's family (1 Sam. 1:20–28). Hannah, his mother, leaves her son entirely in the hands of the high priest Eli at the temple. No more then he belongs to his family. Jesus's behavior both in his teenage years and adulthood seems to be, again, telling us that living under one roof is not going to make the family holy. Very sadly, Jesus abruptly leaves his mom one day, telling her he wants to do the will of his Father. Thus, we see that all those families even four thousand years back have not complied with the right definition of a family. Nonetheless, the church upholds the integrity and dignity of the traditional family system under the guidance of Jesus's Spirit. Therefore, we have to search for the true definition and meaning of a "family with a difference."

The Holy Family of Nazareth became holy not because it was up to the characteristics of a traditional family but rather because it was built and maintained as the meeting place of heaven and earth, where God reached out to us humans in an act of bonding. From the few narrations we read about this family in Luke and Matthew, we observed the strong and indissoluble bond maintained among the members of that family, always tied with God's love and truth.

The family we create or belong to is not just living under the same roof, nor is its togetherness bound by laws and principles, nor is it a place where goods and possessions are distributed evenly and justly. But it is "living together in spirit and in truth." It is a communion of feelings, temperaments, knowledge, and the very self with one another mutually.

Moreover, Jesus's family became holy because he, Mary, and Joseph were bonded, grouped, and united on the basis of one ultimate principle, namely, the will of God. We discovered more of this in Jesus who possessed an incessant obsession of doing God's will from the moment he entered into this world. In the Gospel, he revealed it to his parents (Luke 2:49): "Why were you looking for me? Did you not know that I must be in my Father's house?" When his mom came to visit him while he was performing his public ministry, he was quoted saying: "Who are my mother and [my] brothers?" And looking around at his followers and listeners seated in a circle, he said, "Here are my mother and my brothers. [For] whoever does the will of God is my brother and sister and mother" (Matt. 12:48–50).

This is how Jesus understood and preached the true family concept. Any togetherness other than this is simply fake, deceptive, and sometimes very dangerous.

Jesus wants us to treasure and cherish any kind of family situation we have been led in. As John proclaims in his letter, we should "see what love the Father has bestowed on us that we may be called the children of God. Yet so we are" (1 John 3–1), and we should love one another just as he has commanded us. Some will esteem the appearance of a home more than the happy life within the home. If we are in the habit of passing judgment on a family, community, and people at large, we have probably lost touch with the more central values of love. The Holy Family of Nazareth should be a model of an ideal family life where the fully grown mind-set of loving sincerely, serving selflessly, and sacrificing totally takes origin and grows.

130. Ritual Is Effective
Until It Blends with Homework

Faith of itself, if it does not have works, is dead.
—James 2:17

In the event of Jesus's baptism, we observed him giving publicly a total commitment to his God. It was true he had already given this commitment in privacy as we read in Hebrews 10:5–7: "When he came into the world, he said: 'Sacrifice and offering you did not desire, but a body you prepared for me; holocausts and sin offerings you took no delight in.' As is written of me in the scroll, Behold, I come to do your will, O God." Already, he proved himself as an obedient, humble, patient, and loving human while he spent his most of his youth years with his mother, family, and community at Nazareth.

Now at the age of thirty, we saw him demonstrating it symbolically or sacramentally in front of the public by an available religious ceremony. His personal devotion and interior commitment to his God, Immanuel, inside him was made visible to the God outside him. He used the religious ceremony available at that time to profess his commitment to God and to initiate himself into the community life in the kingdom of God. He dreamed to be a winner in his life. So he used baptism as his first step to immerse himself totally into the hands of God and into the depth of his physical, social, and spiritual life. He was ready to start his winning journey to face the reality of life.

Undoubtedly, Jesus already knew what was in store for him in this journey. With his humble surrender and his simple acknowledgment of his position in his community, he courageously accepted to be a suffering servant. He submitted to the mandate of God to go forward to establish justice in the world and to enlighten men and women with his interior light so that everyone would get freedom from imprisonment and ignorance supplied by the evil force. He willingly agreed to that horrible role filled with hurdles and difficulties. He was ready to take this hard road all the way to Calvary, even to be murdered there.

What we see in this scenario of Jesus's life is that, as he takes his first bold step to his public life, God anoints him on the spot with his Holy Spirit. Plus, God the Father assures him of Jesus's conviction from his early childhood and answers his identity queries: "Who am I?" "What is my relationship with God?" and "Am I God's Son?" As Luke writes, God acknowledges Jesus's worth and identity and shouts out with his thunderous voice from the sky, "You are my beloved Son; with you I am well pleased."

This event of baptism in our Lord's life reminds us of our own baptism either as infants or adults. As John the Baptist has foretold, we—the followers of Jesus—are also initiated into his discipleship by the baptism not only of water but also of fire and the Spirit. Jesus and his church expect that we too might experience at our baptism whatever Jesus has experienced at his. Jesus becomes our pattern and role model in our Christian life.

What Jesus and his church proclaim is that mere ritual baptism won't do justice to its miraculous effects as it has done to the Lord until we do the homework as Jesus has done before and after his baptism. He has been constantly in touch with God inside him by continuous prayers and religious practices; he has been faithful to his commitment to God and religion first in his hidden and private life. Then and only then has he demonstrated it through sacramental signs like baptism, and he has continued to keep it intact by his strenuous obedience to his Father's will.

Most of us have been baptized very early in our babyhood. There have been proxies who have responded yes to God on our behalf. As adults, we should strive consciously to be filled with the Spirit's gifts and try our best to perform all our daily activities as a mom, dad, officer, nurse, teacher, etc., coming out of not mere natural talent, need, or natural love but the commitment we have promised at our baptism. Then we will reap the real fruits as God has designed for us as our destiny. We will be going about doing good with the power of God as Jesus has done. Let us follow the advice of the legendary labor agitator Mother Jones: "Pray for the dead, but fight like hell for the living."

131. Let's Celebrate Life Together

A good heart is a continual feast.
—Prov. 15:15b

In *Gaudium et spes*, the Second Vatican Council's pastoral constitution of the church in the modern world, we read in its introductory note, "Church has always had the duty of scrutinizing the signs of the times and of interpreting them in the light of the Gospel. Thus, in language intelligible to each generation, she can respond to the perennial questions which men ask about this present life and the life to come, and about the relationship of the one to the other. We must therefore recognize and understand the world in which we live, its explanations, its longings, and its often dramatic characteristics."

Enlightened by the bright light of God's Word, we are fully aware of the nature and dignity of humans, who can never be solitary beings. The inner nature of every human is being a social being, holding uninterruptedly genuine interpersonal communion with one another. One of the many signs and symbols humans use for demonstrating and maintaining such honorable communion is conducting together various styles of celebrations of life.

God created all his creation, especially us humans, just to celebrate his life in this universe. As his special investment, he put in us his image and likeness so that we can not only be concelebrants in his party but also be cohosts to continue that life's party until he comes in glory. The celebration of God's life is the only reason we are all affiliated to a marriage-based and bonded family life. Therefore, every family is called a domestic church. Despite our differences in gender, age, and other social variances, we are concelebrants hosting the one and only party of God's life in Jesus.

Jesus's Gospel values are oriented toward such remarkable celebration of human life. In one of the many events in his life, he has underlined what and how this celebration should be held. It is the wedding event at Cana (John 2:1–11) where he has performed an astounding miracle of changing water into wine as the beginning of his signs through which he has revealed his glory.

Let us go back and look around the place where this historical wedding has taken place. We see a variety of people, things, roles, and identities. Jesus and Mary, the disciples of Jesus, and various relatives and friends as guests are sitting there on one side; on the other, we see the bridegroom and the bride, best man and maid of honor, and all the servants and cooks, plus the common folks who have come to witness the wedding event out of curiosity. All are different from one another in their status, relationships, roles, characters, needs, and so on. But one thing that connects them together, and that is the celebration aspect of that moment happening in human life.

Three sudden twists happen during the happiest moment, which seem to be turning points in that celebration. First, it is found that there is no wine to serve the guests. The second turning point is when Mary requests Jesus, her son, to do something about this unwanted happening, Jesus seems to turn down her request. The third twist is water being changed into wine and even with better quality. We know that all the characters participating in that moment of celebration experience different feelings such as sad, shocked, pitying, murmuring, and so on. Yet a few among them—like Mary, the mother of Jesus—follow God's tips to maintain a balanced spirit. Thanks to them, that event again turns out to be a celebration.

This is what every one of us in life encounters in our homes, parishes, communities, nations, and the world. Look at the horrible earthquake, tsunami, tornado, and other terroristic and political wars through which the entire global society has been thrown into a tailspin.

Millions die and billions go without meals, shelters, and medications, and other millions are living in a no-man's-land as refugees. Watch keenly how the celebration in their lives has been destroyed. Yet people there, as well as those around the world, pour out their love and compassion and hold on to God's greatness and goodness, which bring back the celebration spirit once again in that deplorable environment.

As Mary has advised the servers during a critical life situation, our Christian conscience urges us, at such moments in today's world, to "do whatever Jesus tells us to do." Everyone born and bred in this world by the Creator is designed to celebrate a godly life bestowed to us. A genuine celebration of life cannot be realized without being together with our human family. We should not be alone like a lonely man or an island. We should live as a member of a group, family, and community—not as a mere nominal registered member but totally involved in that community—and become an integral part of it. Though we are different in many ways, especially in our IQ, DNA, hereditary, culture, background of formation and education, and talents, we have to work together in times of perils. The more we are involved in assisting the suffering victims in rising and celebrating their lives, the happier will our own life celebration be. We should, thus, go on celebrating God's life in spirit and in truth, in oneness and fullness, in justice and compassion, until he comes.

132. The Tighter the Clinging to God, The Speedier the Flinging of Temptations

Jesus was led by the Spirit into the desert.
—Luke 4:1

The Christian life is a journey, a pilgrimage, a voyage to eternity, a leap into darkness but always in a deserted land. That is how our Lord's life has been

354 | Rev. Benjamin A. Vima

from his very conception up to his burial. As biblical scholars comment, the narration of Jesus's temptations depicts the summary of the entire thirty-three years of the deserted life experience of Jesus.

Unquestionably, no human is exempted from being tempted by the evil forces either to ignore doing good or to surrender to perform evil. Surprisingly, Jesus, the Son of God, has experienced it. The author of the letter to the Hebrews describes Jesus as "one who has similarly been tested in every way, yet without sin" (Heb. 5:15b). We all must be wondering how Jesus could go through the devil's temptations but not commit any sin; in other words, how could he succeed in his spiritual battle?

The practical and realistic answer is found in Luke's portrayal of Jesus's victory over those temptations posed by the devil. The first matter in this regard is to be well understood: every Tom, Dick, and Harry is not commonly taken into the swirl of temptations as Jesus has undergone. Only those who are filled, shaped, molded, and moved by the Spirit as Jesus has been led encounter such hectic temptations. Also, if we observe the event attentively, we find that Jesus has been tempted only at the end of, and not during, his spiritual accomplishment of forty days and forty nights of fasting to attempt to attain an intimate and ecstatic relationship with his God. From this, we are clearly told that most of the temptations of the devil take their express delivery of forbidden apples to boost the human pride, self-satisfaction, and full freedom to exercise even legitimately creative human power against the Creator. This is the truth we discover in Jesus's spiritual warfare with the devil.

Humans are already led by their Creator to toddle, to walk, to run, and to float over or swim against the current of life in this earth. Besides, being reborn in Christ, as his disciples, most of us are again and again led by his Spirit to various deserted situations in life. Unquestionably, whenever we try our best to relate ourselves to God intensely through our spiritual exercises of prayer, penance, fasting, and sharing, we feel happy with Jesus because we have done our best; and spiritually, God guarantees that we are his beloved sons and daughters. It is then and only then that all the problems start, when the hell of temptations is let loose as Jesus has experienced.

What should we do to win over temptations? The one and only suggestion offered to us is to hold on to a persistent faith in God. We should first make sure we have integrated all our torn and broken pieces of life—its different dimensions, the various creatures and creations, and especially the diverse human beings we are related to. Indeed, to choose our priorities in life and lead a balanced life is very much based on the kind of faith we place on the Word of God. The Word and the world must be integrated; the body and soul, the flesh and the spirit must be united as it has been with Jesus's incarnation. And that must be possibly done only when we place all those pieces to the whole—God. He is the past, the present, and the future. He is the beginning, the middle, and the end. He is the giver and the gifts as well.

Second, this God of ours must be heard and believed in his spoken, written words. Third and very importantly, he must be encountered fully and truly by the mutual agape we share with him and our fellow men. Merely celebrating this love once a year as

Valentine's Day won't help us much in this regard. Our heart, mind, and soul must be engaged in every moment of our life in that spirit of love. We notice this threefold strategy applied by Jesus to not succumb to satanic temptations.

Like him, not only should we memorize and speak out God's Word but also imbibe their spirit and truth within us as our blood and bones. Jesus has become a model for us on how to use the Word of God in our journey, our day-to-day life. Our life is like a symphonic orchestra; it is neither a bland unison nor a harsh cacophony but a gloriously dramatic polyphony. Such a polyphonic integration in balance can happen only by total surrender to the Word of God. If this miracle happens in all our spiritual exercises or religious rituals and observances, then certainly we will overcome any temptation.

133. The Breathtaking Hilltop Experiences

Master, it is good that we are here.
—Luke 9:33

The French mathematician and philosopher Blaise Pascal—who has lived over three hundred years ago and, in the closing years of his life, struggled with his own issues of faith and understanding—has written, "In faith there is enough light for those who want to believe and enough shadow to blind those who don't." We plan out our schedule and the beginning, proceeding, and ending of our enterprises and engagements. We almost feel sure we have in our fingertips a beautiful plan of action for our life. The chain of our actions, though many times breed some other reactions as side effects, ultimately has some purpose and goal to be achieved. Even though we are aware that there will be shortcomings, failures, losses, blunders, and dark days in life, still, we try to hide or ignore it and plan for 100 percent full happiness and contentment. Very strangely, in this plan of actions, we don't want to include the ultimate thing—our death and what follows, namely, eternity.

This was how Peter, James, and John pretended to be when they had an ecstatic experience on a hilltop. They did not want it to end. They didn't want this special touch of heaven, this transformation or transfiguration of the Lord, this visit by Moses and Elijah, to end. "Let's put up tents," they said. They wanted to hold on to this moment. But it had to end. It all had to end because the plan had to take place, and they were just mere small things symbolically foretelling what was to come—the ultimate thing.

Living with longing and describing this ultimate thing very enthusiastically, Jesus's disciples, like Paul, were wholeheartedly convinced that God would change our lowly body to conform to his glorified body by the power that enabled him also to bring all things into subjection to himself (Phil. 3:21). Our forebears, like Abraham, were awesome role models of hoping for this ultimate thing. They led their daily life happily, filled with accidents and incidents, with faith in the realization of what was hoped for and evidence of things not seen. Abraham, for example, set out boldly from his native place to a strange land only in the faith and hope he possessed within his heart; he too walked by faith throughout his life despite all the odds and hurdles that upset him and his family. And it was the same with all the genuine disciples of Jesus in the past and at present.

The main source of this amazing life of faith and hope has been, as we read in the lives of biblical heroes and heroines, nothing but the split-second encounter with the striking presence of God. The supreme divine meets with the earthly human spirit in timeless time. To walk in the valley of darkness, this spiritual lightning from the sky to the earth helps humans and strengthens them to go a long way to reach their Promised Land.

The hilltop experience is simply a heavenly encounter with the Supreme Being during this earthly life. In this encounter with God, the human spirit is elevated, connected, related, and intimately presented with their Creator, the heavenly Father. God speaks, and the human spirit listens. During this experience, humans lose themselves but gain God. They become nobody but everybody, they are nowhere but everywhere, they see not one thing but everything, they lose something of them but gain everything of them, and they don't care about themselves but focus only on God. While the human spirit comes across such a heavenly experience, it feels like it is trapped and intoxicated. Everybody who enters into this experience withdraws from the self, held and completely possessed by the divine.

This breathtaking experience with God can be only for a split second, simply a sparkle like that of a lightning strike. Every child, from Adam to the newly born baby of today, is entitled to this experience. So many people in human history have been benefiting from it. Such is the vision all the disciples of Jesus have held in their inner mind, particularly when they have undergone persecution and death. They too have attested to it and proclaimed it joyfully in the dungeon and fire.

Besides many good gifts, Jesus's main purpose in coming down from heaven is just to show his disciples the way to encounter the divine as often as possible. He too has showed us an example of how to get these hilltop experiences. Prayer time and suffering time are the apt occasions to enjoy these spiritual experiences with God. Such moments can keep us going for a long time.

134. The Divine Guidelines on Sin Management

Neither do I condemn you. Go, and from
now on do not sin anymore.
—John 8:11b

We hear about studies in business management, crisis management, life management, time management, family management, and so on. There are thousands of books and research works sold in the market to learn the theories about them. Have you ever heard of sin management? While there are too many courses conducted in hundreds of colleges and universities, there is only one university, the church, and only one textbook, the Bible, teaching the theories and principles of sin management.

Being very smarty creatures as we are, there are some natural tactics we usually apply to manage our sinfulness. As soon as we come to our senses regarding our committing sin, our inner peace is disturbed; we are hurt and therefore act or react against this situation, not able to manage the sinfulness in a productive way. In scrupulosity, we begin to feel always guilty; or in frozen complacency, our naughty brain makes us insensitive to the sins' horror. Many of us distract ourselves from the conscience prick by various hurry-burry, jolly lifestyles or by drifting away from faith and religion with unprecedented justifications. We too have seen some developing a stony heart and hardheadedness and throwing stones at others and thus soothing their own conscience.

Indeed, the Good Book teaches us in detail the horrendous results of human sins. Sin is some kind of attitude and deed that goes against God's love, against our own human spirit, against the wholistic truth, against our relationship with other human beings. But the Word of God also guides us in managing that horrible aftermath of sinning. God's sin management theory, according to scriptures, is "the more we feel guilty, the nearer we go to God, who loves sinners, though he hates sin." He, as the Father, hugs us immediately like the prodigal son's father upon his younger son's return.

When we come to our senses and confess our sinfulness, we must think not about our own ugly past: "Remember not the events of the past, the things of long ago consider not; See, I am doing something new!" (Isa. 43:18–19). As some writers put it, "God has a very bad memory." No matter how many times the Israelites have abandoned their God, no matter how many times they have become stiff necked and refused to do his will, he always comes to call them back. In the whole New Testament, we see God—in the person of Jesus—calling his sinful people to be converted, to put their whole trust in the message he brings, and to follow his way as the way of truth and life.

We also must confess more the marvelous deeds of God. This is what all converted, confessed, and pardoned sinners like Paul have done and do. Paul writes, "Just one thing: forgetting what lies behind but straining forward to what lies ahead, I continue my pursuit toward the goal, the prize of God's upward calling, in Christ Jesus" (Phil. 3:13–14). Also, we must not behave as if we have received cheap grace. We must do something proactively: confessing not merely by words but also by deeds of charities.

Above all, we should remove completely the stones in our spirit and forgive others. We see many sinners around Jesus while he is performing his public ministry, such as the woman caught in adultery and a group of so-called righteous people like Pharisees and scribes (John 8:1–11). They all represent all of us. Usually, we sin in two ways. As the woman caught in adultery, we hurt God and others by indulging our desires at their expense. Also, as the Pharisees and scribes, we hurt others by setting ourselves up as superior to and esteem ourselves better than them.

A valid question arises in my mind: had we been there that day when the adulterous woman was brought to Jesus, what would we have done? Would we have condemned the guilty woman too? Even during the past week, how many people have we condemned in our hearts or in our words? Are we regular readers of newspapers or watchers of TV programs that delight in rubbishing people and destroying their lives? How many people have we ourselves passed judgment on?

On the other hand, to how many have we extended a hand of love and compassion? That is how Jesus has behaved and managed the sinful situations according to his Father's guidelines. When we begin to manage our sinfulness in the light of Jesus's Gospel theory and practice, we too will experience a restful life going through green pastures. And we will ceaselessly sing joyfully with King David, who is another typical sinner of our kind, "The Lord has done great things for us; we are filled with joy" (Ps. 126).

135. The Unbroken Chain Effect of Resurrection

Blessed are those who have not seen and have believed.
—John 20:29b

Once, as I was driving from a town at its outskirts, I found a most captivating ad by the roadside. The sign on it with very big fond read BEFORE PASSING, SEE US. Being a communications student, I loved it. It truly captivated my attention. Since I couldn't read the entire ad, I went back next day and read the whole advertisement. It was an advertisement of a funeral home in town. I was surprised to find the terrific talent of the one who prepared the script. There was a play of words that contained two meanings. It was asking the public to visit the funeral home not only before they leave town but also before leaving this world.

Being a committed preacher of Jesus, whom I believe is the life and resurrection of humanity, I have immediately grasped the invitation of Jesus: "Come, and you will see" (John 1:39a) and "Come to me, all you who labor and are burdened" (Matt. 11:28). While senior citizens, as they get older, feel the nearness of their death, they are overanxious about the things they should do before they die. But I think every Christian elders must focus their attention on how to see the risen Lord, who is present in our midst, even before they die.

Very shockingly, we hear from the risen Lord—expressing his desire to us through his apostle Thomas in one of his apparitions as narrated by John (20:24–29)—that he prefers from us a "faith without seeing." Paul also reminds us, "For we walk by faith, not by sight" (2 Cor. 5:7). How to reconcile the discrepancy found here? On one hand, many critics contend that it is impossible to believe an invisible God and that it is either fake or superstitious. They may be right in telling that we normally recognize, accept, and believe in ourselves, in others, and in other things by hearing, seeing, touching, smelling, and tasting. Yet our Master has contended that the better faith is by believing without even seeing. How do we take his statement?

First, we should accept what the biblical scholars say about Jesus's statement. They say that he doesn't mean that we should ignore or deny our human, normal, and legitimate process of believing. Paul therefore writes, "How can people believe in him of whom they have not heard?" (Rom. 10:14). Rather, Jesus wants his disciples to live and move in the realm of his Spirit. He has assured us that he will be present within us and among us in his risen status as the Spirit: "I am with you always, until the end of the age" (Matt. 28:20b). Such an unfathomable belief has made millions of Jesus's followers, from John up to this day, who have encountered the risen Lord while they are living in this earth. Describing it as he has seen and heard in one of his visions, John writes, "One like the Son of Man . . .

telling him: 'I am the first and the last, the one who lives. Once I was dead, but now I am alive forever and ever. I hold the keys to death and the netherworld'" (Rev. 1:17b–18).

Second, church history had proved that so many disciples of Jesus who were pining and longing for the risen Lord's intimate connections truly encountered his active presence, interacting with them by his marvelous deeds. Jesus himself had asked us, "If I do not perform my Father's works, do not believe me; but if I perform them, even if you do not believe me, believe the works" (John 10:37–38). In that same vein, he encouraged his disciples to abide in him and consequently receive the ability to perform signs and wonders of healing, strengthening, and liberating others. "Whoever believes [your proclamation of the Gospel] . . . will be saved . . . These signs will accompany those who believe: in my name they will drive out demons, they will speak new languages . . . They will lay hands on the sick, and they will recover" (Mark 16:16–18).

Therefore, when we uncompromisingly believe that the same Jesus is alive today in the church, in its authority, in its worship, in its sacraments, and in its preaching, we are undoubtedly encountered by his Spirit through his discipled leaders when they preach, when they touch, when they counsel, when they share, and when they teach us in accordance with their roles in the church. The same is true when we are moving in the risen Lord's Spirit and commit to him our hands, legs, and eyes as his own; those who hear us, those who see us, those who touch us actually hear, see, and touch the resurrected Jesus of Nazareth. This is how Jesus's mission is continued for the past two millennia, and it is going to be through the end of ages.

136. The Shepherd's True Sheep Can Become Good Shepherds

The Lamb who is in the center of the throne will shepherd them.
—Rev. 7:17a

We, the disciples of Jesus, never ceased to address our Master as the Good Shepherd. We should know that this famous Shepherd, who was given by the heavenly Father such a glorious role of shepherding us, first was a hidden, small, innocent, and meek Lamb of God. He was an obedient child of God. Jesus was a sheep to his Father, who was his Shepherd. Like the little shepherd David, Jesus would have been singing every day, "The Lord is my Shepherd. I shall want nothing." He behaved as a Lamb to his Father. He was slain like a Lamb to do the will of his Father. His will and his Father's were so in tune with the same rhythm that he could bravely state, "I and my Father are one." As John the Baptizer named him the Lamb of God, Jesus became a scapegoat and was slaughtered for the sake of his Father's creative and redemptive plan to be fulfilled. John the Evangelist therefore could see him as a Lamb sitting in the throne of heaven (Rev. 7:14–17). This is the stuff with which Jesus breathed, moved, and lived as Jesus of Nazareth, and that was why God exalted him above any other name and entrusted to him the most glorious role of shepherding the sheep of his own flock.

When the same Good Shepherd planned to delegate his power of shepherding to his disciples, he wanted them primarily to behave like true sheep;

he commanded them to be genuine and true sheep, recognizing him, listening to him, and following him. As they continued to humbly and faithfully follow him, they saw themselves—their weakness, strength, status, and destiny. Hence, they could boldly testify as Paul proclaimed, "For so the Lord has commanded us, I have made you a light to the Gentiles, that you may be an instrument of salvation to the ends of the earth" (Acts 13:47). All those disciples were following their Shepherd wherever he led them; even when they felt as if they were in a dark valley, they kept on following him till their last drop of blood poured out for the sake of their Shepherd's creative and redemptive plan. They became, in history, "the ones who have survived the time of great distress; they have washed their robes and made them white in the blood of the Lamb" (Rev. 7:14). Consequently, they were truly recognized by God as good shepherds.

Almost all of us, as we enter into adulthood, for some even earlier, long to be leaders and shepherds. Students prefer to be teachers, staff long to be bosses, laborers dream to be masters, youngsters love to be elders and masters of their own destiny. There is nothing bad about all these preferences and dreams. The question is how to climb up or realize such dreams. Besides, when we have climbed up the top, how are we going to manage and maintain that position intact, productive, and cool?

The only answer to this is to look in ourselves through the mirror of Jesus's personality and behavior. Jesus wants us to live and behave exactly as he has done with his Father. The will of the sheep must become one with the will of the Shepherd. Otherwise, the sheep remain sheep and not a shepherd in fulfilling the responsibility of leading others. The true sheep of Jesus are to be one with him in spirit and in truth. They not only move around the sheepfold, are registered as his sheep in a church, and belong to his sheepfold just for baptism and burial but also are intimately attached to the shepherd, move and stand with him wherever he goes, run after him wherever he takes them, listen to him attentively, act according to his commands, and abide in him as branches in the vine. The will of the sheep must become one with that of the Shepherd. Otherwise, the sheep remain sheep and not a shepherd.

We are sheep only to Jesus, the Good Shepherd. We are weak only before God but strong warriors before Satan. We are humble followers only to the Lamb of God but courageous leaders to our children and other weaklings of society. If we want such identity and dignity to stay within us, we have to then be true sheep of Jesus and not wolves in sheep clothing. The more we ignore and resist our Shepherd, the less powerful and less fruitful we become.

137. The Eucharistic Transformation: Mysterious but Realistic

Every day they devoted themselves to breaking bread.
—Acts 2:46

Every religion is a bundle of ritualistic traditions. And Christianity is not exempted from this. One among those Christian rituals is the Eucharistic celebration, a remarkable ritual that our Lord Jesus has handed down to us through his disciples, as Paul puts it, before has he left from this world (1 Cor. 11:23–26). Through the Bible and church tradition, we are told that this ritual is the source of our spiritual experience. Plus, by participating in this ritual, we will get some incredible experiences, both internally and externally. It is called the Eucharistic transformation, occurring in our life in three ways.

First, we become persons of self-giving. The sacrament of the Eucharist shows how Jesus gives himself in total love, to be eaten by us. His self-giving has been perfected and completed on the cross when he has died, shedding the last drop of his blood for our salvation. Jesus thus gives himself totally for us. He gives until nothing is left to give. He loves his own so much that he has sacrificed everything for his loved ones. Our participation in the Eucharist should make us less selfish and more self-giving, loving, caring, forgiving, and compassionate.

Second, our participation in this ritual energizes us to be life giving. Jesus's self-giving is life giving. The Eucharist is a true food and drink that nourishes us and helps us share in the life of Jesus. "Amen, amen, I say to you, unless you eat the flesh of the Son of Man and drink his blood, you do not have life within you" (John 6:53). He communicates his life to his dear ones by sharing his own flesh and blood with them. He becomes one with us so that we may be transformed into his body. St. Augustine has heard the words of the Lord once in his prayer thus: "You will not change me into yourself as you would food of your flesh; but you will be changed into me." We become what we eat. The life that the Eucharist gives is, of course, eternal life as Jesus is the eternal Son of God. Our participation of the Eucharist challenges us to love, to promote, to uphold, and to defend life in all its forms, from the moment of conception to natural death. Just as the Lord shares himself in the life-giving sacrament, so we need to share our own lives, talents, time, and resources with the needy.

Third, the Eucharist also enables us to be a unified community. The Eucharist is the sacrament of unity. Jesus has given himself up for us to unify and reconcile humanity with God. Our participation in the Eucharist—which is a sacrament of forgiving love, unity, and reconciliation—should make us long and work for reconciliation, peace, and harmony in our own families, communities, and the world at large. Thus, by participating in the Eucharist, we will possess an amazing ability to see dualities—the pros and cons of situations as change approaches—and to quickly and efficiently think them through before making any decisions. We will dare to look deeply into our desires, regenerate self-awareness, and recognize psychological ambiguities. This will bring balance into our home and family life. We will pay attention to the details as we bring our inner and outer life into unity and harmony. Surely, we will enjoy the changes occurring within us.

As we come to terms with ourselves, we will be able to see a more fulfilling purpose in life, and our field of experience broadens. That has been the experience the disciples of Jesus from the day of his death and resurrection as they have participated in the Eucharist, which they have named splendidly "the breaking of the bread" (Luke 24:35). We will focus on matters that affect us most deeply, and like magic, our life will become easier, and things will seem to take care of themselves. We will have all the necessary resources and motivation to make tangible changes and achieve results in all our endeavors. We will become self-giving, life-giving, and surely unifying persons. In every step of our lives, we will develop into peacemakers and peace lovers. In sum, through regular participation in the Eucharist, we will be energized—like those of the early church (Acts 2:42–47)—to live as true champions of Eucharistic unity at home, in the community, and in the world around us.

138. Our Faith Calls Us to Be Doubly Anointed

Whoever loses his life for my sake will save it.
—Luke 9:24b

We always admire the people who proclaim their staunch faith that Jesus Christ is the Messiah as Peter has responded to Jesus's question "Who do you say that I am?" In the same vein, most of us continue to assure ourselves and others, declaring the same profession of faith. We love to insert in our prayers and hymns to Jesus such wonderful faith-filled terms as the psalmist uses in Psalm 63: "O God, you are my God; you indeed are my savior and I will bless you as long as I live."

Very surprisingly, in the Gospel passage of Luke, we read Jesus rebuking Peter for such profession (Luke 9:20–21). In narrating the same event, Matthew (16:13–23) and Mark (8:27–33) in their Gospels offer us another version and background of the heartbreaking rebuke of Jesus against Peter. According to them, Jesus has appreciated Peter for his profession of faith in him, but then he has vehemently chided him, saying, "Get behind me, Satan," when Peter has rebuked Jesus for foretelling his suffering and death.

In the light of the above-mentioned passages, we can draw a breathtaking lesson for our Christian life. The faith we uphold in Jesus as Christ the Messiah should be based on the understanding of the twofold messiahship of Jesus as anointed by God.

In the culture of Judaism, we read there were so many leaders anointed with the oil either of kingship or of priesthood. Since Jesus had come to fulfill God's law, he alone possessed the twofold perfection of kingship and priesthood. Being the Messiah, from his conception, he had been anointed by the Holy Spirit as he himself claimed, "The Spirit of the Lord is upon me because he has anointed me."

In like manner, Jesus also declared that the godly anointing he got from his Father was not only of power and glory but also of suffering and death, only through which he would covet God's glory. We heard him in the Gospels sharing with his disciples frequently, "The Son of Man must suffer greatly and be rejected by the elders, the chief priests, and the scribes, and be killed and on the third day be raised" (Luke 9:22). All OT prophets, like Zechariah, prophesied so about Jesus: "When they look on him whom they have thrust through, they will mourn for him as one mourns for an only child, and they will grieve for him as one grieves over a firstborn" (Zech. 12:10b).

Those prophetic words summed up the twofold identity of Jesus, namely, he had to go through rejection, condemnation, and horrible suffering from the humankind, who would at the end salute him and honor him as their leader. When Jesus asked the question "Who do you say that I am?" he wanted Peter to say, "You are the kingly but suffering servant Messiah." It was for such identity that Jesus came to this world, took the form of a slave, and underwent ignominious death—death on the cross. He came, suffered, and died so that disciples like Peter could know his immense love for them and appreciate his unbearable sufferings, bleeding, and death for the sake of their salvation.

Most people in the world today acknowledge Jesus as the founder of the largest religion, a revolutionary Jewish reformer, a great teacher, and a man of peace. Undebatably, Jesus's teachings have transformed the lives of an innumerable number of people. He can indeed be termed as the single most influential person who has ever lived in world history. No other person in history has occupied so much space in books, poetry, paintings, and sculptures. Yet all these do not make him what he truly is: the Savior of the world and our personal Savior. But we the disciples of Jesus do.

Jesus has exclusively called the discipled leaders to be doubly anointed in the way he has coveted. He demands us to purify our faith in him, to identify him not only as a glorious Messiah but also as the suffering Servant. He too invites us to embrace truthfully his boldness and stamina to bear the bitter consequences of following his footsteps of justice and love, namely, unprecedented suffering and even ignominious death. "If anyone wishes to come after me, he must deny himself and take up his cross daily and follow me" (Luke 9:23). If we begin to live in his way, at times, it may bring to us unbearable sufferings and hardships. Christ demands that we have to bear them willingly

and smilingly with him. Its amazing result is winning
the win of eternal life, for which we have been destined.

139. Do the Works of the Lord
According to His Word

I have become all things to all . . . For the sake of the gospel.
—1 Cor. 9:22–23

One of the Gospel events that I, as one of the discipled
leaders, love to read and reread and to cherish its
lessons and impacts is the story of Martha and
Mary hosting Jesus at their home (Luke 10:38–42).
In that narration, we notice that while the former is
shown busy with the work of the Lord, the latter is
more interested in knowing the Lord of the work.
Traditionally, this story has been interpreted as if
Martha is busy only with how to serve Jesus as her
priority; but as for Mary, her priority is to hold and
maintain a personal relationship with him. The bleak
part of this interpretation is—quoting Jesus, "Mary
has chosen the better part"—esteeming erroneously that
any person choosing a religious or ascetical vocation is
holier and better than those taken up with the activities
of everyday life in the world. This sort of thinking has
come out of dejecting the Gospel value proclaimed on
this occasion—a quiet life of contemplation and prayer,
personified in Mary, is superior to a busy life of activity
and action, personified in Martha.

Jesus indeed loved to visit the Bethany home of
these two sisters who were considered by him the best

hosts with TLC. They followed exactly their Jewish tradition of hospitality, perpetuated from the time of Abraham and Sarah, who believed every guest coming to their home was a godsent proxy (Gen. 18:1–10). In the person of Jesus, these ladies recognized an extraordinary Messenger of God. Both of them pleased the Lord, and that was why he chose them as signs to witness one of his most promising values of the kingdom. He therefore did not intend to disparage Martha and her activity but rather to show that hearing the Word of God is the foundation of all action and that the Word of God must permeate all other concerns.

For example, it is right and just that parents be entirely concerned and completely involved in the activity of raising and rearing their children; however, in the light of the Word of God, we are told those parental activities should not be purely from natural human urges but much more from the wisest words that flow from the Supreme Parent, God—that is, all our secular activity must flow from, be based on, or be an expression of the Word of God. Therefore, to hear the Word of God is the absolute prerequisite for right action; the daily action of doing what Jesus has said is the one thing necessary, namely, the building up of the kingdom of God in the world. In other words, prayer is not better than action in the sense that they are contrary or contradictory realities, one to be chosen over the other; but rather, prayer is primary in the sense that it is like the source of a stream, while action is like the flow of that same stream. They are continuous, complementary, and mutually dependent. Prayer without action is sterile, and action without prayer is empty. Ultimately, scripture is calling us not to deem one as better than the other but rather to embrace both.

Only one who has become the hearer of the Word can truly become a sincere doer of the Word.

Jesus likes his disciples to respect this inner and intrinsic connection between closely attaching to God's Word and intensely serving his people. Paul has been the most praiseworthy role model in this regard. Writing to Colossians, he testifies his seamless striving to uphold this connection: "Now I rejoice in my sufferings for your sake, and in my flesh I am filling up what is lacking in the afflictions of Christ on behalf of his body, which is the church . . . It is he whom we proclaim, admonishing everyone and teaching everyone with all wisdom, that we may present everyone perfect in Christ" (Col. 1:24–28). And the same holds true for all our saints. St. Therese of Lisieux, a contemplative nun, has written, "To give the Lord a perfect hospitality, it is necessary that Mary and Martha must be joined as one."

140. The "Faith-Filled" Share Alike Blessings, plus Dangers

Be doers of the word and not hearers only.
—James 1:22

Our life is made of both day and night, joy and sorrow, blessings and curses, uphill and downhill. Every human experiences it, and willy-nilly, they have to go through this paradoxical life path. Whenever we come across in the scriptures words like "night" and "day," most of the time, they mean the darkness-filled and light-encircled situations we meet in day-to-day life.

When Jesus is talking about the vigilance of his disciples waiting for their Master, he points out that they should be ready—as Mark explains—in the evening, at midnight, or in the early morning. While most of the NT writers refer to the waiting for the Parousia of the Lord, they never ignore that these night experiences are the metaphors signifying the disasters, calamities, dangers, and tribulations humans undergo. To us, the discipled leaders of Jesus, Luke very well spells out that this sort of waiting is not merely for the end-time arrival but much more for being faithful to Jesus's instructions in the period of Parousia.

In these life difficulties and perils, God in Jesus invites us not to be agitated but to strive to be cool and maintain our mental and emotional balance like our holy ancestors; even in their dark days, they are celebrating the Lord's name and their life with him. "For in secret the holy children of the good were offering sacrifice and carried out with one mind the divine institution, so that your holy ones should share alike the same blessings and dangers" (Wis. 18:9). To encounter both blessings and dangers in our life with smiling faces, God instructs us through his scriptural words about an effective tool that is called faith.

Faith is considered by our church tradition as one of the theological virtues. The book of Wisdom tells us that faith is simply a human ascent of intellect and will. "That night was known beforehand to our Fathers; with sure knowledge of the oaths in which they put their faith" (Wis. 18:6). And the letter to the Hebrews expounds it: "Faith is confident assurance concerning what we hope for, and conviction about things we do not see" (Heb. 11:1). Faith, therefore, is a reality of the human capacity to dream dreams. It is an ascent of human intellect and will about a reality that is not there at present and is unseen and unheard, a virtual reality. It's simply a human thing.

Faith also is a virtue of perseverance in pursuing certain things that are not available at present. It is chutzpah, the human spirit of impudence, a certain nerve or guts to put out into deep water to launch some daredevil activities without any tangible hold. As the Lord Jesus states in the Gospels, faith is the spirit of a faithful and farsighted steward waiting and waiting for great things to happen. "Let your belts be fastened around your waists and your lamps be burning ready. Be like humans awaiting their master's return from a wedding" (Luke 12:35).

Moreover, faith is a virtue maintained and grown by human efforts. Simply storing certain truths and values in our intellect, even showering certain emotional kudos or appreciation toward them, will not nurture faith. Rather, with the seed of faith, humans have to work. Interpreting our Lord's words (Luke 12:35–38) about our vigilant services even at the time of darkness, the biblical scholars underline that "the vigilant waiting that is emphasized in the Gospel is a faithful accomplishment of duties at hand, with awareness that the end, for which the disciples must always be ready, will entail the great judgment by which the everlasting destiny of all will be determined."

Once our faith gets mature and stronger, then it does a marvelous job in our lives. Faith is a powerful instrument to handle the unfairness of life successfully. According to the study done some years back by the Gallup Institute's religious research center in New

Jersey, about 13 percent of believers are found to be most religiously committed. They are fully engaged in doing something with their faith seed, very faithful in their religious practices. The empirical evidences show that the benefits of faith in those people's lives are numerous. Their vibrant faith has transformed them to be more ethical and honest; more tolerant, respectful, and accepting of persons of different ethnicity, race, or social, political, or economic background; more apt to perform acts of kindness, offer charitable services, volunteer, and so on; and far happier than those with little, weak, or no faith to sustain them.

141. True Peace Only by Blazing Fire

*Can you . . . be baptized with the baptism
with which I am baptized?*
—Mark 10:38

In the Gospels, we hear from Jesus many alarming statements, among which is a very provoking one: "I have come not to bring peace but division" (Luke 12:51). The critics of religions will cynically agree with it because it is a common opinion, plus a global and historical reality, that religions are the major source of division, suffering, and war disturbing our world. This statement of the Master may also shock all his discipled leaders of peace.

Very surprisingly, it seems to contradict the whole message of the Gospel. At the Last Supper, Jesus has told his disciples, "Peace I leave with you; my peace

I give to you" (John 14:27a). Matthew quotes Jesus declaring in the Sermon on the Mount as one of Jesus's beatitudes, "Blessed are the peacemakers for they shall be called the children of God." Can we believe that such a peace-loving Teacher and a Prince of Peace could utter such controversial words?

Indeed, we need to pause before our crude judgment and try to go deeper into his statement, by which he might have meant something other than what we understand at its surface level. In the light of the Spirit and of the works of the church fathers and biblical scholars, we discover that Jesus hasn't said anything negative about peace; rather, positively, he has been concerned about true peace.

We should know that no human being can survive even a single moment without some sort of inner peace. Physically, emotionally, and mentally, a person should be in balance. Every bit of our human system within us must be at its balanced level. This is called tranquility. If that normal level is lost, a problem starts in the body, mind, and soul. However, this tranquility can be disturbed or distorted by many of our unwanted activities. No human person can say that he/she passes through daily life with no disturbance whatsoever. Thus, our peace is gone. During that critical situation, we are used to resorting to many strategies to bring back that mental and emotional balance.

We think we can bring back our peace by inducing undue and uncontrolled physical pleasures and excitements through alcohol, drugs, perverted sex, even unlimited food, etc.; by disturbing other people's peace through fighting against them and including them into our company of miserable, low-spirited people; by being busy in our pursuit of money, becoming workaholic, and turning out to be too extreme in our worldviews; by becoming fake champions of community causes through making use of religion and devotion as a cover-up to avoid any trouble at home or in the office; by trying to bring peace in other people's lives or other neighborhoods, even other nations, through waging wars and violence; and above all by compromising and being complacent. Sure, we will establish peace by such endeavors, but that peace is always temporary and fake.

Jesus came to proclaim about true peace, not as the world and earthly gimmicks offer. He coveted that remarkable peace within himself by using some right tools for it. He asserted that it was his lifelong goal. He tried to be immersed (baptized) totally into it. He expressed it by saying, "I have come to set the earth on fire, and how I wish it were already blazing! There is a baptism with which I must be baptized, and how great is my anguish until it is accomplished!" (Luke 12:49–50). He also shared his tactics of achieving true peace. He exhorted us to be burned with his fire of truth, justice, and love.

Once this fire is burning within us, surely, there will be lots of things and even persons, our near and dear ones, who have to be knocked out (Luke 12:52–53). Division starts there between the spirit of committed disciples and the spirit of complacent and indifferent people. He wants us to meet such chances as challenges of faith in him and stand in the battle and never quit.

In this struggle, the Word of God encourages us, pointing out that there have been, in our midst, millions of witnesses who have followed this unique way to peace. The author of the letter to the Hebrews cheers us (Heb. 11:1–38) by giving us a long list of those ancient witnesses who have been role models in being burned with Jesus's fire, blazing but dispelling darkness in the world, and enlightening every one of God's children.

They have put their lives on the line in defense of a way of life that they passionately believe in. They have fought for truth, justice, human rights, and basic freedom, which is everyone's sacred right. Jesus joins that blessed cloud of witnesses. And he too has been demanding all his followers to join the club of those baptized in his fire. Let us take his amazing fire of justice, truth, and love in our hands; let us run the race of life while keeping our eyes fixed of Jesus, who has already won the race.

142. Narrow Gate to the Wide Chamber of Bliss

Many are invited, but few are chosen.
—Matt. 22:14

Once, someone asked Jesus, "Will only a few people be saved?" Jesus's reply to this question was one of his hard sayings: "Only those who go through the narrow gate will be saved" (Luke 13:22–24). What is a narrow gate?

"Narrow gate," according to Jesus's Gospel, is nothing but an earthly human life led in discipline. It is a life that is groomed, shaped, tamed, molded, and disciplined by the spirit of his beatitudes of the Sermon on the Mount. If we reflect over those beatitudes in the light of what Jesus has upheld and preached continuously till his death, we can discover the three dimensions of this narrow gate, which discipline our lives and make us worthy of walking in the right path to our blissful destiny of salvation.

In factual truth of our earthly life, there had been—from its onset—a palpable narrow gate being restrained with limitations, mainly those of our weak and fragile body. And so was Jesus. But he hugged it, loved it, and did the best he could despite its limitations. Scriptures quoted him, saying when he came into the world, "Sacrifice and offering you did not desire, but a body you prepared for me; Then I said, as is written of me in the scroll, behold, I come to do your will, O God" (Heb. 10:5–7).

With Jesus, we are aware of the fact that this earthly body is so limited that, at any time, it can betray or disown us. It is unpredictable in its cooperation with us but always predictable that it will meet its own disintegration, namely, death. We—though rational beings, only little less than angels—are blindfolded by our ignorance. Our ways are not God's ways. His thoughts are not our thoughts. His way is the high way. He makes his own choices. Those who are first here will be last there, and those are last now will be first in heaven. We may try to accomplish all sorts of things here in our own way. But God has his own way of judging them. As Jesus underscores, our judgment about our undertakings and achievements can easily be thwarted by the all-wise God on our Judgment Day.

There is another constituent of the narrow gate. It is the burdensome bundle of our day-to-day sufferings. We come across so many sufferings and pains in every dimension of our life—physical, mental, emotional, psychological, and spiritual. All of them hurt us very badly. All of us carry for life so many of the scars of such wounds. Why are all these happening to us? Scriptures candidly respond to this question: "My son, do not disdain the discipline of the Lord or lose heart when reproved by him; for whom the Lord loves, he disciplines; he scourges every son he acknowledges. Endure your trials as 'discipline'; God treats you as sons" (Heb. 12:5b–7a).

The third element of the narrow gate is nothing but the intrusion of others into our lives. To be alone is much better than to be squeezed by others. Both in our family and our community environment, we encounter such troublesome "squeezing" of others in our safe and restful territory. Though it isn't right, we still dream of being let alone as a lonely island. At least we can put up with the pain of being squeezed by family members who are both blood and law related.

But it is so excruciating when we face the same squeezing in a community environment, which we call neighborhood, town, parish, church, nation, and the international order. In that situation, almost all who screw us are strangers. Our life is intruded by them as refugees, migrants, and unwanted people of different opinions, different colors, different faiths, different values, and so on.

Yet God's eternal dream is that his entire creations, specifically humans, live together as one family of his sons and daughters. He has prophesized his dream through Isaiah: "I am coming to gather all nations and tongues; they shall come and see my glory" (66:18). The old Israelites have hated such dream of God, and so today we do the same because many times it hurts us. God invites everyone to his banquet of blissful life. Individuality is not the best source of salvation.

The only source of salvation is living and moving as a community member.

Unquestionably, a community life is a pain in the neck. Bringing everybody together to work with us is so hard, and it is simply a martyrdom to be undergone in common works. We have to, by all means, accept everyone in our life, though it pricks and hurts us. That is the way to be disciplined to go through the narrow gate. We must be convinced that we can perfectly walk through the narrow gate if we do it with Jesus, who is the Way, the truth, the life, and the gate. While many of us are invited to take this challenge, only a few have the guts to pass through it. Let us be one among those blessed few.

143. The Code of Conduct in God's Banquet

Everyone who exalts himself will be humbled;
the one who humbles himself will be exalted.
—Luke 18:14

Any sophisticated and civilized community-bonded life demands some codes of conduct like dress code, table manners, bodily gestures, even tone of voice and restrictions in words uttered and the quantity of food inducted. Those who observe such etiquette will be honored highly, given a warm welcome, and offered high places in those gatherings. Most of us base our security on either how we join an elite group of society or what the world offers us like riches, possessions, education, titles, good names, social praises, and well-groomed appearances. Almost all of us succumb to such bad attitude.

Surprisingly, Jesus has recommended a different base for our security. He has proposed a unique etiquette to be observed in the kingdom of God he has established as another option for his fellow men. We can call it "the kingdom manners."

For the hosts, Jesus promulgates an etiquette of equality. The kingdom of God is the perfect society in which God's spiritual meals are provided for everyone, not just as a private dinner for two by candlelight. All the dishes on the table are for everyone equally. There is enough and more for every person's needs. It is an occasion of sharing and joyfulness. Those who act as hosts must not show any discrimination whatsoever in inviting and feeding the guests. "When you hold a lunch or a dinner, do not invite your friends or your brothers or your relatives or your wealthy neighbors, in case they may invite you back and you have repayment. Rather, when you hold a banquet, invite the poor, the crippled, the lame, the blind" (Luke 4:12–13). Jesus wants them to be polite and kind to their guests, strangers and loved ones alike. They should never judge them according to their outward appearances or backgrounds. All are the same as God's children and friends of Jesus.

As for the guests, Jesus proposes the etiquette of humility. He admonishes the guests to be modest, humble, and simple and wait until their hosts take them to the prescribed tables. "When you are invited by someone to a wedding banquet, do not recline at table in the place of honor . . . Rather, when you are invited, go and take the lowest place . . . Then you will enjoy the esteem of your companions at the table"

(Luke 14:8–10). Humility is plainly and simply the proper understanding of our own worth. It is neither to overestimate one's worth nor to underestimate one's self, for that will be self-contempt. To feel self-contempt is to feel worthless and to live without any hope for improvement or achievement. Instead, we simply admit the truth about ourselves: we do not know everything, we do not do everything right, we are all imperfect and sinners.

Nevertheless, genuine humility directs us not to forget our worth, recognizing that we are made in the image and likeness of God and that we are called and empowered to help build the kingdom of God with our God-given gifts. Confirming this truthful fact in God's kingdom, the book of Sirach exhorts, "My son, conduct your affairs with humility, and you will be loved more than a giver of gifts. Humble yourself the more, the greater you are, and you will find mercy in the sight of God" (Sir. 3:17–18).

The basic element behind these codes of conduct is the belief that our survival and security in this life depends on our Creator God, and the only status that counts is one's relationship with God. Our real status is measured not by our rank or occupation but by the level of love and service offered to God through our relationships with those around us. This calls for a strong inner security, which is independent of an arbitrarily conferred status or position. This inner conviction is generated from the believable fact that we, as Christians, already have come to Mount Zion and the city of the living God, where our position gets stronger and all fears are smashed (Heb. 12:22).

We are always both guests and hosts in God's banquet of life not only in this world but also in the life after death. The ultimate reason for observing the kingdom manners Jesus has proposed is this as he himself has stated: "For you will be repaid at the resurrection of the righteous" (Luke 14:7–14). Thus, we become guests of honor as we share God's gifts and blessings in everyday life; at the same time, we too turn out to be hosts when—for the sake of God and in Jesus's name—we share the same blessings with our needy brothers and sisters in our family, community, and entire human family.

144. Detachment Is the Offshoot of Attachment

There is no one who has given up . . . for
the sake of the kingdom of God
who will not receive back an overabundant return.
—Luke 18:29–30

Our life is a bundle of relationships through which we are made what we are. Once, we have been in the womb of our mother, a lump of mere flesh and bones. But later, as we grow, we have become humans, thanks to the connections we have established with God and our fellow men. Religions, as any other natural helps, are there to make those relationships stronger, more fruitful, and more successful. And so does our Christianity.

However, it shocks us when we read certain demands Jesus puts to his would-be followers. We hear Jesus telling us, "Whoever wishes to come after me must deny himself, take up his cross, and follow me" (Mark 8:34). At least we can bear with this requirement. But he has added another requisite that seems terrible and hurting us, namely, "If any one comes to me without hating his father and mother, wife and children, brothers and sisters, and even his own life, he cannot be my disciple." In other words, he seemingly expects from us an uncompromising behavior of detaching ourselves totally from our dear and near ones. To many of us, these words of Jesus may seem a heartbreaking and an undoable demand to be followed in our daily life. But if we go deeper into it in the light of the Spirit, we discover the most useful and fruitful strategy in maintaining our human relationships.

Let us be very clear about one thing: when Jesus arrived on this earth, with a striking note, he taught us how to sustain the remarkable relationship established between God and ourselves and among ourselves. He claimed and proved himself as God with us, Immanuel, and demanded from us the same kind of relationship with him. "You have faith in God; have faith also in me" (John 14:1b).

This is what his religion is all about. It is a new religion with a new life—a new life with a new idea of relationship. In this new relationship with Jesus, we are commanded to be total and wholistic in giving up our very self to his love. Most of the time, we are tempted to be half-hearted or even to back off from obeying this command.

In our discipleship with him, Jesus doesn't just want a bit of us. He wants all of us. Any love game in life demands a total claim on the Beloved. Love claims the Beloved totally. He has given himself totally to us. For our relationship with him to flourish, we have to accept his gift of himself and give ourselves totally to him. The relationship with the Lord demands living his life and even following him in sacrifice. "You cannot be my follower unless you take up your cross." The relationship with the Lord means putting him before our possessions. "You cannot be my disciple unless you renounce all your possessions."

When Jesus says, "Leave your relations and even your very self," he does not mean to desert everybody at home and all our friends and become a lonely person or an isolated island in the universe. On the contrary, he expects us to build up all our relationships in this world not by mere natural bases of blood and flesh, human laws, contracts, or racial, creedal, national, regional, tribal, civic, and social foundations but on love for Jesus, justice of God, morality of innocence, human dignity of God's child, freedom of God's Spirit, peace, forgiveness, and joy of heaven. Any relationship we create in this world—such as spouses in marriage, parent and child at home, leader and follower in any social and political arena—should not lack this Gospel foundation.

To explain such Gospel-oriented human relationship, there are many events and sayings found in a beautiful event described in the letters of Paul. One is the shortest letter to Philemon, where Paul writes from prison to his friend, urging him to take back a slave who has apparently done something wrong but who, under Paul's influence, has become a Christian. Paul exhorts him to accept the converted slave as he relates to the slave as an affectionate father, brother, and even part of himself (Philem. 9–17). This suggests that, in the kingdom of God Jesus has preached, if some of our natural relationships obstruct us to embrace such macrofamily spirit of Jesus, we should detach them to gain an indestructible eternal life. We are born for such destiny, though we are vulnerable to become dust and be annihilated like all other creatures (Ps. 90:3–6).

However, those of us who adhere to the words of wisdom that have come from our Creator, Jesus Christ, about whom the book of Wisdom has prophesied, "Who can know your counsel, unless you give Wisdom and send your holy spirit from on high? Thus were the paths of those on earth made straight, and people learned what pleases you, and were saved by Wisdom" (Wis. 9:17–18). Indeed, the God whom we worship and surrender to is love with wisdom and power.

145. Come, Let Us Destroy First Our Own Molten Calves

Those who are well do not need a physician but the sick do.
I did not come to call the righteous but sinners.
—Mark 2:17

Our God is one of love, compassion, forgiveness, goodness, justice, and peace. He is a God of life. As Pope John Paul II has once said, "When God gives life, he creates it for eternity." Indeed, by going through the marvelous deeds of God to his people as narrated in the Bible, we notice him being very much vexed and disturbed by the people's misbehavior and infidelity. "When the Lord saw how great the wickedness of human beings was on earth, and how every desire that their heart conceived was always nothing but evil, the Lord regretted making human beings on the earth, and his heart was grieved" (Gen. 6:5–6). He has been so heartbroken, especially when his own chosen people— for whom he has performed numerous good deeds for their survival and victory—being impatient of waiting for God's messenger, have created their own idols and begun worshipping it (Exod. 32:1–10). As we often hear preachers contending that God loves the sinners but hates the sins, the "thrice holy" God can never bear unholiness smeared on his image and likeness he has created humans with.

We humans, up to this day, have been demonstrating the same kind of blindfolded and ungrateful tendency to create our own god as Israelites has created by their own hands. There are people among us who are slaves to the molten calf of fanaticism, death, violence, hatred, violence, and terrorism. Many others surrender to the molten calf of hatred, retaliation, and vengeance. And so many in the world worship the molten calf of secularism, materialism, licentiousness, worldliness, and immorality. These kinds of worshippers of the molten calf can be found in all present-day life situations— developed and underdeveloped, educated and uneducated, poor and rich, religious and irreligious.

The greatest problem hidden under the carpet of these man-made devotions is nothing but the ignorance and arrogance of fake-self-dominated humans. That is why God calls them "the stiff-necked generation," and he cries out sternly, "Forty years I loathed that generation; I said: 'This people's heart goes astray; they do not know my ways.' Therefore I swore in my anger: 'They shall never enter my rest'" (Ps. 95:10–11).

Saul, who has become Paul, has confessed this truth about his past sinful life: "I was once a blasphemer and a persecutor and an arrogant man, but I have been mercifully treated because I acted out of ignorance in my unbelief" (1 Tim. 1:13).

Very fortunately, we know the God we worship never keeps his resentment against us. He rather is a God who hates sin but loves the sinner. He has shown himself as the Lord of both justice and mercy. So in the scriptures, we read, "The Lord changed his mind about the punishment he had threatened to inflict on his people" (Exod. 32:14). The forgiven Paul testifies to the amazingly forgiving God: "I was mercifully treated, so that in me, as the foremost, Christ Jesus might display all his patience as an example for those who would come to believe in him for everlasting life" (1 Tim. 1:16).

Jesus, coming from his Father, has preached a gospel of mercy and acted it out in life, telling us, "I came to offer forgiveness to sinners." If we browse all his sayings in the Gospels, we can notice that two-thirds of them proclaim that the God of Jesus is eternally merciful. His three parables about the lost and found coin, the sheep, and the prodigal son cover the central message of his mercy proclamation. He underlines at the end of each story how his Father will be happy when he forgives and accepts the repentant sinners. "I tell you, there will be more joy in heaven over one sinner who repents than over ninety-nine righteous people who have no need of repentance" (Luke 15:1–32).

Almost all disciples of Jesus today, together with many religious leaders, shout out the truthful facts of sinful humanity. Many may try to take efforts to eradicate the grim situation. But God in Jesus expects us, before waging war against evil forces outside, to humbly submit to the supremacy of our God of love and fight against the molten calves we ourselves have created or cooperated in making. Let us start disciplining ourselves in accordance with the commandments of the Lord.

146. Earn and Spend Justly, But Save and Store Heavenly

*The person who is trustworthy in very small matters
is also trustworthy in great ones.*
—Luke 16:10a

The naked truth of earthly life is that no one can survive in this world without money in any form. Money is a means of bargaining for our livelihood among one another. It is only a symbol of what we give and what we get. It is a basic instrument for any human interaction. Therefore, money is as good as our body. It stands as a symbol of our own identity and worth. We work hard in our jobs, and through the wages and salaries, our labor is acknowledged.

Being Jesus's discipled leaders, we are not asked to hate this money. When the Lord has said, "No one can serve two masters . . . You cannot serve God and mammon" (Matt. 6:24), he never intends to put a conflict between God and money; rather, he points out the war to be waged between the Supreme God and the avaricious possessor of money. We can derive this conclusion from the manner Jesus has treated money and money owners or moneylenders in his life. Money, by itself, is not the root of all evil. Paul verifies it, writing, "The love of money is the root of all evils" (1 Tim. 6:10a).

The Word of God teaches us how we should handle money with care both in acquiring and using. Prophets like Amos have been warning, with curses from God, those rich people who acquire wealth by exploiting the innocent, the poor, and the ignorant of society (Amos 8:4–7). Jesus has cautioned rich people, telling sadly, "How hard it is for those who have wealth to enter the kingdom of God!" (Luke 18:24). Sometimes he has cursed them for their misusing riches: "Owe to you who are rich, for you have received your consolation" (Luke 6:24). He too has used many parables to teach humans how to use money, such as the parable of the dishonest steward (Luke 16:1–8), the parable of the rich man and Lazarus (Luke 16:19–30), and the parable of the rich fool (Luke 12:16–21).

What about Jesus's personal handling of money? Indeed, he acquired money, provided by his own friends out of their resources (Luke 8:3), and he also carefully used it for different purposes (Matt. 17:24–27). He was praising those who used their money, be it a dime, for good causes and with a cheerful heart: "But she [widow] from her poverty, has contributed all she had, her whole livelihood" (Mark 12:41–44). "If you wish to be perfect, go, sell what you have and give to the poor, and you will have treasure in heaven" (Matt. 19:16–30).

From his living style and through his sayings, Jesus wants us to acquire money in the right and just way, by our sweat and blood, by our toil and talents, by our sincere efforts and smartness. At the same time, he demands from us to start using this money in his ways, as his faithful stewards, because he is the giver and owner of all our resources. He advises us to use this money to make numerous friends so that they can assist us in reaching our home—heaven. Money should help us not in buying people for our own gratification and self-glory but for the greater glory of God and in earning our dues in the life to come.

147. Blessed Are the Poor in Spirit And Rich in Mercy

Blessed are you who are poor, for the kingdom of God is yours.
—Luke 6:20

In the Gospels, we find Jesus dividing humanity into two principal categories, for example, the goats and the sheep, the blessed and the cursed, and the first and the last. One of the most intriguing divisions he made is the poor and the rich. To expound this division, he has narrated the parable of the rich man and Lazarus. In this story, we read Jesus introducing his two dominant characters with a single note. About the rich man, he says, "There was a rich man." Note well that he does not say, "There was a man who made lots of money" or "There was a man who started with nothing and made a fortune." Also, regarding the second notable character, he doesn't describe him as "Lazarus lost his money in the market" or "He was too lazy to earn a living." But he presents him plainly, saying, 'There was a beggar."

This gives us a clue about what message our Master intends to convey to us. His story is not about a particular rich man and a poor man but about the general state of being rich or poor. That means, in a biblical way, that Jesus divides humanity into two principal categories: the Lazaruses (in Hebrew, the term means "God is my help") and the Diveses (in Latin meaning "the rich man"). This difference is maintained throughout the scriptures to stress that God can help and support only the category of poor people, who are also called *anawim*.

Our Teacher invites us to notice how the Diveses behave when they are feeling full. They go to the front of the line and look down on others. They consider themselves better and deserving of respect. They also are certain their rich status will remain forever. Even if they face some loss or failure in maintaining or increasing their wealth, positions, and properties, they are confident by their IQ and shrewdness that they can earn them back. With this sort of "rich" attitude of satisfaction, they don't care to depend on others, including the Creator.

They too deal with life as a business of buying and selling everybody and everything around them only for their success and self-gratification. Jesus emphasizes that even this "business dealing" attitude continues after their death. According to Jesus's story, while the rich man is burning in hellfire, he makes certain deals and negotiations with Abraham. "I beg you, father, send him [Lazarus] to my father's house, for I have five brothers, so that he may warn them, lest they too come to this place of torment" (Luke 16:27–28). He never gives up his pride, hardheadedness, or arrogant self-imposing personality. He behaves the same way as he has been used to being listened to and making deals. And when he cannot save himself, he tries to keep the money in the family by using Lazarus as a servant-messenger to warn his brothers. God, with Moses, giggles at his pathetic effort.

On the contrary, the *anawim* group of people, the Lazaruses or the poor in spirit, tend always not to have what they want or even what they need and therefore depend on others, especially God, whom they esteem as their champion. We hear in the canticle of Mary, who has burst out singing praises to the Almighty Champion, who sides forever only with the poor people but thwarts the malicious attitude and behavior of the rich ones, "He has shown might with his arm, dispersed the arrogant of mind and heart. He has thrown down the rulers from their thrones but lifted up the lowly. The hungry he has filled with good things; the rich he has sent away empty" (Luke 1:50–53).

That is what Jesus expects his discipled leaders to uphold about God's mighty deals among us. As humans, we are prone to either dreaming of becoming members of the social elite club or feeling envious of those who have already reached their puffed-up position, and we too dislike being beggars in the hands of God because of our pride and self-prestige. We try all we can to covet it and to be ordained permanently and hold it up to our death. This attitude must be diverted for us to see the people who are standing behind us who are poorer. Today, very pitiably, to become richer, the rich manipulate the poor; and in the process, the poor become poorer.

The world around us provides us with countless opportunities to change our lives. We seldom make use of these chances. We are overburdened with selfish needs and ends. Though we are unfaithful, God continually—by sending his messengers and prophets like Amos—pours his grace on all his disciples and calls us to repentance and conversion. For this, we need to live out each moment of our existence as an act of love.

148. We Need an Increase of Faith in Its Quality

Why could we not drive the demon out?
Because of your little faith.
—Matt. 17:18–20

The first team of Jesus's disciples often placed before him certain petitions for their life. One among them was "Lord, increase our faith" (Luke 17:5). There was a plausible life background behind their request. We always thought the disciples experienced crises, persecutions, rejections, and tribulations only when they were left alone to preach, teach, and witness to Jesus's Gospel after he went to heaven; but in fact, they faced many problems also while they stayed and walked with Jesus while he was alive. They should have been psychologically overwhelmed by Jesus's conditions and demands in following him as his disciples, such as to leave everything, including properties, relationships, and even their very self.

Those discipleship requirements were too hard to be digested and fulfilled. Hence, they needed the virtue of faith. They realized they did not have enough faith to cope with Jesus's Gospel demands. Hence, they begged Jesus to increase their faith. Jesus understood their request. Discovering a certain flaw in it—namely, while Jesus always expected his followers to have an enhanced quality of faith, the disciples prayed for the quantity of faith to be enlarged—he answered to their appeal by pointing out the mustard-seed kind of faith. "If you had faith as a grain of mustard seed, you could say to this sycamore tree, 'Be rooted up, and be planted in the sea,' and it would obey you" (Luke 17:6). He meant that the strength of faith does not depend on its outward largeness but rather its inner content. To explain the latter and how to enhance the quality of their faith, he used the parable of the master and his slave (Luke 17:7–10).

If we keenly go through this parable, we can discover Jesus emphasizing three ingredients of faith that should be developed and nurtured by every disciple. Faith in God first must be approached not merely as a bundle of creeds to be known, memorized, and recited regularly but also as some enrichment of our inner spirit of trust and confidence that our God is near us, even when he seems so far away, and that he will take care of his own.

Second, a deeper and well-developed faith contains the spirit of total love. In a true love relationship, one does not say, "Well, darling, I have loved you for three hours. Now it is your turn to love me back for three hours." The same is true in our loving relationship with God; the genuine joy and satisfaction consists in unconditional giving and sharing.

And third, Jesus has underlined that our quality faith must be enhanced by a continuous service to

God and our neighbors. Our relationship with God is not about buying and selling but one of total and unconditional love and service. The very energies with which we serve him are his gift to us. We are "merely servants." We can never do more than "our duty." Our attitude must be that of a humble servant. So Jesus has said, "When you have done all that is commanded you, say, 'We are unworthy servants; we have only done what was our duty.'"

We all need now more and greater faith than ever before. The main reason is that, worse than ever before, our present life is in very critical situations. Problems, crises, confusions, wars, terrorism, and violence are found in every corner of the world. Some are bad, others worse. Often in these life-threatening situations, we are reduced to a sense of helplessness and hopelessness.

One thing is sure: such problems concerning the survival of human lives are not anything new to humans. It has all started at the onset of humanity's evolution. But there is a vast difference between what humanity has faced in olden times and what we do at present. Whereas the tribal people have had a restricted outer vision about the happenings around them, the civilized humans have got a larger vision of the entire universe. What is happening even in the little corner of Africa or Asia comes into the homes and hearts of all residents in the globe and knocks them down. There is an astronomical enlargement of their outer vision of human life because of modern technology and communication.

In those days of tribal life, humans have managed or coped with the crises of their time with the little inner vision they have had as faith. But postmodern age people, having a greater vision of life and an enlarged understanding of what is going on around the entire globe, cannot handle it with the same tribal faith, which is very narrow and small. Today this is what Jesus invites us to possess—an enlarged inner vision, which God has described to the prophet Habakkuk: "For still the vision awaits its time; it hastens to the end—it will not lie. If it seems slow, wait for it; it will surely come, it will not delay" (Hab. 2:3–4).

149. In God's Kingdom, Power Comes Only by Humility

Whoever exalts himself will be humbled;
whoever humbles himself will be exalted.
—Matt. 23:12

Throughout the scripture, we come across thousands of references to highlight the importance of humbling ourselves to our Creator in our life journey. Though he allows us to call him Abba, Father and though he calls us spouse, we cannot deny his holiness and greatness and certainly our own fragile creatureliness. Besides, we are drawn by God's deeds toward the humble, meek, poor, and sinful humans. He acts as their champion.

In the book of Sirach, we read, "Those who serve God to please him are accepted; their petition reaches the clouds. The prayer of the lowly pierces the clouds; it does not rest till it reaches its goal; nor will it withdraw till the Most High responds" (35:20–21). Here, we should remember that God, who hates sins, always loves the sinner. And we should be well aware of the kind of sinner he likes and the kind of poor he listens to. God becomes the champion only of the sinners who accept truthfully their sinful status. When they begin to humble themselves in front of God sincerely, their cry is surely being heard by the Creator.

Jesus never missed even a single moment to spread such a consoling Gospel message to the downtrodden. His only portrayal of his Father was as an eternal friend and champion of the needy and sinners. When he noticed there were certain bullheaded and hardhearted people moving around God's holy places, including a few of his own disciples, he offered them a stern lesson how to be humble of heart to covet God's blessings; he narrated the simple parable of the Pharisee and the tax collector (Luke 18:9–14).

In that story, he used the character of the tax collector to exemplify the group of sinful but contrite people who suffered from the loneliness caused by their sins. This tax collector had many things in life. He was rich. But he was alone. He had no friends other than other tax collectors, people as despicable as he was. His people hated him. His family hated him. He hated himself. Surely, he would have thought God would hate him. So he slipped into the temple and sincerely sought God's forgiveness. And Jesus asserted that his Father heard the cries of this abandoned one.

On the other hand, we noticed in Jesus's story a Pharisee as an epitome of the self-righteous men and women. According to the Master, this stiff-necked religious person clearly had evidence to prove that he was the "good" person. He carefully kept the law of the Jews and the commandments of God. He faithfully observed the obligations of a good Jew; he prayed, he fasted, and he gave alms. What he really said to God was "God, you should be deeply grateful that you have someone like me, someone who is so faithful in following your commands." Yet Jesus's verdict was God was not happy with him because, basically, this rotten self-righteous man was a totally self-centered person.

In the light of Jesus, what we learn is that any humans with humility are always pleasing God in whatever situation they are in. Humility is plainly and simply nothing but the proper understanding of our own worth. Humble persons never overestimate their worth; however, it does not presuppose that they need to underestimate their self-worth, for that will be self-contempt. To have humility is to be true to oneself. Those who are truly humble believe themselves to have nothing when, in fact, they have everything because they possess God. In a word, those who humble themselves, God justifies. Humility is not denying the truth but affirming it without pride and self-assertiveness as Paul alleges loudly, "I have fought the good fight. I have finished the race, I have kept the faith" (2 Tim. 4:6–8).

One of the rare virtues we do not find today in the world is humility. Sadly, this is a fact observed even in many of the so-called chosen elite group of Jesus in this age. This may be because our forebears have misinterpreted it as against self-esteem. We are told again and again to be proud of ourselves, our culture, our nation, and our racial backgrounds and thus keep our self-esteem boosted. The vice of pride takes a dominant role in every step of our lives. Unfortunately, we have lost the beautiful virtue of humility, especially in our relations with God. So many blessings, therefore, turn out to be curses to our children and nations.

We, as discipled leaders, may hilariously sing every day, "I am proud to be a disciple ordained for leadership." It may be a nice song. But I suggest to alter the lyric to make it better and fruitful: "I am indeed blessed to be Jesus's discipled leader." That is what God in Jesus expects of us in doing the remarkable role of being his leaders in his kingdom.

CHAPTER IX

AT END OF THE DAY, REST IN THE PEACE OF CHRIST, OUR LIFE'S CLIMAX

150. Restful Settlement in the God We Trust

Do not worry about tomorrow.
—Matt. 6:34a

All of us are overwhelmed with so many worries that intensify our stress. We are worrying when jobs are scarce and when homes with overdue mortgages are being repossessed in record numbers. Yes, there are a lot of difficult situations swirling around us nowadays. Yes, there are many things we need to make it through each day—food, clothing, shelter, and so on. One author very truly compares worry with a "human god, invisible but omnipotent."

Jesus was fully aware of these injurious results of worries in his disciples. As a human being, he himself had gone through such intensive worries and stress. If we looked back at his life as narrated in the Gospels from his early days, he was snowed under with stress. So he knew well what humanity's fate is. He had great concern for us. He didn't want to leave them in that stressful situation and also never allowed them to use their own devices to solve it. He desired that his disciples learn from him the ways to cope with worries and stress as he applied in his own life. He found deep rest even in the midst of such deplorable life situation.

First, he reminds us emphatically that worry is futile. Worrying about life cannot add a single moment to our life span. It is sheer useless to worry about tomorrow because "tomorrow will take care of itself. Sufficient for a day is its own evil" (Matt. 6:34). We cannot, by worrying, add anything to our lives and improve our situation. It is said that today is the tomorrow we have worried about yesterday."

Second, we should never worry about ourselves and our limitations and sinfulness because our judgment won't be as correct as the Lord's. Nor should we be worried about the complaints, remarks, and other gossips from others. Again, it is because they are not our true judge; it is only God (1 Cor. 4:1–5).

Third, after offering those wise and reasonable facts of human life, Jesus asks us to trust in God because we are God's precious children. He loves and cares for us. God to us is more than a parent: "Even should a mother forget, I will never forget you" (Isa. 49:15). This means we are worth a lot in God's eyes, and he loves us deeply. We are forever engraved in the palm of his hands. Therefore, Jesus counsels us to stay put in God's trust. It means to settle oneself single-heartedly. "You cannot serve two masters." Those masters are God, who has established his kingdom already in us, and Satan, who—trying his best to destabilize God's kingdom—longs to establish his own. In continuation of this advice, Jesus adds that we should keep God as our priority. "First seek the kingdom of God and everything will be added unto" (Matt. 6:33).

God in Jesus confirms to us constantly that when we settle in him with trust, we become very restful, safe, secure, and peaceful. The restlessness we feel many times is generated by our imbalanced way of approaching our life issues, especially our human relationships. As we are journeying toward an unpredictable and critical future of our nation and the world, let us look up to the North Star and firmly move and live in God, whom we trust as our Rocky Mountain.

151. Get Away Alone with Jesus
For a Genuine Rest

*Come to me, all you who labor and are
burdened; I will give you rest.*
—Matt. 11:28

We are used to read and hear many "get away today" promos and ads in social media. Most of us surely make the best use of the discounted vacation travel packages to go around the nation's historical, awesome, and entertaining resorts. It is all, we think, for our rest and refreshment. But many times, I know by experience that after those tiresome and hectic travel planning and executing, when we come back home, we cry aloud to our soul mates or business partners, "Honey, I am so tired. Please excuse me. I cannot attend my duties today!" This is how most of us misuse the times of leisure, rest, and holidays.

Jesus too invited his tired disciples to take some rest, saying, "Come away by yourselves to a deserted place and rest a while" (Mark 6:31). And by this, he taught all his disciples how to make the proper use of resting time. First, he demonstrated it by his life and then through his instructions.

Our scriptures and tradition prove the eternal fact of God the Creator as the Supreme Shepherd to humanity, and therefore, we are proud to sing with David, "The Lord is my shepherd; there is nothing I lack" (Ps. 23:1–4). We too are convinced by God's Spirit that God, the generous Shepherd, has handed over his shepherdship to his beloved Son, Jesus, as the prophet Jeremiah has already prophesied: "See, days are coming, when I will raise up a righteous branch for David; as king he shall reign and govern wisely, he shall do what is just and right in the land. In his days Judah shall be saved, Israel shall dwell in security. This is the name to be given him: The Lord our justice" (Jer. 23:5–6).

Jesus never argued against it, and he willingly accepted that role to shepherd humans in God's name. He imitated the Supreme Shepherd and showed mercy and compassion to the needy and hungry people. As the Gospels spelled out, "His heart was always moved with pity for the humans, for they were like sheep without a shepherd" (Mark 6:30–34). He discovered they were full of problems, issues, and desolate experiences in life. He did, within his limited and restricted physical power and environmental situation, all that he could. He was a round-the-clock missionary of preaching, teaching, and healing. Since he was fully aware that "the spirit is willing, but the flesh is weak" (Matt. 26:41), he withdrew from the hurly-burly of the world and spent so many hours alone frequently on either hills or deserted places.

Besides, when he chose a team of humans to cooperate with him in his Gospel endeavors, his main goal for them was to act exactly like him as compassionate shepherds for the needy and the downtrodden people. He sent them to do the same missionary works in and around Palestine (Mark 6:7–13). When they came back full of joy and enumerated to him all the experiences with excitement, Jesus noticed they were obviously famished and exhausted of their tedious missionary journey. At this juncture, the compassionate Master wanted them to go with him to a deserted area to be refreshed for their next move of shepherding.

Jesus was fully aware of the importance of rest and solitude for humans, where we would allow God to refresh us. Hence, he truly wanted them not just to enjoy leisure time but also to be with him alone. This was to get back more spiritual energy they lacked. Hence, with Jesus, they went off in the boat to a deserted place. However, as Mark narrated, people saw them leaving, and many came to know about it. They hastened there on foot from all the towns and arrived at the place before them. Jesus saw the same crowd from which he purposely wanted he and his disciples to be freed. So the Master and his delegated leaders joined hands together and began once again their ministries.

Here is the lesson Jesus offers us in conducting our human life. He exhorts us to be balanced in working and in resting. We can sum up that lesson in one single biblical term—justice. That is the identity-name the prophet Jeremiah has given to Christ in his prophecy. The term "justice" literally means "balance; to stand in balance." All our mental, physical, and spiritual problems come out of the imbalanced handling of our own lives and roles. We should know we are divided within ourselves; human life is a very risky business to deal with, especially when that business is full of responsibilities such as leading others as shepherds. While we place more attention or emphasis on one side of us, the other side takes its own toll.

Our human spirit can be transformed into God's kingdom only when we accept and appropriate its rare blend of justice and peace and of work and rest. Jesus, who has been identified as "justice" by his Father, is also peace to himself and to the world (Eph. 2:13–18). Let us then obey the Lord of justice, go and stay with him alone, and enjoy our total, restful peace.

152. Blessed Are the Grateful Hearts, Where God Settles

Dedicate yourselves to thankfulness.
—Col. 3:15b

The best times I felt tremendously happy and fulfilled in my adult life are two: whenever I openly and wholeheartedly acknowledge my gratitude to my friends and supporters and benefactors and when many of my adult friends thank me with a sincere heart for whatever I have done for them and for the community. Unfortunately, the worst hurtful thing I have experienced has been seeing most of our loving and cute children and grandchildren lacking in the basics of gratitude, such as looking adults in the eye to thank them. Many parents will surely feel as I have on this holiday season as it starts with Thanksgiving.

Jennifer Breheny Wallace, in her well-thought-out and well-researched article "How to Raise More Grateful Children" published by the *Wall Street Journal* on February 23, 2018, exposes this crisis of ingratitude among modern people. She writes that "every generation seems to complain that children 'these days' are so much more entitled and ungrateful than in years past." She too augments her argument by one of her research study, saying, "In a 2012 national online poll of 2,000 adults, commissioned by the John Templeton Foundation, 59% of those surveyed thought that most people today are 'less likely to have an attitude of gratitude than 10 or 20 years ago.' The youngest group, 18- to 24-year-olds, were the least likely of any age group to report expressing gratitude regularly (only 35%) and the most likely to express gratitude for self-serving reasons."

The main reason for such overlooking is, as the author claims, the selfie culture our generation is endowed with, which often praises and rewards bragging and arrogance over kindness and humility. "Feeling grateful" is simply the outcome of how we develop within ourselves a mind-set, a way of viewing our life and the world around us. As David Rosmarin, director of the Spirituality and Mental Health Program at McLean Hospital in Belmont, Massachusetts, says that it is "a spiritual emotion, whether it's implicitly or explicitly expressed." This is why almost every world religion includes gratitude as part of its value system.

At this juncture, it is good we should be reminded of the beginning of the great celebration of Thanksgiving Day in our country. On October 3, 1789, when George Washington, the God-fearing president of America, assigned Thursday, the twenty-sixth day of November, as Thanksgiving Day, he spelled out splendidly the why and how of this celebration. He underlined, "Whereas it is the duty of all Nations to acknowledge the providence of Almighty God, to obey his will, to be grateful for his benefits, and humbly to implore his protection and favor—and whereas both Houses of Congress have by their joint Committee requested me to recommend to the People of the United States a day of public thanksgiving and prayer to be observed by acknowledging with grateful hearts the many signal favors of Almighty God especially by affording them an opportunity peaceably to establish a form of government for their safety and happiness."

The first dutiful thing any spiritually grown and levelheaded human should do, not only on this remarkable day but also every day, is to praise and thank loudly and boldly our God—the Creator, the Redeemer, and the Sanctifier—for his wonderful creation, for his eternal mercy, and for all his blessings abounding in day-to-day life. Jesus has reminded us to be grateful as one of our discipleship duties when he has appreciated the healed leper who has come back to thank him, saying, "Ten were cleansed, were they not? Where are the other nine? Has none but this foreigner returned to give thanks to God?" Then he has said to him, "Stand up and go; your faith has saved you" (Luke 17:17–19).

In this regard, we are fully aware of the fact that we pray not for God's sake but for our own. Among the prayers I recite in church services, I love the most heartening one, which is "Father, you have no need of our praise, yet our desire to thank you is itself your gift. Our prayer of thanksgiving adds nothing to your greatness but makes us grow in your grace." This prayer underlines the truth that we pray because voicing our praise, expressing our need, and offering our thanks and prayers help us know who we are before God and all others.

We should also remember that we are to bless others through the witness of our own family life. During this Thanksgiving, I encourage every family to ask themselves and the Lord what they can do this year so that, by next Thanksgiving, others will have experienced God's blessings through their efforts.

Just think of children's trust on their parents and parents' attitudes toward them. There is a beautiful lullaby of a mother that depicts parental goodness:

"Hush, little baby, don't say a word. Mama's going to buy you a mockingbird. And if that mockingbird won't sing, Mama's going to buy you a diamond ring." As it continues, this popular lullaby expresses the unquestioning willingness of parents to satisfy their child's every need and desire, whether these are as necessary as food and shelter or as frivolous as a mockingbird and diamond ring. That is a truly amazing and praiseworthy parental love. At the same time, we also must understand that such fervent love and sharing will do no good to our children if they don't pick up from their childhood a certain attitude of gratitude toward whatever they would receive. That will make our children really great persons in the kingdom of God.

153. Be a Daring Child To Enter into God's Chamber

Ask and you will receive; seek and you will find; knock and the door will be opened to you.
—Luke 11:9

Every religion is nothing but a pool of ways and means, values, and convictions to unite humans with God. As Christians, we believe that God has created humans in his likeness and that our first parents have walked in the Garden of Eden with God and talked with him face-to-face. We also know that because of the sins of humanity, most of them fail to be on the road with God; they are dissipated. Some take the wrong route, others stop their journey in between for their own gratification, and many are even rejected by God because of their injustice and infidelity.

However, a few strived to be loyal to God, followed his directions, did their homework promptly, and tried to walk with God till their death. Abraham was one such faithful person who persevered in his deals with God, and we read in the Bible how both conversed with each other with so much intimacy and confidence. There was a wonderful relationship between them; there was a give-and-take policy and a friendly but justice-based negotiation going on in their conversation (Gen. 18:20–32).

This is nothing but pure interpersonal communion between two persons, in which we find emotions, rationality, and intimacy meeting together. Both parties enjoy a spiritual intercourse. The same amazing experience is also found in the lives of Jacob, Moses, Joshua, and many other patriarchs, judges, prophets, kings, and queens.

When Jesus lived in this world, he never missed even a single moment without communing with God. He esteemed God as his beloved Father, and superbly, his conviction was affirmed directly from God, many times in private prayer time but a few times publicly with a loud voice: "You are my beloved Son in whom I am well-pleased." This spiritual communion with his Father put him at rest and sanity in the midst of sufferings, oppositions, and failures. Except sin, he experienced every bit of life challenges as all of us. He too knew what human frailty is and how each one of his followers would be tossed by life-threatening tsunami of perils and afflictions. Hence, he offered us an action plan of prayer. As he tasted and experienced this marvelous communion in prayer, he desired his disciples to also benefit from such encounters.

Jesus not only showed how we can relate ourselves with God in prayer but also, as Paul exclaimed in his letter, "brought us to life along with him, having forgiven us all our transgressions, obliterating the bond against us, with its legal claims, which was opposed to us, he also removed it from our midst, nailing it to the cross" (Col. 2:13–14). By his bleeding death, he brought reconciliation between God and humans, and he succeeded in making us as the adopted children of God and bestowed to us an amazing ability to call him Abba, Father.

He taught us how to pray a quality prayer, which can be performed in spirit and in truth and in trust and in hope and which would be spiritually beneficial (Luke 11:1–13). He wanted us to follow him in using the prayer tool he gave us. We should relate ourselves to God not with fear or any strangeness but more by being intimate, close, and personal. He asked us to demand our Father, to persist in asking, to persevere in petitioning, to show confidence and dependency like a child, and to never lose heart. "Don't leave the Father," Jesus exhorted us, "without His saying 'O.K. my child; let it happen to you as you desire.'"

This means prayer is not to be taken as a mere bundle of prayers to be recited or as some religious ceremonies to be enacted; rather, it is a constant and intimate communion with God. We should never think of God as white-bearded Santa delivering our blessings and gifts at our appeals, nor should we make him appear as a judge and face him in his court; rather, we should dare to go into his private chamber. We must always remember Jesus's advice that we deal in prayer not with a power, an energy, or an idol and surely not with a sleeping beauty but with a loving parent.

154. Tough Times Don't Last, but Tough People Do

Of that day no one knows . . . but only the Father.
—Mark 13:32

Through his scriptures, his church teachings, and our daily experiences, God demonstrates his longing for us to be fully aware of our end and that of the universe so that we walk in line with him and reach our glorious destiny.

In the synoptic Gospels and the book of Revelation, we hear so many frightening factors regarding the end of the universe, including the last breath of every human being. Such magnified rhetoric about the end times has been interpreted positively by church fathers in the light of scriptures themselves. While Jesus describes the occurrences at end times, he actually quotes two OT prophecies uttered by Daniel (12:1–3) and Joel (3:3–4). We find in those prophecies two dimensions of the end-time happenings. One is negative prophecy: "Those days will be a time unsurpassed in distress since nations began until that time." And the other are some positive points we hear from the prophets. Jesus sums them up: "And then they will see 'the Son of Man coming in the clouds' with great power and glory, and then he will send out the angels and gather his elect from the four winds, from the end of the earth to the end of the sky."

Biblical scholars advise us not to take those negative prophecies literally. They are like stories and parables placed before us to straighten out our lives and feel the urgency of getting back the image of Jesus Christ within us. In human history, we observe similar calamities mentioned in the scriptures that have happened in the past, happening today, and will continue in their own styles and forms. We may not know when and how those calamities will happen to us and to the entire universe. Jesus says, "But of that day or hour, no one knows, neither the angels in heaven, nor the Son, but only the Father."

Therefore, God in Jesus expects us not to panic or be overanxious about these things. The main reason for this is he has drawn an indelible mark on our forehead through his grace at our baptism, and we have confirmed it in our confirmation. John writes about the identity of those remnants: "They will look upon his face, and his name will be on their foreheads" (Rev. 22:4).

We should assume that when we try to transform ourselves into Jesus's image, we feel we're putting on a mask. Down deep, we know we're not the person we appear to be. Remembering such unique status, Jesus wants us to wait for him with unwavering hope. He has promised he is with us till the end of the world. With his presence, we should live our faith, even in the trials of life, not in fear but in firm hope, for we are people of hope in a loving and saving God.

The more we read these end-time stories and the more we experience such calamities and disasters in our lives and at our backyards, the greater our efforts should be in becoming like Jesus Christ. Every kind of end brings us to the conclusion that we will be judged according to our cooperation with God's grace. We may have tough times to go through—like death striking our family, accidents, terrorist attacks, job loss, and so on. But because Christ has already won the victory for us, we will not let these tough times defeat us.

The one and only prophecy from the Spirit uninterruptedly ringing in our minds and hearts should be "This is the covenant I will establish with them after those days, says the Lord: 'I will put my laws in their hearts, and I will write them upon their minds,' he also says: 'Their sins and their evildoings I will remember no more'" (Heb. 10:11–18).

155. On Earth Peace, Goodwill toward Men

This will be a sign for you:
An infant wrapped in swaddling clothes, lying in a manger.
—Luke 2:12

Though Jesus's birth is as any other human birth in Palestine, it has its specialty. First, Jesus's birth is history. In the Gospel of Luke, we are given a tiny historical background of Jesus's birth. According to him, Jesus's birth has occurred at the time of Augustus Caesar as the Roman emperor and Quirinius as governor of Syria.

Second, Jesus's birth is a story. In every human's birth, except their parents, all others do not know fully the real fact of one's birth. Parents know all the things that have happened in conception and birth historically.

All others are able to get only some glimpse of it through its stories as told by parents or relatives.

In the same way, in Jesus's birth, though it was historical, only Mary—his mother—knew well its entire historical facts. When she and Joseph joined together and shared the history of their son's birth, it surely reached others, like us, as stories. And that too was only through two evangelists, Matthew and Luke.

Third, Jesus's birth is a mystery. It contains too many truths and issues that cannot be easily digested or accepted by ordinary human beings. Jesus has been conceived by the Holy Spirit in the Virgin Mary's womb (Luke 1:26–38). Pointedly, from his conception, Christ's humanity has been filled with the Holy Spirit, for God "gives him the Spirit without measure" (John 3:34). Professing this incredible essence of baby Jesus and calling it as grace from God, Paul writes, "For the grace of God has appeared, saving all and training us to reject godless ways and worldly desires and to live temperately, justly, and devoutly in this age" (Titus 2:11–14). Another breathtaking dimension of mystery is that such a prosperous and glorious Son of God has been born in a humble stable into a poor family, and simple shepherds have been the first witnesses to this event. Startlingly, we discover that only in this poverty is heaven's glory made manifest.

Jesus's birth—though it has been a history, story, and mystery—informs us of an important lesson regarding our need of the day. If we desire to get God's fuller life in this world and the world to come, we should read between the lines of these stories of Jesus's birth and find out what condition God puts before us to receive his life. Luke, in his narration, mentions one event that is very normal and ordinary at any poor baby's birth, that is, "an infant wrapped in swaddling clothes and laid in a manger." It is three times repeated by the evangelist to emphasize its importance as a perfect message announced to all who celebrate Jesus's birth.

Glory belongs only to the Supreme Being, God. With angels, we love to sing, "Glory to God in the highest." We want our God to be all in glory, in power, and in victory. We like to see him always stand erect—no failure, no lack of anything. When we want him to come to us in our midst, we look for him in the same glorious status. But the Bible tells us we will rather die if we see him that way in our mortal body, so he has taken an ordinary human form.

He came as an infant—helpless, vulnerable, weak, simple, and poor. God asserted that, until we digested this intolerable revelation of God's glory, we cannot get peace or remain in peace. He knew it would be hard for us; therefore, he presented a positive message again through the angels, who added a verse to their hymns: "Peace to the people of goodwill."

Only good-willed people who dream of greater things in life from above will accept this hard truth of seeing a God as an infant, finding his glory in poverty and love. God's unique glory at the birth of Jesus shines. He highlights it as being poor in spirit, being committed to life out of love, and reciprocating love for hatred, forgiveness in place of retaliation, and truthfulness in times of trials.

156. With the Inner Drive of Our Call, We Inherit Our Victory

We are ambassadors for Christ, as if
God were appealing through us.
—2 Cor. 5:20a

Some among us consider that life is unfair, and so they dare to die soon; many others believe that there is nothing to gain after death, and so they plan to live. This kind of confusion, distortion, or negative view about life is a pest bugging all humans at one time or another. However, God does not want us, his disciples, to live in that suffocating mind-set. His Spirit instructs us to go deeper into some scriptural passages to help ourselves erase these negative thoughts and live our earthly life contently, smilingly, and fruitfully.

One of the best advice the scriptures offer us for our life's survival and success is to clearly understand and uphold the glorious vocation of our life. Paul elegantly portrays our life's vocation in his writings (Eph. 1:3–14). Our essence and existence, he writes, are already predestined by God the Creator, who has chosen us even before the foundation of the world. The purpose behind this startling deal of God to us is to accomplish all his endeavors fully and realize all his intentions totally in his Son, Jesus. God's main intention for calling us is for every one of us to be holy and without blemish before him, like his Son, and he has chosen us so that we might exist for the praise of his glory and to sum up all things in Christ in heaven and on the earth.

This was how all God's friends and disciples esteemed highly their vulnerable lives. Let us take for example the prophet Amos. He was a humble shepherd, but he was fully convinced that he had been called by God to prophesy. He narrated challenging the king that he was in no way a professional employed to prophesy to earn his livelihood; rather, he insisted the One upstairs urged him to do this hectic job, and he obeyed him (Amos 7:12–15). When he was threatened by his king, who ordered him to flee from his territory, he challenged him with his audacious tenacity, "I am not a prophet, nor do I belong to a company of prophets. I am a herdsman and a dresser of sycamores, but the Lord took me from following the flock, and the Lord said to me, 'Go, and prophesy to my people Israel.'"

Of all the prophets, Jesus had been the best role model for us in handling life's problems by our inner conviction. He showed it first in his own life and then taught his disciples the same. He kept in his heart and mind that only God the Father called him to perform his prophetic role as the people's Messiah; as Amos, he claimed it in public quoting Isaiah 61:1–2: "The Spirit of the Lord is upon me, because he has anointed me to bring glad tidings to the poor. He has sent me to proclaim liberty to captives." And at the end of this quote, he too confirmed his inner conviction: "Today this scripture passage is fulfilled in your hearing" (Luke 4:16–21). Therefore, being too zealous of God's will and his kingdom values, he esteemed God's will as his food and life.

In the Gospels, we read that Jesus chose all his disciples first to abide in him, meaning to fully imbibe his inner convictions of their godly predestination, and then to be sent out as the proxies of his prophetic role to bear witness to God's love by preaching and healing. "He summoned the Twelve and began to send them out two by two and gave them authority over unclean spirits" (Mark 6:7–13).

He bestowed to his disciples authority and power to drive out unclean spirits, first from themselves and then from others; knowing how humans can easily be subdued by those unclean spirits, he commanded his disciples that they should detach themselves from worldly things, instructing them to take nothing for the journey but a walking stick—no food, no sack, no money in their belts—but to totally cling to God for their needs. He too advised them to shake the dust off, perhaps referring to the dust of feelings like resentment, anger, hatred, and revenge to be free enough to let their faith in Jesus Christ shine not just in words but also in our actions. Then he wanted them to drive out the demons from other people.

Even though we are proud to be born and bred in the postmodern age, we are living in a world that is still in desperate need of prophets and apostles sent by Jesus. Our human race continues to be enslaved by so many unclean spirits. The saddest happening today is many of his modern-day disciples are indifferent to Jesus's reasons for choosing us. Let us fully believe in the truth that we have been called and destined from all ages to come and to be born and reborn at this hectic period to continue the work of Jesus, joining the team of messengers sent out by the Spirit to walk the walk of Jesus (being intimately connected to him), to talk the talk of Jesus (preaching his values), and certainly to work the work of Jesus (casting out unclean spirits).

157. Death Has No Final Say over Our Life

He will destroy death forever.
—Isa. 25:8a

The core message that God's Spirit proposes to us through the Gospel story of the miraculous event of Jesus raising Lazarus from his death (John 11:1–45) is a remarkable, positive stroke to our vulnerable life. It instructs us to never give up hope even in the most hopeless of situations in which we find ourselves as individuals, as a community, or as a nation. It is never too late for God to revive and revitalize us.

Scriptures state it is possible to hold such hope if we have strong faith in Jesus as the living Word who has come from God, who has demonstrated himself as a merciful and compassionate Father, plus has made promises of revival and renewal of life. He is the Son of a God who shouts out that he does not desire any human to die. And he is the one who uninterruptedly promises us, "I will open your graves and have you rise from them; I will put my spirit in you that you may live, and I will settle you upon your land" (Ezek. 37:12–14).

Jesus reclaimed his godly identity of having a life-giving ability. Jesus expected Martha, the sister of Lazarus, to believe that he has the power not only to give eternal resurrection on the last day but also to revive and revitalize the darkened lives of humans who believe in him. "I am the resurrection and the life; whoever believes in me, even if he dies, will live, and everyone who lives and believes in me will never die."

We should be convinced that Jesus continues to perform such miracles of revival in our lives. The wonder of wonders is that we, the baptized disciples of Jesus, have already risen from ungodliness, darkness, and filthy wickedness because of the living presence of the risen Jesus within us. Paul expounds this marvelous deed of God repeatedly in all his letters. While he underlines that all of us have been dead in our transgressions and sins in which we have once lived after the age of this world, he too insists that "God, who is rich in mercy, because of the great love he had for us, even when we were dead in our transgressions, brought us to life with Christ, raised us up with him, and seated us with him in the heavens in Christ Jesus" (Eph. 2:4–6).

Unfortunately, as Paul bemoans (Rom. 6:2–8), forgetting the glorious status we have been bestowed with, most of the baptized children of God today are still living in the tomb of hopelessness and decay in the bondage of sinful habits and attitudes. Thus, we walk around more dead than alive. However, we should never be discouraged and frustrated or get angry against ourselves. The Lord constantly inspires us to keep on trusting and loving him and let our friendship with him be evergreen.

According to Jesus, any deviation or wrong choice that makes us dead spiritually is not totally to be considered as death; rather, Jesus wants us not to be squirming on our spiritual downfalls but to believe that it is an occasion, as he has told his disciples about the death of Lazarus, to glorify more God's immense love and patient compassion for us. "This illness is not to end in death, but is for the glory of God, that the Son of God may be glorified through it." He highlights that any evil things happening in our lives are very temporary. All the sufferings we undergo are not the end of all; they are all simply stepping stones to the ultimate fullness of eternal life.

If we suffer or die enduring in our friendship with Jesus, we can hear his commanding but compassionate voice: "Lazarus, come out." Immediately Lazarus wades his way out of the tomb, and the Lord urges other disciples to help him be untied. God calls us today to come out of the tombs of our hardness of heart, out of the graves of our fears and selfishness, out of everything that keeps us imprisoned. Let us always lend our hearts and minds to Jesus, who is our life and resurrection.

158. Ritual Resurrection Is A Lead to Actual Resurrection

You were buried with him in baptism,
in which you were also raised with him.
—Col. 2:12

According to our religious faith, God will survive even without us, but we cannot survive without him. The mechanism to survive with God is what we call religion. In life, there are 1,001 unsolved mysteries, millions of unresolved bad times, and incalculable unfulfilled dreams. The world seems to move on today in that same darkness as any other centuries. This human experience of darkness and gloominess about life is so universal that one humorous person has noted, "Life is just one damn thing after another."

Then how do we survive through this grim darkness? It is all by stories, fantasies, fairy tales, daydreams, and memories of the past. Those stories are not only read or heard but also remembered, believed, and celebrated. Undebatably, that is what any religion is all about, and so is our church. The story of resurrection is one among many. It is not at all to be listed in the top ten stories like Santa's. It is a story not to enjoy temporarily by reading and listening or to be pretended. It offers amazing benefits to our life when it is also remembered, believed, and celebrated and much more lived and experienced.

Our NT books proclaimed this fact of Christianity. They all enumerated what went before and came after the resurrection of Jesus. Who was this Jesus before he was resurrected? We noticed that the book of Acts and the letters of the apostles, especially Peter, kept Jesus's resurrection as the core of their preaching (Acts 10:36–43). They testified that this risen Jesus was an ordinary human, full of God's Spirit, and went through the challenges of his life but never drifted away from the higher ideals he imposed to himself for his life journey. We can even say that, as he was dying and being buried, his spirit would have continued to whisper with hope and conviction in his beyondness with the psalmist's words, "I shall not die but live and declare the deeds of the Lord. The Lord chastised me harshly, but did not hand me over to death. The stone the builders rejected has become the cornerstone" (Ps. 118).

As for the aftermath of resurrection, we read in the Bible that whoever visited or reflected over the empty tomb where Jesus had been buried and believed that his resurrection was a true but heavenly event in human history, they were historically empowered, renewed, and rejuvenated and began witnessing to this resurrected "human being." The only testimony they submitted was "We have encountered the resurrected Lord. He urged us to live and preach his gospel of mercy and joy."

Paul reiterates in all his letters the real effects of Jesus's resurrection. According to him, what happens ritually in baptism is not the real effect of resurrection. Rather, it must occur actually in life. If it is true that we have been resurrected by the belief in the risen Jesus, the only sign for such miracle is nothing but the living of our daily life. "If then you were raised with Christ, seek what is above, where Christ is seated at the right hand of God. Think of what is above, not of what is on earth. For you have died, and your life is hidden with Christ in God. When Christ your life appears, then you too will appear with him in glory" (Col. 3:1–4).

In the midst of so many debates going on for and against Jesus's resurrection, the main source of the present-day disciples' belief in it is what they personally experience its aftermath. Our personal experience of the living Jesus is his unending Gospel and unfinished task. The resurrection story is not at all for being proved by an outsider or any outside technique or strategy. It is to be lived and experienced by each and every one of us. We are that team, that family, that community of which every member has been experiencing the resurrected Lord in our daily lives. If what we say about the resurrection of Jesus to others, especially to our young ones, has not been accepted and believed, it is because—I am vexed to say this—we ourselves have not got that experience of the resurrected Jesus in our lives. The story of resurrection is not like that of Santa. Santa can be pretended and faked but not the resurrected Lord. Let us never forget that ritual resurrection is only a startup of actual resurrection.

159. Death Is a Passage to a Better and Fuller Life

Whether we live or die, we are the Lord's.
—Rom. 14:8b

Every one of us longs to live a life of peace, joy, freedom, peace, and justice, plus certainly an unending one. Whenever we do not possess such fulfilling life, we wish for a better tomorrow, a better future, a better life. This desire and dream is innate in us because we know we have been created by a God who is life. When Moses has asked God what his name is, God has replied, "I am Who Am." In other words, he has been, he is, and he will be a living God forever. We, his creatures made in his image and likeness, are naturally inclined to possess such life too. If we don't get it or lose it, we are disappointed, confused, and tensed. To add to this struggle, human death comes in between to worsen our problem.

In this precarious life, the Spirit of Jesus exhorts us not to be afraid of facing death because we will be resurrected surely from it. Death has a very short duration. It is only a means and not an end in itself. Final resurrection as the goal of all humans is the central concept of our Christian faith. It is very much a matter of faith and trust in God's Word as we have no proof or experience of such a life, nor can we say very much about it. Paul puts it well, quoting Isaiah, "What eye has not seen, and ear has not heard, and what has not entered the human heart, what God has prepared for those who love him" (1 Cor. 2:9).

In an exuberant faith, being influenced by the images found in the book of Revelation, we lead a hope-filled life that will take us one day after death to heaven, a place where we wheel on clouds, play harps, and sing the praises of God all day long and every day forever. In explaining the heavenly life of humans after death, Jesus has ascertained, "They can no longer die, for they are like angels; and they are the children of God because they are the ones who will rise" (Luke 20:36). Though there are too many explanations and religious dogmas around this world, we adhere firmly to what Jesus's teaching on this issue. We will enjoy a fuller and better life than anything we have dreamed of, totally different from what has been touched and explained with our limited human brain.

There is no problem in longing and dreaming for a better future and life. The real issue is what kind of means we use to attain that better tomorrow. In scriptures, we find our God of love handing out to us the means to achieve such better life through many events and examples. One of them is the life and death of the Maccabees, narrated in 2 Maccabees 7:1–14.

Up to the end of earthly life, the entire family had strived to fulfill all God's laws. As the psalmist sang, "They indeed kept their feet firmly in God's paths;

there was no faltering in their steps" (Ps. 17:5). Even in the critical moment of their life, they had never deviated themselves from their adherence to their God and his demands. When they were tortured and bleeding to death, they shouted, "We are ready to die rather than transgress the laws of our fathers." They burst out to the torturers, "You dismiss us from this present life, but the King of the universe will raise us up to an everlasting renewal of life, because we have died for his laws." They too bravely stretched out their hands to be slain, unflinchingly exclaiming, "I got these from heaven, and because of His laws I disdain them, and from Him I hope to get them back again."

We need not wait for such religious war or persecution, as in the time of the Maccabees, to demonstrate our steadfastness to God. We, the committed disciples of Jesus, are already martyrs to the existing social order, social upheavals, social injustice, and other problems. Our human life is stifled, disintegrated, disabled, and chronically vulnerable to sickness because of ignorance, carelessness, and sinfulness of our own parents or grandparents. We undergo self-immolation caused by others' selfishness and hardheadedness. We are caught up in a self-imprisoned life situation because of natural and artificial causes. We need to pass through this valley of darkness and tears in adhering very firmly to God's love and service with steadfast faith that "our God is not of the dead, but of the living, for to him all are alive" (Luke 20:38).

160. Let God, Let Go

I am the Lord . . . there is no God besides me.
—Isa. 45:5

In the Gospels, we found the Pharisees and the enemies of Jesus ruthlessly trying to trap him in his words and attitudes as a religious Jew, plus to make him politically incorrect and get into the bad book of Romans. However, our Master always prevailed by his godly wisdom. One such incident was vividly narrated by Matthew (22:15–21). In that event, he was asked, "Tell us, then, what is your opinion: Is it lawful to pay the census tax to Caesar or not?" Jesus responded, "Give to Caesar what is Caesar's and to God what is God's".

Through this statement, Jesus—with all his God-given Jewish smartness—brings out very clearly his continued theme of life, namely, God and God only. According to him, there can be other political and social priorities in life, like paying taxes, but it is God who should be number 1 in our attitudes and actions. This saying of Jesus is reflected in his entire life and teaching, thus restoring the right relationship between the Creator and the creature.

Educated Jews like Pharisees, Sadducees, and scribes knew very well what Jesus was referring to. It was the supreme command of God: "Love your God with your whole heart, whole mind, whole soul, whole body and strength; and the addition to it was: love your neighbors as yourself." Scriptures profusely proclaimed the supremacy of God over all his creations, particularly humans. Through the prophet Isaiah, he claimed, "I have called you by name, giving you a title, though you do not know me. It is I who arm you, though you do not know me, so that all may know, from the rising of the sun to its setting, that there is none besides me" (Isa. 45:4–6). Paul continued to live in the same spirit of faith in the sovereignty of God and never ceased to preach about it in all his letters. "Give thanks to God always knowing, brothers loved by God, how you were chosen. For our gospel did not come to you in word alone, but also in power and in the Holy Spirit and with much conviction" (1 Thess. 1:2–5).

As the disciples of Jesus, our first and deepest loyalty must be allocated to God. Any of our attitudes, any of our plans, any of our opinions, any of our suggestions, and any of our personal, social, religious, and political activities regarding the development, management, and maintenance of our life must be generated, influenced, presented, and implemented on the basis of that truthful fact. If not, our Master will be reprimanding us as he has done Peter: "Get behind me, Satan! You are an obstacle to me. You are thinking not as God does, but as human beings do" (Matt. 16:21–23).

Therefore, we should "give to God what is God's." God is the Lord, and there is no other; we are to worship him alone. Let God, let go. I mean our whole body, whole soul, whole mind, whole strength, and whole life. Not just 5 percent, 10 percent, or 50 percent but 100 percent of everything we own and do should be handed over to our Creator. This is the challenge that God presents to us, especially now when we are divided politically, religiously, and socially because of our self-inflicted isms and prejudices.

161. The Wild Dream of New Heaven and New Earth

Christ will appear a second time to bring salvation to those who eagerly await him.
—Heb. 9:28

Wild dreams of today are the practical deeds and enterprises of tomorrow. All of us have dreamed so many wild dreams about our lives in our childhood. And that is what we experience, express, and live in today. Only our dreams have made us create beautiful choices for life. We have grown, developed, and achieved because of our dreams.

Customarily, all religions are based on certain fairy tales and wild dreams. Christianity is not exempted. Our God always invites us to dream dreams and live through them. We Christians live on wild dreams about God and about life after death. All our dreams are enlisted in our creeds and dogmas. At the end of our regular creed, we recite one of the most admirable, though unknown, dreams of our life's ultimate end: "He will come again in glory to judge the living and the dead, and his kingdom will have no end. We look for the resurrection of the dead, and the life of the world to come."

These are indeed wild dreams about our future. Though such dreams may sound weird, we are convinced of their authenticity because of their basis resting on the wild but real dreams of Jesus and the prophets. Jesus's prophecies and predictions about these ultimate things have been his wild dreams about human life and the entire creation. Along with his forebears, like the prophet Malachi (3:19–20), Jesus has spelled out very lengthily (Luke 21:7–28) his own version of our final end, which he calls "the great day," "the Day of Judgment," and "a day of wrath."

In biblical verses about the ultimate moment of the universe, we observe that its first phase is about the horrible and stunning disasters and perils. Generally, preachers love to name this event as "rupture." Unfortunately, many of us stop with only the first portion of the prophecies to frighten their hearers. God has another goal for such description of end times. We can observe that in every prophecy, as its second part, uttered on this "ultimate thing," there is a specific and vivid note given about a positive and hope-filled message.

For example, at the end of Malachi's prophecy, we read, "But for you who fear my name, the sun of justice will arise with healing in its wings." Also, in Jesus's exposition of this great day, we get a positive stroke from him. First, he advises us not to be fretting over or tossed around by cheaters: "See that you not be deceived, for many will come in my name, saying, 'I am he,' and 'The time has come.' Do not follow them!" Then he adds an encouraging word: "When you hear of wars and insurrections, do not be terrified." He too promises during those terrible days that he will bestow his power to do what is right and to testify to him properly. Above all, at the close of his description about the end, he emphasizes our responsibility of persevering in him, with him, and for him. "By your perseverance you will secure your lives."

As a matter of fact, all spiritual writers claim that these wild prophetic dreams are perfectly necessary for us to go through this valley of tears. In their view, which we can surely agree with, these dreams make our lives meaningful and our today's burden light and sweet. The prophetic predictions of the big bang events are not at all nightmares. They are the source of strength and guidance for making proper decisions in our daily life. When we see and experience these wild dreams coming true, maybe partially, in day-to-day life, we should stand erect, raise our heads, and be alert not only for the external attack of the evil but also for our demoniac internal violence.

These dreams and realities, if they are not connected with Jesus's dreams, many times turn to be dangerous to ourselves and society. They too will stifle our good works and services. Other times, these dreams take us off the ground, frighten us, and keep us in complexes, being faithless in the future, ending up in depression, and making eating and drinking as the only goal in life.

Let us keep dreaming wild dreams. Human dreams come out of learning the dreams of others through stories. We should allow ourselves to dream the most meaningful dreams of Jesus: "There will be new heaven and new earth," "There will be one flock and one shepherd," and "They all may be one as you and I are one." Also, let us get the help of God in Jesus to realize all our dreams, however wild. But those dreams must be in accordance with his own dreams about his reign. So let us dream the wild dreams of Jesus about that day of wrath, that Day of Judgment, and that day of victory. At any time, that day will be ours. Besides such far reality of creation's end, Jesus has also dreamed about us, who are still crawling and groping in the dark. Let us make his wild dreams about us come true in us.

Printed in the United States
By Bookmasters